THE
GAME
OF
THEIR
LIVES

THE
GAME
OF
THEIR
LIVES

Dave Klein

Random House
New York

Grateful acknowledgment
is made to *Saturday Review—World* Magazine for permission to reprint
excerpts from an article by Dr. Arnold Mandell, October 5, 1974.

Library of Congress Cataloging in Publication Data

Klein, Dave.
The game of their lives.

1. Football—Biography. 2. Baltimore. Football
club (National League)—Biography. 3. New York (City).
Football club (National League)—Biography. I. Title.
GV939.A1K53   796.33'2'0922 [B]   76-14177
ISBN 0-394-40923-X

Manufactured in the United States of America

2 3 4 5 6 7 8 9

FIRST EDITION

For Carole, Aaron and Mindy,
Always

Author's Note

ONCE UPON A time, Pete Gent wrote a marvelous book. And Harold Rosenthal asked me to attend a press party honoring that book's paperback publication. I went because Pete and Harold are old friends.

At the party, I met Herb Schnall, the president of New American Library, a new friend. And he introduced me to Mike Seidman, an editor. Through Herb and Mike, I got the chance to write this book.

So I'd like to thank Pete for writing *North Dallas Forty* . . . Harold for thinking of me . . . Herb for believing in my project . . . Mike for his reassuring voice on the telephone through one long summer . . . and the players who agreed to let me talk to them about the game and their lives.

And for moral support, it is important to say thanks to Willie and Butch, Lew and Larry and Craig.

I wanted to do this book, but at first I didn't know how. Why, I asked, would anyone care about the left end, or the right tackle, and what they did to each other in a game played nearly twenty years ago? I have covered pro football for fifteen years, and I remember too many games, too many names. But I knew that most of them didn't mean a thing to anyone else. Yet how zealously we guard those gossamer moments. How stubbornly we cling to them. They are our futile grip on immortality. We may not be here tomorrow, but sure as hell we were here yesterday.

It has been said that men's souls turn to nostalgia. Which is reason enough for a book on a championship game in 1958. Because we want to remember more than we want to learn. And because the game brings a flood of other memories. It recalls the feel and the taste and the heady exhilaration of yesterday's youth.

But the book is not really about the game at all. It is about the men who played it. I chased across the country to find them, and I was welcomed into their homes and offices. I have met them in bars, in hotels. I have taken their time, putting their words down on tape. Then I went away with my little cassettes and put their lives and their feelings on paper. I haven't done full justice to any of them—they are complex and private, and no mechanic armed with tape recorder and a typewriter can ever plumb all the depths. But I did my best.

Many of these men were my friends, and they were easy to talk to. And those who began as strangers are strangers no more, thanks to their courtesy and cooperation. I had no idea at the beginning that there would be so much of private feelings, of non-football victories and disappointments. There were times when I felt uncomfortably like an interloper, a Peeping Tom of inner thoughts. Whatever strength the book has is due to their willingness to talk and their qualities as individuals. I want to thank each of them and to caution the reader that they are not responsible for my judgments, whether charitable or otherwise. And to all the others who played in the game but who are not in the book, my apologies. There just wasn't room.

I have written parts of this book on airplanes . . . in hotel rooms with four screaming walls . . . in places such as Cleveland and New Orleans, Acapulco and Antigua, San Diego and Cape Cod. Mostly at home. I think I liked it best at Cape Cod. The house in Welfleet didn't have a telephone and I managed to finish four chapters there. I worked each day, and when I was empty, I went to the beach with my kids and my dog.

I would rather do that than anything else.

At first I wanted to know about the game. But after a while I didn't give a damn about it, except that it gave me a hook, a reason to come to know some truly outstanding people. I am grateful to them and I hope they will approve what I have done.

Scotch Plains
July 1976

Contents

The
Game

. . . they were bent
On paths coincident
On being anon twin halves of one august event.

—"The Convergence of the Twain,"
Thomas Hardy

IT WAS NEARLY twenty years ago, on a December Sunday. A group of men played a football game, a championship game, perhaps the most memorable ever played.

This is a book about those men.

With the simplicity that comes with hindsight, we call the game memorable and the players famous. We recite plays and statistics and the final score.

That is the easy part.

This game, the 1958 National Football League championship between the New York Giants and the Baltimore Colts, was played in Yankee Stadium, in New York City. That fact alone helps explain its lasting impression. New York was and is the center of the nation's news media, and the game was covered in a different spirit than if it had been played in Cleveland or Miami.

The game deserves to be remembered. It went into sudden-death overtime—the first time ever in a championship. Its drama and excitement grabbed the nation by the nape of the neck, and shook and shook. When it was finished, nothing about pro football would ever again be the same. Once the parochial entertainment of the dozen towns that had teams, pro football emerged as a national pastime and, within a decade, a national passion. Tickets became a commodity beyond reach. People carefully deeded them to favored survivors in their wills.

Television and football were married that day, and the union has outdone even the wildest hopes for its success. Rates for advertising minutes on TV games have risen halfway to the moon. Rates for the purchase of Super Bowl minutes have orbited well beyond that. Players now receive salaries unheard-of, unthought-of, by the players of 1958.

But what of these men—as men? While the game grows in our memories, the players take on a wooden sameness as good soldiers who made that mock battle come out as it did. We forget that they still think and feel, and that they were alive long before and long after that legendary afternoon. The men who lined up for the kickoff that day could not foresee the game's significance. They were concerned with the future of pro football only as an assembly-line worker might view the future of the steel industry.

Johnny Unitas played in this game. So, too, did Frank Gifford. And Gino Marchetti. And Sam Huff. But in 1958 these names were not household words. For every sports fan who recognized them, there were five who more readily identified with Mickey Mantle, Willie Mays, Warren Spahn. Baseball. The World Series. Eight of the players in this game have already been elected to the Pro Football Hall of Fame, and others will follow. But they became household words only later, because we came to know them through television and the press.

In 1958, these men were workingmen, tradesmen, glamorous only when compared with the miners and factory workers who were their fathers and brothers. They were men without great expectations. But they were hungry, hungry enough to hide serious injuries so as not to place their positions in jeopardy. They were individualists, but they submerged their identities for the sake of the team.

"We got along so well," said Baltimore's fabled pass receiver, Raymond Berry, "because there was a deep and real respect among us, each for the other. We were very different people then . . ."

Today they are people of middle age. Today they are just men, not superstars. They are prey to the same doubts and problems that mark our own lives.

They were asked to look back at that game; indeed, to look back to what they were, in that time and place. They judge the game not only by its impact on the media and the fans, but by their personal successes and failures then and later. Many of them profited from football's burgeoning popularity, but only one, Unitas, got rich as a player. The rest simply paved the way for a new era and a new type of athlete. Since leaving the playing field, they have faced the ego-bending shock of becoming has-beens. Thrown into the more conventional world, many were ill-prepared. When football values no longer mattered, some could not cope. Yet surprisingly few became coaches, and fewer than half the men interviewed here still possess a direct tie to the game.

Now, in middle age, their memories are mellow, sometimes somber, often frankly nostalgic. They are no longer young, no longer perfect physical specimens with football talent beyond the rashest dreams of the sandlot player. And football is no longer what it was in 1958. Their youth and the game's will not come again.

These thirteen players were participants in a small piece of history —one legendary afternoon nearly two decades ago. By telling us how it looks now through their eyes, they help to fix the moment in a way no one else could. They are, by and large, proud to have played in such a game, proud to be able to say, "It was mine, I was there." But they are clear-eyed, and they tell us what the game was not, as well as what it was.

For many of them, it was not their most memorable game. For some, especially the losers, it might have been best forgotten. It was not a metaphysical confrontation between good and evil. It was merely a game played by tough, determined professionals for one year's championship. And since that Sunday afternoon they have all lived through five hundred more Sundays. Some have sons and daughters as old as they were then. Some are grandfathers.

This, then, is about men, more than about football. It is an attempt to re-create an event through memories of its participants. And it is a study of middle age, of a group of men who achieved a kind of fame early in life and for whom the middle years have been a time of often painful adjustment, different from yours and mine in degree, but not in kind. They are presented here not as heroes larger than life, but as witnesses. They are men with human flaws and failings, but men deserving of respect and sympathy.

So come . . . to 1958. Dwight Eisenhower was our president. Our Vice-president was destined to be with us for a long time, on and off. Senator John F. Kennedy was preparing to run for the presidency two years hence. Joe Namath was fifteen years old. O.J. Simpson was eleven. Don Shula was an assistant coach at the University of Virginia; the Miami Dolphins were yet unborn.

Of the twelve teams in the National Football League, the best were the Giants and the Colts. And on December 28, eleven from each team lined up for a kickoff.

They were about to play the game of their lives.

. . .

The New York Giants had won the NFL championship in 1956, defeating the Chicago Bears 47–7. In 1957, they had lost out to Cleveland. Now, in 1958, they slid through the early season without particular distinction: four wins, three losses.

"We had to win our last five games," said Frank Gifford, who in large measure was responsible for whatever offense the Giants generated. "We did . . . and we had to come from behind in each one of them in the last two minutes. I've never seen pressure like that, and I've never seen a team respond to it quite that professionally. But anyway, the last game was against Cleveland. If the Browns won it, or even if they tied us, they'd have the championship. We had to beat them.

"And we did . . ."

The game was tied at 10–10 with 4:30 to play when Pat Summerall came on for a thirty-eight-yard field goal attempt. There was a raging, blinding snowstorm swirling in Yankee Stadium, and Summerall squinted through the dusky light, swung his right foot—and missed.

But the New York defense got the ball back, and when it was fourth down it all fell to Summerall again. This, indeed, would be his final chance, the team's last gasp. And the kick would be from forty-nine yards out, a heroic attempt even in ideal weather conditions.

He kicked. The ball soared just past the reach of the massed and frantic Browns. It gained altitude, began to arc, then dipped triumphantly behind the goal posts, cleanly through.

"And you know something?" Summerall said later. "It surprised the hell out of me. I never thought I'd make it."

By winning, the Giants forced a playoff game with Cleveland to decide the Eastern Conference champion. That game, too, was in Yankee Stadium. It was a study in ferocity. No one favored the Giants, not even the home fans, who by now had grown crazed with the weekly drama and the ever-increasing intensity.

"We had already beaten Cleveland twice that season," recalled head coach Jim Lee Howell, "and nobody figured we could do it again. Hell, even I had some doubts. They had Jim Brown."

And Sam Huff beat his brains out.

This game belonged to Huff. The middle linebacker, dogging Brown's every move with the fury of an assassin, limited the fabled fullback to a net gain of eighteen yards for the game. The rest of the defense took everything else away. The Giants won, with inconceivable, impossible ease, 10–0.

And when the game had ended, with darkness already enshrouding an emptying Yankee Stadium, thousands of frozen fans lined up to buy tickets for the championship game the following Sunday. Until well past midnight, they waited there, shivering, still cheering up into the cavernous stadium, which echoed back their yells of jubilation.

The Giants were ready for the Colts. They were bruised and sore, injured and exhausted. But their pride was whole.

Baltimore had finished with the same regular-season record, 9-3-0, a single game ahead of the Chicago Bears and the Los Angeles Rams. The Colts, never having won a championship, had scrambled frantically.

"We could have won it the year before," said defensive end Gino Marchetti, "but we blew it. We collapsed in the last two games. But we knew . . . dammit, we knew . . . that we had a championship team. I think losing those two games set us up for '58. We came back that summer, and from the first day of training camp all we thought about was the championship. We had never played at that level of confidence for a full season. When I saw what we had, I knew we'd win it."

The deciding game came late in November against the San Francisco Forty-Niners. That performance showed what the Colts could do.

"We were down, twenty-seven to seven, at half time," recalls halfback Lenny Moore, "and in the locker room Weeb [Ewbank, head coach of the Colts] told us we were playing just a terrible game. We were giving up anything San Francisco wanted, and we weren't doing a damned thing on offense. I can remember, I think, that he did most of his yelling at Unitas, and John got terribly quiet and flushed. He didn't say a word, not one word, but when we came back for the second half, he played maybe the greatest half of football I've ever seen. And so did our defense. I mean, that day we could have done anything, beaten anybody. There was something magical about it."

The Colts scored four touchdowns in the second half. San Francisco was shut out.

"And when Weeb took out most of the starters," Lenny said, laughing, "we still had time for another couple of touchdowns. We were angry when he wouldn't let us go get 'em."

The Colts lost the final two games of their season. But, unlike a year before, it didn't matter. They had clinched their Conference championship, and Weeb was resting the regulars, giving the injured time to heal, girding his team for the onslaught of the Giants in the championship game.

The New York defense had limited its twelve opponents to a total of 183 points, a low figure in the league. Baltimore's defense had surrendered 203 points, the second lowest figure in the league. But the difference in offensive firepower was clear. The Colts scored better than 30 points a game, far outdistancing the rest of the teams with 381 points. They had beaten Green Bay, 56–0; Detroit, 40–14; Los Angeles, 34–7. The Giants, on the other hand, scored only 246 points. Only three of the twelve teams in the NFL had scored fewer.

And so the game began.

A crowd of 64,185—a people-packed, standing-room sellout—crammed into Yankee Stadium. It was the twenty-eighth of December, but it was mild. It was "Mara weather," named for the Giants' family ownership, so called because the Giants always seemed to receive unusually pleasant weather for their home games, November and December notwithstanding.

First Quarter

Both teams came out feinting, groping. For the first few series, neither side was expecting much. Baltimore kicked off. Don Heinrich, the second-string quarterback, started for New York. It was coach Jim Lee Howell's habit to keep Heinrich in for the first few series of downs while the Giants were feeling out the opposition. But there was no doubt that Heinrich was the warm-up. The main man, Charlie Conerly, New York's wise old veteran, was not the best quarterback in the league, but he was one of the shrewdest. He stood on the sidelines, conferring with Coach Howell and offensive coach Vince Lombardi.

Heinrich was not an unarmed reconnaissance foray. He wanted to strike, to wound, to achieve by sudden surprise. If an early attack was successful, he would not be removed. He would be a championship quarterback.

So he came out throwing. But his first attempt, to flanker Kyle Rote, the Giant captain, was batted down—scornfully, almost—by

Gino Marchetti. Heinrich's second attempt connected with halfback
Alex Webster for seven yards, putting the Giants on their own twenty-
seven, third and three. Would Heinrich look now to Frank Gifford,
the running back who had kept the Giant offense going? No. Now yet
another pass, a crisp, across-the-middle route by Rote. Incomplete.
The punt was to Baltimore's thirty.

And now the Johnny Unitas offense trotted onto the field. It was
already clear that Unitas was special, that he could throw the football
like few men alive. But his offense ran into the Giants' defense, which
was playing for a championship at home. Halfback Lenny Moore got
the first handoff, but the Giants' Carl Karilivacz came up from the
cornerback position, forced the play and smeared the flyer for a
three-yard loss. Now fullback Alan Ameche bulled up the middle,
gaining seven, putting the ball on the Colts' thirty-four. And then, for
the first time, Unitas danced back to pass. But Sam Huff, the Giants'
middle linebacker, charged past unprepared linemen, and crashed
into the quarterback with his own brand of fury. Unitas fumbled.
Giant Jimmy Patton was there to recover on the Colts' thirty-seven.

This was Heinrich's moment. The ball was close. The Colts were
stung by this early setback. Could he fool them? Sure. They would
expect him to pass, to go right for the jugular, to take advantage of
the sudden uncertainty.

He tried to cross them up. He sent Webster on a slant, guard Jack
Stroud leading with a block. But Webster was stopped for a one-yard
loss on the thirty-eight.

Now Heinrich had to pass. But, as Unitas had done, he tried to drop
back too quickly. He fumbled the snap. A split second after the ball
hit the ground, Marchetti landed on it, and gave Baltimore new life.

And Unitas blew another chance. He hit L.G. Dupre for four yards
on a swing pass. Dupre went up the middle for a yard. And on third
down, Unitas went to tight end Jim Mutscheller on a sideline pattern.
But Karilivacz cut across the tight end's body and snared the ball on
the New York forty, returning it five yards to the forty-five. Karilivacz, who would be exploited so ruthlessly later, was a hero for a
moment. The crowd cheered lustily.

Then the Giant offense screwed it up again. Gifford lost a yard.
Fullback Mel Triplett was held for no gain. Heinrich threw to Triplett, but the pass gained just six yards. For the second time, Chandler

punted. The Colts' receiver was tackled by Ed Hughes on Baltimore's fifteen.

This was where the Giant defense lived, rising up when the other side was struggling near its end zone, denying all hope of escape, forcing either a fumble or an interception or, at best, a punt.

But Unitas arrogantly stood behind a wall of blocking on the first-down play and threw the bomb to Lenny Moore. Sixty yards were gained on that play. Moore hauled it in on the Giants' forty and ran to the twenty-five.

Now the New York defense had been stung. It was confused and frantic, right? Wrong. The warriors fought back.

Ameche made five yards up the middle to the twenty. Then a swarm of Giants stopped Dupre for a one-yard loss. When the Colts came out for the next play, the Giants were moving—stunting, looping, distracting Unitas. He went to his memory file of audibles, but the Giants kept shifting. The whistle blew, and the Colts were moved back to the Giants' twenty-six on a delay-of-game penalty. It was third and eleven. Moore gained two. It was fourth down.

Steve Myhra came in to try for a field goal from thirty-one yards. It was wide. But the Giants were offsides. Now the ball was on the nineteen. Myhra was closer. He wouldn't miss again, would he? No one will ever know. Huff roared through the line on the left side of the center and blocked the kick. Katcavage recovered the ball. It belonged to New York, on the twenty-two-yard line.

The defense left the field to a standing ovation, great waves of sound cresting and breaking on the field from the triple-tiered stadium. And seconds later the din only increased, for Conerly was coming in.

He had seen enough. Now he wanted to taste it.

His first call was a simple slant on which Alex Webster gained nothing. But now he threw to Triplett, who swung out of the backfield behind the linebacker. Triplett caught the ball and gained nine yards. Now, finally, the Golden Boy, Frank Gifford, swept left end. Blocks by Rosey Brown and Kyle Rote left the path open. Gifford danced down the sideline for thirty-eight delicious yards, to Baltimore's thirty-one.

Now Triplett charged up the middle for two more. But a pass to Rote fell short, and another to Webster was aborted from the start when Webster slipped and fell running his route. It was fourth and eight. Summerall came in and kicked a thirty-six-yard field goal.

The Giants led, 3–0, at 12:58 of the first quarter.

The quarter ended four plays later. Unitas hit Moore for five. Dupre made three on a trap. But Unitas to Moore was incomplete, the Giants' Linden Crow in the way. And Brown punted to the New York twenty-eight. Crow received the kick, circled back to find room to run and was caught from behind on the eighteen.

But still, the Giants had the lead. The defense was unyielding. Even the offense had life this day. All was well.

The hell it was.

Second Quarter

How quickly this game changed.

Conerly, looking for more big yardage from Gifford, threw him a sideline pass to the left. It was complete. The wall of blocking was there. But Frank fumbled the ball and the Colts' Big Daddy Lipscomb joyfully threw his three hundred pounds on the ball. The Colts had it on the New York twenty.

There was not a sound as the Giant defense once more trudged onto the field. Only the small core of Baltimore fans who had made the trek north cheered. It was a lonely noise.

Moore ran for four yards. Ameche ran for five. Third and one. Unitas was taking no chances now. Ameche up the middle, the pop-sock-scream of the short-yardage play, and he made one. It was first down on the ten. No stopping them now, these fired-up Colts. Unitas faked to Ameche up the middle, and then spun to hand the ball to Lenny Moore, who danced around the left end. Only Jimmy Patton saved the touchdown, making an ankle-tackle at the two.

But he had saved it for just one play.

The signal was barked . . . the snap was made . . . Ameche came roaring up behind Unitas, took the ball and crashed into the end zone. The Horse had done his work. The Colts had scored. Myhra's conversion made it 7–3, Baltimore.

Bert Rechichar kicked off for the Colts. Triplett took the ball on the twelve and returned it to the New York thirty-three. Trailing now, Conerly had to move quickly.

Triplett gained a yard. Conerly flicked a pass over the defensive line to the sure-handed Rote, a fourteen-yard gain to New York's forty-eight. The Giants were moving. It would be one of those games.

No, it wouldn't.

Conerly was smothered by Marchetti and Donovan at his thirty-nine, a nine-yard loss. Webster gained four yards on a trick play that really didn't work. On third down, Conerly tried the swing pass, the flare to Gifford. It was incomplete. So Chandler came out to punt, and he boomed it. High and spiraling, far and deep, it came down in the hands of Jack Simpson.

Time for another reversal. Simpson fumbled, and New York's Mel Guy recovered. By God, the Giants were on the Baltimore ten. They were about to recapture their lead, and the crowd exploded in a roar of ear-splitting noise.

On the first play, Gifford fumbled again. Joyce of the Colts recovered on the fourteen. Deathly silence now, the crowd watching in disbelief as the teams changed. Not again. Not so close. That damned Gifford.

"I felt really bad about that one," says Gifford now, "because it was a fourteen-point fumble. The touchdown we were going to get, and the one the Colts got when they took the ball away. If I had to pick a spot where the game began to turn, there it was. And it was all my fault."

And Baltimore did, indeed, score. It was Unitas at his best, putting on a fifteen-play drive that consumed eighty-six yards and ate up most of the rest of the second quarter. It was beautiful.

From the fourteen, John went for broke. He tried a deep pass to Dupre. Incomplete.

Then he hit Raymond Berry (for the first time) for five. Then he hit Ameche for ten. The Colts were on their twenty-nine. Now Moore skirted right end for ten more. Ameche roared through the middle and added six before Huff poleaxed him at the Baltimore forty-five. The Giant defense was breaking down.

Moore tried the inside route and found room enough for four yards. Then Ameche slammed for two more, putting the ball in Giant territory, on the forty-nine. It was first down.

Unitas hit Berry on the forty, but it was ruled out of bounds. Dupre ran a slant for three. Unitas, back to pass, saw his receivers covered. So he dodged a tackler and ran it himself, startling the Giants with a sixteen-yard gain to their thirty.

First down again. Moore made one. The Colts were flagged for illegal motion in the backfield, and the ball went back to the New York thirty-four. But it was only a temporary setback. Unitas went to his bread-and-butter, Berry. The pass was good for thirteen yards to the twenty-one. And on third down, Ameche cracked through for six to the fifteen. Another first down.

No more running now. Unitas had seen his opening. On first down, he sent Berry to the left corner of the end zone. Berry found the seam —behind Patton, in front of Em Tunnell. It was a touchdown. Myhra converted. The Colts led 14–3, and the Giants were dying. Perhaps not dead. Not yet. But sure as hell on their way. Baltimore's defense was stifling, and Baltimore's offense was a smoothly-oiled, piston-propelled machine. It was just a matter of time. Everyone could see it.

The shaken Giants took the kickoff and ran out the clock in three plays—King, Conerly and Webster carrying—too shaken to take another chance on putting the ball in the air.

The crowd was hushed.

Half Time

That the score was "only" 14–3 would have been surprising to one studying the statistics amassed during the first two quarters.

Baltimore had registered nine first downs; New York, two. Baltimore's total yardage figure of 198 was far superior to New York's 86. The Colts had passed for 115 yards, the Giants for 39. Eighty-three rushing yards by Baltimore overshadowed the 47 by New York. Unitas had hit on 8 of 12 passes, Heinrich 2 for 4, Conerly 3 for 6.

There was strategy brewing in the New York locker room during the break. It revolved chiefly around Gifford, but not because of his fumbles. Vince Lombardi had decided that because Frank was the Giants' most feared player the Baltimore defensive plan was to keep him cornered. It had worked, but only because the Giants had not compensated.

What if the same plays designed for Gifford were used as fakes? Decoys could pull the Colts out of position for counter-plays, motion going against the grain, away from where the overanxious Colts were going each time Gifford moved.

They were all in on it now. A subtle excitement built and sustained itself on hope. The defense? Hell, the defense wasn't worried.

"Stop fucking it up," said Huff, "and we'll bring you their fucking heads."

And so, armed with new optimism, trailing 14–3, the Giants hit the field. The Colts were there, buoyed by their lead, confident of victory, more ferocious than ever because a trailing team does desperate things that lead to still more errors.

Third Quarter

Before the "new offense" could get in gear, the defense was tested again.

The Colts' first possession resulted in just one first down before Huff and Company caught Moore for a seven-yard loss and forced a punt. Huff and Don Shinnick came to blows on this series and had to be pried apart. Had this not been a championship game, both might have been ejected.

The Giants took over but got nowhere. Three plays netted minus-eight yards. Chandler punted, and Moore took the ball with a fair catch on the Baltimore forty-one.

Excellent field position. The game was about to crack wide open. Unitas, on the first play, dropped a bomb to Mutscheller, whom the Giants had nearly ignored in order to cover the faster Moore and the more precise Berry. So Big Jim took the ball for a gain of thirty-two yards, to the Giant twenty-seven.

Here they came.

Dupre ran for one. On second down, Unitas to Berry was incomplete, but Unitas to Berry on third down was good for eleven, and a first down on the Giant fifteen. Unitas threw to Moore down the right sideline for another dozen yards. First down on the three.

Good night, Giants . . . Good night, Giants.

But Huff remembers this as the turning point. "There was just no way they were gonna score," he said. "We were like wild animals out there. They weren't gonna get a damned thing."

Ameche drove up the middle for two yards, setting the ball three feet from another touchdown. Unitas tried for it on a sneak and got nothing, Grier, Huff and Modzelewski burying him at the line of scrimmage. But surely Ameche could get the one yard. He tried the middle, too, and was nearly ripped in half by Grier and Huff.

It was fourth down, but Baltimore wasn't going to settle for a field goal. Not from the one-yard line.

Unitas got cute. He looked up at the bunched New York defense, which was wisely waiting for Ameche's blast up the middle, and called a play that would send Ameche wide to the right with a carefully timed pitchout.

No sooner had Ameche touched the ball than he was pulled down by Livingston, who had seen the play coming. The Giants had held. The defense had prevented the touchdown, and now the offense came out on its own five-yard line. The score was still 14–3, not 17–3 or 21–3. There was one more chance.

Zap! Gifford ran for five. Webster ripped open the middle for three more. It was third down, two to go, on the New York thirteen. Run now, because passing is dangerous that close to your own end zone. Run now, with Gifford on the right. Or with Triplett up the middle. Or with Webster slanting off tackle.

Run now.

"They thought so," said Conerly. "So we passed."

It was perhaps the most spectacular play of the game to that point. Conerly faked that pitch-right to Gifford, and the Baltimore defense reacted violently. But Charlie still had the ball, and Rote was breaking across the field. Now Rote had Conerly's pass tucked under his arm, alone, in the clear.

Rote ran. Baltimore chased. Rote was tackled on the Baltimore twenty-five. Then he fumbled.

"I didn't really fumble," he insists. "The guy pulled the ball away. But there it was, on the goddamn ground, and I just went numb. You know what? Thank God for Alex Webster."

Big Alex, who had trailed the play to provide a block, ran down the ball. He picked it up in huge, meat hook hands, and ran. He was hauled down by an army of crazed tacklers at the one. But there were the Giants, eighty-six yards downfield from where the play had begun. Now there would be a game. Now the Giants were alive.

Webster was stopped for no gain. But then Triplett bulled his way up the middle on the next play for the touchdown. Summerall kicked the extra point. Baltimore's lead had been shaved to 14–10. Now the momentum was New York's. Now, as Huff says, "They were waiting to see what we would do; they were the ones who were worried. We had it going."

The noise in Yankee Stadium was a very real weapon. It was incredible, wave after wave cresting in the rafters, hurtling down and smashing on the field. You never heard noise like that. Certainly the Colts never had. They froze.

Chandler kicked off, and the Colts had three plays. On the second play, Modzelewski sacked Unitas for a seven-yard loss. The fourth play was a punt, Don Maynard taking it for the Giants and returning to the nineteen.

And here they came, in a drive that would bridge the third and fourth quarters. Webster slashed for three. Conerly did the "yes-Gifford-no-Gifford" number again, and spun around to hit Schnelker breaking over the middle for a seventeen-yard gain to the New York thirty-nine. The quarter ended. But not the din.

Fourth Quarter

No one, no team, no defense was going to stop the Giants now. As the defense looked on almost disbelieving, the offense moved like a machine.

The first play was from the Giants' thirty-nine.

Conerly came right back to Schnelker, and this time the play was even more successful. The hulking tight end took the ball down to the Baltimore fifteen. It was a gain of forty-six yards, and the Colts appeared stricken by a sudden paralysis. The game was being wrested from their hands. They were being blasted out of the stadium by a second-class offense.

From the fifteen, with Conerly now sure that Baltimore was befuddled, the Giants went back to their first-half game plan. Gifford broke with the snap of the ball, threw out his hands as if to take the pitch, then kept going into the right corner of the end zone. The ball was there. He made the catch. Touchdown.

The Giants had taken the lead, 17–14. The defense was all fists and knees, forearms and shoulder smashes. Still, the Colts took the ball and moved from their twenty to the Giants' thirty-nine. Ameche lost one from there. Unitas failed on a long pass to Dupre. He tried one to Moore, and Huff batted the ball down out of the air. On fourth down, Rechichar tried a forty-six-yard field goal. (He was used on the long ones, not Myhra.) The attempt was short.

Now the game turned cautious. The Giants had the lead and the ball, and the clock was working for them. Reserve fullback Phil King made four to the twenty-four. Conerly hit Ken MacAfee, an old pro in his final season, with a fifteen-yarder to the thirty-nine. First down. But Gifford lost three. Then Triplett, crossing up the defense, skirted left end for seven to the forty-four, and Gifford flashed for ten more to the Baltimore forty-six. First down. Touchdown drive gathering steam.

Gifford made four more.

And Phil King fumbled on the Baltimore forty-two, and the ball squirted away from several hopeful arms. It was kicked backwards, toward the Giants' end zone, and it was finally recovered by the Colts' Ordell Braase on the New York forty-two.

Unitas, keenly aware of the dramatic shift of the tide, struck for everything on the first play. It was that fly pattern to Moore, the one Giant defensive coach Tom Landry dreamed nightmares about. The pass carried to the corner near the New York goal line, and Moore was there, forlornly chased by Crow and Tunnell.

And Moore caught the ball—out . . . of . . . bounds. Moore ranted and raved. Moore was nearly thrown out of the game. But he could not change the decision. No play. An incomplete pass. The Giants were saved.

Unitas threw to Berry, but Karilivacz broke it up. On third down, he hit Berry for eleven, to the New York thirty-one. First down.

Dupre slammed off right guard for four, to the New York twenty-seven. It seemed the game was turning again, but the Giant defense struck back, awesome and awful in its determination.

Unitas went back to pass, and Giant end Andy Robustelli beat Jim Parker off the ball. He flew toward the quarterback and crunched him to the ground for an eleven-yard loss.

Again Unitas faded back, and from the middle of the line came Modzelewski. He cracked him down for another loss, this one for nine yards. The Colts, who had been so close, were now too far. They were on the Giants' forty-seven. It was fourth and twenty-six. They punted.

"We just had to keep the ball, run out the clock, and they'd never get another chance," said Webster. "We were so hot . . . everything was working so well . . . it sure looked like our game."

And so, for perhaps the last time, the Giants took the ball on their nineteen. And Conerly, aware of the clock, kept the ball on the ground. Webster drove for five, and after Gifford was stopped for no gain Charlie had to pass. He threw to Webster, who had circled out of the backfield, and it was a ten-yard gain, and a first down. No first down had ever been as crucial.

Webster ran for one to the thirty-five. Gifford added five more to the forty. It was third down, four to go. Just two minutes remained. With a first down now, the Giants could kill the clock.

What to call? Conerly, in the huddle, surrounded by his tough, experienced players, offered up a run for Gifford. No one dissented. But Gifford didn't like the play.

"Charlie wanted to call a Power-47, with me taking the ball and Trip leading me into the tackle hole. But I changed it in the huddle myself, to our '69' play. I wanted Trip going up the middle, for some kind of a distraction to Baltimore."

The ball was snapped. Gifford took Conerly's handoff. Triplett, though, had first faked getting the ball, driving up the middle. It worked. Some of the Colts tackled him viciously. Gifford had the ball wide to the right.

At some point in the play, someone screamed—Gino Marchetti was down on the ground, writhing in pain. His leg was broken. A moment later, Gifford was tackled. Had he made it?

"It was close," Gifford says, "but listen, I've been playing football all my life. There was no question that I made it. By the time they untangled everybody . . . and I looked where they put the ball . . . Christ, before I could even gripe about it, Ronnie Gibbs [the referee] said, 'Fourth down.' And you can't argue about it. It was never in my nature to begin with, and it wouldn't have done any good. That was the play when Marchetti broke his leg, and in all the confusion, with him laying on the ground screeching and all, the ball did get kicked around. I just know, in my mind, I made it. Unquestionable.

"In fact, I confronted Gibbs after the game. You know, it's hard. I wouldn't want to indict him. But he was . . . as I recall, without trying to quote him, it was, 'Well, I blew it.' Which is understandable, with all the confusion and Marchetti and all that. And besides, it wasn't that big a deal then. We had Chandler to punt and he was the best in the league."

Several of the Giants, mostly the offensive linemen, fought with Howell, pleading with him to go for the first down. "We only needed four inches," says Jack Stroud. "We would have run through a brick wall at that point. Besides, Marchetti was out, and whoever they put in for him couldn't have been as good. And he would have been nervous, tight, ready for it to happen to him. And it would have gone at him, and dammit, it would have worked."

But Howell chose to punt the ball and Gifford agreed: "Chandler led the league that year in punting . . . and we were tired, dead tired. I'm not sure we would have made it, anyway. Besides, the percentages were all on our side. Baltimore had to come a long way in a short time, with only one time-out left."

Chandler punted. He boomed it high and deep, and it was fair, caught by Taseff on the Colts' fourteen. Baltimore was eighty-six yards away, though, of course, they would need less for the tying field goal. But time was running out.

What happened next is the stuff of legend, and the hero was Johnny Unitas.

"Two things were important here," he said. "We had to concentrate on getting the ball up the field, which meant we had to pass, not eat up the clock by running. But the Giants knew that. So we had to pass in a way they wouldn't expect."

The New York defense was primarily concerned about the long pass that would snatch away the game. The defenders played off the Colts' receivers in a "prevent" alignment. And they tried to guard the sidelines, because a completed pass stops the clock only if the receiver gets out of bounds after making the catch.

So Unitas threw over the middle. His first two passes—to Mutscheller and Dupre—were incomplete, thrown into the howling asylum of the Giant defenders. But on third down he found Moore for eleven. The first down kept him alive.

He threw incomplete to Dupre. But then it began to break. He dropped back and found Berry isolated on Karilivacz. Berry made Karilivacz disappear. Complete for twenty-five yards to midfield. First down, less than a minute to play.

Again to Berry, again Karilivacz disappeared, again a completion. Fifteen yards this time, to the New York thirty-five. First down. Clock running. The crowd in agony.

Certainly now he would throw to someone else. Wrong. Berry

again. Deep, across the middle of the field, Giants scurrying to find him, to arrest his unique and ruthless moves before he was open. Too late. He was open. He caught the ball on the New York thirteen, a gain of twenty-two yards. Three straight passes had gained sixty-two yards, had moved the Colts from their twenty-five to New York's thirteen.

In came Myhra, shaken with the prospect of what he had to do. Myhra hadn't been one of the more reliable kickers during the season, having made just four of ten field goal tries. And he was tired, having played much of the game as a reserve linebacker.

The clock was running. One of the fans in the stands remembers that Myhra ran onto the field with nineteen seconds remaining, and when his foot touched the ball there were seven ticks left. The referee's hands went up. The kick was good. (Some say it was not, that it sailed inches to the outside of that left upright.) The score was 17–17.

Never before had a championship game ended in a deadlock. For a moment, the crowd remained hushed, as if wondering what would happen next, what additional torment lay in store for them. There was no voice not hoarse, no throat not raw, no body not spent.

The team captains walked back to the middle of the field, a coin was flipped and the Giants won. They chose to receive.

And from somewhere, from some perverse spirit that knows no other way, the cheering began again. Louder, but more unsure. Wilder, but less confident. A cheering, perhaps, in anticipation of defeat. A cheering that said "Well done" no matter what else took place.

Sudden Death

The Giants, totally without energy, kept the ball for three plays. Gifford ran for four yards to the New York twenty-four. Conerly tried a pass to Schnelker, but it was incomplete. On third and six, Conerly ran it himself and made five. But five was not six. And the New York twenty-nine was not the New York thirty.

Chandler punted, and the Colts took over on their twenty. And Unitas was coming back out.

Could he do it again? We know he did, taking thirteen plays to score the winning touchdown. There was no time pressure now, but that's not to say there was no pressure. Starting from the twenty, he sent Dupre on a sweep for eleven yards and a first down. But then he got into trouble. A long pass to Moore was incomplete, and Dupre got two on the ground. It was third and eight. But once again Johnny found the play. He threw to Ameche on a flare pattern. Complete for eight yards to the forty-one. First down.

Again the Giant defense looked like a winner. They held Dupre to three yards. Then Modzelewski roared past the Colt line to get Unitas in the backfield for a loss of eight yards. Third and fifteen, and the crowd began to roar again.

But whatever decides ball games like this one—luck, intelligence, stamina—was now with the Colts. Unitas later said that the ground plays had set up his next call. It was a pass to Raymond Berry, complete to the Giant forty-three-yard line—twenty-one yards and a first down. Then, before the defense could recover, Ameche came up the middle on a draw play for twenty-three yards. The ball was placed on the New York twenty, and the fate of the Giants was sealed. The defense had finally come apart.

After a pile-up at the line of scrimmage, Unitas went to Berry again. Complete for twelve yards to the Giants' eight. On first down, Ameche gained a yard. Then Unitas hit Mutscheller at the one on the right sideline. First they would try for the TD on third down, then perhaps kick the field goal on fourth.

No decision was necessary. On third down, Alan Ameche took the handoff and scored. The crowd was no longer screaming as the defeated home team and new champions left the field exhausted. Three-score men and six had played the game of their lives.

Postscript

Marchetti, his leg broken, had ordered the stretcher-bearers to put him down in the end zone while the Colts drove for the tying field goal. "I didn't want to be inside someplace," he said. "This was my game, too." But he was carried off when the sudden-death period began, and lay alone in the visiting team's locker room for its duration. "When I didn't hear much noise, I knew we were moving," he said. "Then the door flew open, and one of our safeties—Ray Brown, I think—came running in. Before he yelled, I knew we had won it. The crowd was very quiet."

Statistically and artistically, the Colts deserved the game. But for the Giants, older and tired, it was a hard one to lose.

"I remember sitting on the bench next to Charlie," says Frank Gifford. "Man, we were really beat. Charlie . . . I never saw him like that, he was just exhausted. And we watched it happen and he says, 'Wow, I can't go any more,' and we watched it and then, just before they scored to tie it up, I said, 'Boy, you're gonna have to go some more,' and he said, 'I can't, I just can't.'

"When it went into overtime, we just didn't have any life left. They were a better ball club, and we had played well above our heads to come back and take the lead in the second half. When they tied us, they had the game won. I knew it. Charlie knew it. And deep down, I think we all knew it."

The two teams played again a year later for the championship, with virtually the same players. This time it was not as close, at least in the fourth quarter. The Giants were ahead 9–7, but then Unitas and the Colt pass defense scored 24 points to win the game, 31–16. After that, although both teams appeared in later title games, they were never "up" in the same season. Within five years, the nucleus of both teams began to drift away. The offensive and defensive "geniuses" who worked for the Giants under Coach Jim Lee Howell departed to pursue their own careers—Vince Lombardi in Green Bay and Tom Landry in Dallas. In 1963, Weeb Ewbank, fired from the Baltimore organization, became coach of the New York Jets in the new AFL. Ultimately, he beat his old team in the third Super Bowl (and, incidentally, beat the Giants again, this time in the contest for the hearts and dollars of New York fans).

As for the players, most of them drifted quietly out of the fans' range of view. Like other players before and since, they came back to camp a step or two slower and lost their jobs to a younger candidate. Or they got hurt and never really recovered. Or they were traded. Except in the memories of the hard-core faithful, they just faded away.

Today, out of uniform and out of the spotlight, some of these men seem different; others are nearly unchanged. But they are still vividly alive, men of middle age with experiences and maturity that make them more interesting now than they might have been the day after the game. Time dulls the reflexes and slows the legs, but it can sharpen the mind and round out the character. These men may have faded away as football players. As men they are still very much here.

Sam Huff

. . . Unitas fumble recovered by Patton after *Huff* tackle
on 37

. . . Myhra field goal from 27 blocked by *Huff*

. . . Unitas to Moore broken up by *Huff*

. . . Ameche plus 6 to 45, *Huff* tackle

. . . Unitas no gain on quarterback sneak, *Huff* tackle

"In football, you take on a guy across the line, and you know if you defeat him you can win the game. It's basic. You know where you stand."

SAM HUFF PLAYED middle linebacker for the New York Giants for eight years. In that time, he became the beneficiary, the focal point, the identity, for the Giants' vaunted defense. If Andy Robustelli was deadly and sinister, if Rosey Grier was massive and gargantuan, if Emlen Tunnell was the classic safety, if Tom Landry was lean and mean, if Harland Svare was a smiling assassin, if Jim Katcavage was a glazed-eyed killer, then Sam Huff was the depository for all the glory.

He was the middle linebacker in a time and place when entire defenses were based on the concept that a 4-3 alignment was a funnel, and that the neck of the funnel was the middle linebacker.

He had a football player's mentality—brutal and brutish, quick and clever—and he even had a football player's name.

Huff.

Short. Hard. Harsh. The stands would ring with the chant of the faithful: "Huff, Huff, Huff, Huffhuffhuffhuff." He captured the aura of that defense. He was its identity. If the tackle made a magnificent play to cut down a ball carrier, it was Huff who finished him off. If the end forced, and turned the ball carrier in, it was Huff who nailed him. If the cornerback took away the pass pattern, forcing the receiver to cut for the middle, it was Huff whose forearm leveled him, flat.

Arnold Mandell, a psychiatrist in San Diego, in a study of football players, has characterized the middle linebacker as follows: "In time of war, he is the ideal man to be sent on an infiltration assignment behind enemy lines. He will be intelligent enough, believable enough and charming enough to get past the guards; and he will be ruthless enough to assassinate his target swiftly, cleanly, and without a touch of remorse."

And that was Sam Huff, a wily country boy, something of a braggart, a con man, a self-server. In short, the classic middle linebacker. He had the drive to excel, a drive thrust forth from an insatiable ego. He loved the adulation; he adored the notoriety. He reveled in the glory; he worshiped the fame.

He is charming. He is quick. He is able to hold up his end of many far-ranging conversations. He smiles quickly, easily. He is a perfect host. But deep underneath, the listener gets a feeling he is being used, being had. At bottom, Huff is somewhat reserved, somewhat skeptical of other people's claims.

And he is still the middle linebacker, though long since retired to a desk. He still defends his kind, still lashes out at others. And some of "the others" are teammates—offensive teammates. He knows now, as he knew then, that the defense was the heart of the Giants, and he is blissful in his knowledge that he was the heart of the defense.

Sam will bridle noticeably when it is suggested that he was a manufactured hero, that perhaps no other player in the history of the professional game fell into just such an ideal set of circumstances at just such an ideal time.

He was in New York. That meant a great deal.

He was a middle linebacker, the quarterback of the defense, the name.

He was with a team that needed a strong defense to compensate for a sometimes sluggish, unspectacular offense.

He had the right name. Huff. Not Nitschke, not George, not Grabowski or Cherlawicz or Federspiel. Huff. Short and hard and tough and simple. Basic, elemental.

Being in New York, and being a middle linebacker, and being possessed of such a perfect name, he became the star of a 1960 CBS documentary on defense, entitled "The Violent World of Sam Huff." It was he who was wired for sound, he who was followed by cameras during a game. It was his voice barking commands, cracking expletives, screaming at the enemy. It was he who suddenly became a household word, at the very moment when pro football was on the brink of its golden, glittering age.

It was not "The Violent World of Ray Nitschke," nor "The Violent World of Bill George." It could have been. Many say it should have been. But the overriding truth is that it was not. It was "The Violent World of Sam Huff." Short. Hard. Basic.

And Sam Huff, today a vice-president for Marriott Hotels, Inc., talks about the 1958 NFL championship game as a member of that New York defense. And only that.

"I think we played a great game . . . yes, defensively. We played the same type game we always played. And it was two great defenses going at each other. And the fact that we gave them so many breaks in the early part of the game even said a lot for the Giant defense. We were able to hold the Colts, and they had a lot of opportunities. It was a very hard-hitting, hard-fought game. Defensively. It was much more hard-hitting than you see in today's games, because in those days everybody considered himself a hitter, took great pride in their hitting. The physical contact in that game was as great as you'll ever, ever see.

"The execution was so much greater than what you see in . . . for instance, today's Super Bowls. I mean, I've never seen anything like the one where Tarkenton hands off and fumbles the ball and it goes into the end zone and is recovered for a safety . . . I mean, that's a very rare thing. I never saw that in a championship game.

"Hell, we saw fumbles once in a while. In that '58 game, we were the ones that fumbled."

But he didn't mean "we." He meant "they": the offense, Frank Gifford.

"It seemed like he used to carry the ball kind of wide all the time. Seemed like he used to have more fumbles . . . I don't know, maybe it's just my imagination.

"And we had Mel Triplett, who didn't have the greatest hands in the world.

"But I guess the best team won that game . . . the reason I say that is their defense was just about equal to ours . . . I don't think it was quite as good as ours . . . but I think their offense was better than ours.

"But that had been our trouble all through those years. The offense was never quite as good as the defense. And whenever we came up against the Green Bay Packers or the Baltimore Colts—who had great balance both offensively and defensively—the edge would go to them. They could control our offense to where our offense couldn't score, and if they got a break or two their offense would be right there in field goal position.

"The games we won . . . we shut a lot of teams out, like we went three games in succession and never scored a touchdown, and we won two of them just by kicking field goals and playing great defense. We never had high-scoring games. If I had to rate any team as being the finest club ever put together, I'd have to say it was the Baltimore Colts of '58 and '59, because it was offense and defense. And for a long period of time, it was the Green Bay Packers under Vince Lombardi. And now, I guess, it would be the Miami Dolphins and the Pittsburgh Steelers.

"Our teams . . . well, you'd have to rate the defense up there with any defense in history. Perhaps it was the finest defense ever put together. But the offense didn't have great speed . . . it had a good offensive line . . . and Charlie Conerly at quarterback didn't have the rifle arm of Unitas or the accuracy of Y.A. Tittle; he knew what he could do and he did it, very well, much like Fran Tarkenton . . .

"And he certainly didn't have the fast receivers that Tarkenton has, a backfield without great speed. But don't get me wrong, he had some great players. Alex Webster . . . you know, boy, if you needed three or four yards, he was tough to stop.

"But maybe if we would have had the '61, '62, '63 offense with the '58 and '59 defense . . . those combinations might have ranked right up there with the Packers, with the Colts. But we didn't have the offense-defense combination."

Huff's attitude in the 1958 game was fatalistic once the tying field goal had been kicked with seconds left.

"I felt we had lost it then. Myhra wasn't the greatest field goal kicker in the world, but he made that one, the biggest one of his life. And a ballplayer can feel momentum changing . . . and when they marched down from their fourteen, momentum changed. And in the overtime, well, they just kept marching and we couldn't stop them. Even great defenses can be beaten, by a great offense, and that Unitas-Berry team was maybe the greatest for pass gains. Also, we got a guy that year, Carl Karilivacz . . . he's dead now . . . from Detroit. The Giants liked veteran ballplayers then. But it was very difficult . . . they called it a 'clique,' in New York we called it 'togetherness' . . . it was a defense that was really together, enjoyed playing together . . . enjoyed the game . . . and it was very difficult for Carl coming into our system. He really could not make the transition into our system in one year. And I felt this was a weakness, and the Colts felt this was a weakness.

"Carl did not have the greatest speed in the world, and he was playing against Raymond Berry, who had the greatest moves in the world. When you have a slow receiver, the best thing to do is take his timing away from him. The bump-and-run is what put Raymond Berry out of football, I think. You know, a fast defensive back will belt him, run with him, step on his foot, hit him with an elbow . . . anything to distract him. I think Carl played off Berry, gave him too much room . . . and I think Berry was one of the few receivers in all of football who would really sacrifice his life to catch the football. Lot of guts . . . lot of courage.

"He'd come across that middle knowing the linebacker was going to hit him, and if he got past that linebacker the next one was going to hit him. Most receivers will not come across the middle like that and catch the football. Berry was one who would do it, and Unitas knew it. When Unitas needed the yardage, he'd go to Berry.

"But we had Carl and that was that. We only had thirty-three players on the roster, and who were they going to put in there? There wasn't anybody else. Hell, we played those years with only four defensive linemen, and I think in '59 somebody got hurt and we had to put in Frank Youso, an offensive tackle.

"So we tried to help him with the linebackers. You know, you loosen the linebackers up, and you have to give up something when you do that because you can't play the run hard and play the pass hard, too. We tried to get myself and Harland Svare into those passing zones to take that quick slant away from Berry. When we did that, of course, Unitas would counter with those quick traps, with Alan Ameche coming up the middle.

"That's the way he worked it. He was a master at it. When you expected a run, he'd pass. When you expected a pass, he'd come with the run.

"But I can't say that was my most memorable game. So many things affect a player's mind, little things. When I came to the Redskins . . . I think we talked about this once . . . and I came back into Yankee Stadium the next year, and sixty-five thousand fans gave me a standing ovation, that was a memorable time. Nothing will ever replace that. One thing happened in Washington here, too. I had played eleven and a half years and never missed a game, never missed a practice, and I got hurt in a game, one of my own men, big defensive tackle named Spain Musgrove, hit me instead of their quarterback, and really sprained my ankle severely, ripped the muscles away from the ankle bone. So I missed four games, and I was very depressed about it.

"I wanted to play. I could run, but I couldn't walk. I'd take a pain pill, a Darvon, and it wouldn't bother me. Then, five games later, the defensive coach asked me if I could play. We were getting behind and we had to stop them. I said, 'Certainly I can play.' And the fans in Washington realized I was back, and they gave me a standing ovation. And at least we turned it around and tied the Eagles, twenty-eight to twenty-eight. It was a big moment in my life. It was a tremendous feeling, to feel that you can lead a group of guys, that you have the charisma to change a game around. It's like being in the Army . . . one guy can change a battle, turn things around.

"It wasn't like that in those days [before The Game]. If you remember, they didn't even introduce the defense. It was just the offense. And when they drafted guys, it was for the offense, and if they couldn't make it there they'd send them to the defense. The guys on offense were the heroes . . . but when we got successful, they started introducing the defense to stop the offensive from being booed in Yankee Stadium.

"In those days, we felt the defense on the Giants was like a separate team. It's true, and maybe to a ridiculous degree. We even had our own dressing room in training camp . . . there was a lot of competition between units. We really went at each other. We even had pre-scrimmage talks, pep talks . . . guys would get up and, you know, say things. Like, 'That Frank Gifford, he walks around here like he's making a movie, like he's in Hollywood, and he's making all that money.' Agitating things like that, just to get up for scrimmages."

It takes a particular psyche to excel at defense. It requires a peculiar twist of mind, a desire to inflict pain, to hurt, to punish. Can background be a factor? Can conditions of youth play an important role? Is Sam Huff the product of a specifically structured childhood? There is a streak of meanness, not very subtle, in this man, as there is in every defensive standout. Some have called these traits aberrations. Mike Curtis, who for a time in the early 1970's was the game's top middle linebacker, freely admitted, "I like to hit people, and if it wasn't for football I'd be in jail. I couldn't do on the street what I do on the field."

The defensive player is the hunter; the offensive player, his prey, his victim. In 1960, Hall of Fame middle linebacker Chuck Bednarik leveled Gifford with a blind-side tackle. Gifford almost died from severe head injuries. And frozen in an unforgettable picture is Bednarik jumping up and down with joy, while Gifford, unconscious, lay on the field. Furthermore, most older coaches insist defensive players do not need the intellect of offensive players. It is simpler to tell the defensive player to kill, far more difficult to teach the offensive lineman, for instance, the intricate steps and moves and disciplines necessary for unity of motion.

"First thing I look for in a defensive player," says one veteran scout, "is nastiness. Is he mean? Is he arrogant? Does he like to hit people? Does he enjoy racking a guy? I don't want a defensive player with a conscience. It's almost as if I'm looking for a hit man, a killer. I want somebody with guile, with cunning, with a cocky, cruel attitude. I want an assassin. If I find a guy with all that, I'll make him a defensive player on the spot."

And the middle linebacker is the epitome of such a man.

He must have quickness and instant recognition. He must be big enough to fight off linemen, quick enough to stay with backs and receivers, mean enough to hurt all of them. No middle linebacker flinches, or turns his head at the point of contact. And no man can hurt like the middle linebacker, because here is a dedicated athlete, dedicated to violence, who is six-three and perhaps 235 pounds, running with a full head of steam, often catching a ball carrier or a quarterback unawares—blind-side—and hurtling the full measure of momentum and frenzy into the other man's body.

"The thing I dream about," says Claude Humphrey, one of today's finest defensive ends, "is the blind-side tackle. I don't intentionally try to maim anyone, but if he has to leave the game . . . well, that's a bonus, I guess."

"I was brought up in a coal-mining area of West Virginia," says Huff. "We were poor. A lot of people now would call us poor whites. My father worked in the mines. But I was happy. That song by Tennessee Ernie Ford . . . you know, load sixteen tons of number nine coal, always in debt to the company store . . . that tells the story of what my life was. Payday was every two weeks. They didn't make enough money for me to go to college . . . I was the only one of two sisters and an older brother who went to college. I owe everything in my life to football. If I didn't get a scholarship, if I didn't play football,

I'd be there now, in the mines. My brother works in the mines . . . all my relatives . . . they enjoy it. My dad always thought I was crazy to play such a game, in the middle, no less. But I felt secure there. I was secure with the guys around me, and that's how they felt about the mines. They were secure. They knew where to look for the danger signs, what to do all the time. Me, I'm scared to death of the mines. I guess the greatest fear is of something you don't know, something you're not familiar with.

"But we were poor. As a kid, I didn't have but one pair of shoes. I'd go barefoot most of the time, and I couldn't wait for May to come so I could take my shoes off. I had T-shirts and jeans . . . hey, I dressed like the kids today, but they think it's stylish. I didn't have any choice. Pocket money? Are you kidding? My mother used to slip me twenty-five cents sometimes to go to the movies. The town was real small . . . Farmington, it had about seven hundred people.

"But those were good days. Kids are at such a fast pace today . . . in such big high schools . . . they lose their identity. Kids from my town are all successful, and they all have a solid foundation. I wouldn't mind for my kids to be raised the way I was raised. Matter of fact, they would be better off.

"One of the reasons I was a competitor, why I wanted to excel, I guess, was my childhood. I was always a little embarrassed because of the kind of furniture we had in our house . . . and we didn't have indoor plumbing, we had an outhouse . . . so I always wanted something better. I felt I wanted to be a high school football coach . . . I love sports, it's my life. Sure, I'm in the business world now, but I'm always into something with sports.

"My mother and dad didn't understand that. They were always working so hard. But I remember once, I got them to New York. There was a fan club called Huff's Club, and it held annual meetings, and I was able to get my parents to come. It was their first airplane trip . . . and what I had to do was drive them to Washington and take them on a plane that wasn't taking off . . . and once they saw it, saw all the seats and everything, like a living room, then they weren't afraid any more. It was money well spent, to see them enjoy themselves.

"Sometimes I go back there, to Farmington, but it's not the same now. You can't ever go back . . . you would like to, but you're not a part of it any more. It's different. Most people there look at me like

I'm an outsider, a big-city slicker. And I look at them and I can't understand why they don't try to do better. We don't relate like we should. I'm not a part of the scene any longer."

Huff's first encounter with organized football was as a sophomore in high school. "Only time that we played tackle in grade school was when our teacher, Blair Wolf, went away for a while," he says, smiling.

"I lived in a four-room mining row-house, we called it. It had four rooms . . . living room, kitchen and two bedrooms. And we had a big stove in the middle of the living room . . . and we used to go down and throw coal off the coal cars and put it in sacks and haul the coal home to keep warm with. I never had my own room . . . not even my own bed. I shared a bed with my brother.

"I never knew what a filet mignon was until I went to college. My mother would usually cook a big pot of vegetable soup, and my God she could make the greatest soup you ever tasted. She'd go get an old bone from the store and cook potatoes and tomatoes and peas in there, and it'd come out as fine a soup as you ever tasted. Put Campbell's and Heinz to shame. We'd have a pot of soup for three days. And we'd make our own bread and plant our own garden . . . and dammit, what is so bad, being poor? Why is it so bad? If you have to, you can dig up that ground and grow the finest garden.

"Now I have a farm in West Virginia that I go back to . . . it was something I always wanted as a boy, and now I have it. I remember, my first year with the Giants I made seven thousand dollars, but that was big money. My dad worked in the mines from the time he was thirteen to the time he was sixty-three, and the most he ever made, I think, was ten thousand. My highest salary was thirty-seven thousand, and that only happened after I was traded to the Redskins. Today it isn't much, but at the time I think I was the highest-paid linebacker in football. Most I ever made with the Giants was nineteen thousand."

Sam Huff got that football scholarship, from West Virginia University. And he became an All-America player, along with teammate Bruce Bosley, an offensive lineman. And he was drafted on the third round in 1956 by the Giants. The country boy was in the big city.

And the country boy couldn't handle it.

"I never dreamed about pro football. Never did. I had heard about it. My hero when I went to grade school and high school was Gunner

Gadski. He played with Cleveland, and sometimes I'd see the Pittsburgh Steelers, once in a great while, and hear about Ernie Stautner and Lynn Chadnois and Dale Dodrill. But suddenly the teams were calling, asking me if I'd like to play pro football. I said yes. Why the hell not?

"So the Giants drafted me . . . because of Al DeRogatis. We were playing against North Carolina State, and DeRogatis came down to scout Bruce Bosley. And he saw me play. DeRo said he liked Bosley, but he liked Huff just as well.

"The Giants drafted me . . . but they never did call me before, which I thought was odd. Anyway, I went to play in the College All-Star game in Chicago against the Cleveland Browns, and I was scared to death. But I went out there and played. We had guys like Joe Marconi and Bobby Moss and Bruce Bosley and myself . . . all from the same team. Bruce and Joe had been first-round picks, but I was the only one of all the West Virginia players to start. I worked my tail end off.

"But anyway, the Giants. I got to training camp . . . it was Winooski, Vermont . . . and the Giant players at that time really treated the rookies bad. I'll never forget it. They wouldn't even talk to you. I didn't like it. I thought Jim Lee Howell picked on the rookies . . . he'd yell at you, scream at you, shout at you . . . and I just didn't feel comfortable. I was running as fast as I could go, always had great pride in my speed, and hell, I was outrunning everybody else my size, and he's still yelling at me.

"I was on defense and Chandler was on offense, and I had a tremendous scrimmage. As a matter of fact, we won because Chandler was punting and I slipped the center . . . I was always great at that . . . and nobody touched me, and I took the ball right off his foot and went sixty-five yards for a touchdown. And we won. Howell said we would have a day off if we won. And do you know he made me practice the next day? To me, as a twenty-one-year-old kid, that wasn't fair. I was down on Jim Lee Howell.

"I just couldn't understand it. So I went to Don Chandler . . . he was a rookie, too . . . and I said, 'I don't feel welcome at all, let's get the hell out of here.' He said, 'Okay, let's go.' I said, 'I'm not kidding, I'm ready to go.'

"But we had to turn in our notebooks, and we go downstairs to the coaches' office . . . well, Lombardi used to share a room with Jim Lee

Howell, and Howell wasn't there but Lombardi was, on the bed, sleeping. We walk over and shake him, and he wakes up and says, 'What the hell do you want?' and we said, 'Coach, we quit.' "Well, I'm telling you, I never heard such carrying-on in my life. He scared Chandler to death, he ran. I couldn't get out . . . I had a bad knee. But he's calling us cowards and s.o.b.'s and everything . . . and I said, 'Coach, you can call me anything you want, but I just can't take this any more.' And he said, 'Dammit, we've got so much time invested in you . . . you can make this team, all you've got to do is stick it out.' And I said, 'No, I just don't like it, and I'm not going to hack it.' And I leave and I go upstairs and pack my suitcase.

"And there was this other rookie . . . I forget his name, but he was from Ohio State . . . and he had a car . . . I don't know how he got a car, maybe everybody from Ohio State had a car . . . he was going to drive us to the airport. But Ed Kolman, who was the line coach, he came into my room, and he said, 'Sam, I'd like to talk to you a little.' Okay, fine. But I'm still packing, and he asks me why I'm leaving.

I said, 'Coach, I'll tell you. It's not the football, I can play football. First of all, I'm homesick. And next, it's Jim Lee Howell, he's just on me so much I can't take it, I really can't. I had pride in my attitude here. I'm running and I'm struggling and he's still on my back, and I don't need it. So I'm getting out.'

"And Ed said, 'I'll tell you what. You stay, and I think you can be one of the great ballplayers in this game. And if you stay, he won't say anything else to you. Stick it out, and you won't be sorry.' Well, I thought about that. Then I told him, 'Okay, if you promise me he'll leave me alone, then I'll stay.'

"So I went to Chandler to tell him I was staying, but he was mad because nobody came to talk to him. He said he was still going, and I couldn't talk him out of it. So we all went out to the airport, me and Babe and this kid from Ohio State. And we're sitting there, and here he comes, Lombardi. I mean, Lombardi just loved Chandler, and lucky it was such a small airport, only one flight a day.

"To Lombardi's dying day, Don Chandler was one of his favorite people. He even traded for him after he got out to Green Bay. And Howell left me alone after that, and Chandler, too. But I have to say this: Jim Lee hurt some good football players. I know the effect he had on me. You had to know personalities. Like Phil King . . . you could yell at Phil King and he didn't give a damn, just went on doing things. Lombardi had a feel for it. He knew who he could chew out, and who couldn't take it. He never pushed the wrong guy. That was the difference between him and Howell. He knew when to stop, when not to do it."

Huff, indeed, was close to Lombardi, from that day on. It was a teacher-pupil relationship, and Huff worshiped the gruff Italian. Years later, when Lombardi was dying, Huff was there.

Huff has an amusing mix of modesty and confidence. "I don't think any athlete should evaluate himself," he says, "because it's too personal . . . too prejudiced. That's where kids today get themselves in trouble. They say, 'I'm the greatest,' and they really believe it. They think they're better than O.J. Simpson and . . . bullshit, they're not. But they think it, and then they want the same kind of money. I knew when I did a good job . . . and when I did, I knew I was the best middle linebacker around.

"I played in five Pro Bowls, but I never picked myself for those teams; others did. I never picked myself for the All-Pro team; other people did that. I didn't pick myself to be on the cover of *Time* magazine [in 1959]; other people did that. I never went to CBS and said, 'Hey, would you make a film of my life and entitle it "The Violent World of Sam Huff"?' They came to me [in 1960].

"I knew about Joe Schmidt in Detroit, and Bill George in Chicago. I knew the three of us were the best. Bednarik was a little earlier, but I think he was a tremendous football player. I always felt I did my best in games Schmidt and George were in.

"I blocked a kick once against Detroit in Yankee Stadium . . . a big game . . . and we won, seventeen to fourteen. They don't keep records of how many blocked kicks a guy has, but I think I blocked as many as anybody. I had something I wanted to prove. And you don't play that way for money.

"Even now, working for the Marriott company, I don't go out and work my butt off just for the money. I feel like I can get some business that the Hyatt corporation doesn't have, that the Hilton corporation doesn't have. It's pride. And I had a very difficult period adjusting to not playing. Still do. Oh God, when I get around people in sports, I just get the shakes. When it comes time for summer camp, man, I just feel like I should get ready and go.

"I never did get an offer as a head coach. I don't know, in sports it's a case of somebody having to put in the right word. Best thing I can say is, Don't hold your breath. In sports, most of the owners of teams are tremendous fans . . . read the sports pages . . . that's how guys get jobs, the owners think they're going to sell tickets by bringing in a coach with a name.

"I find myself second-guessing everybody. I do it all the time. I become involved. I can't watch a football game with a crowd of people. I watch it analytically, technically. When a coach makes a decision to go for it on fourth and four . . . my God, the guy is leaving things wide open . . . have to be very lucky . . . even if you make it, it's not a great decision. Guys playing the game are as smart as the ones coaching, and when a coach makes a bad move, the guys say, 'Jesus, what in the hell is he trying to do?' You lose morale that way.

"I would like to be a head coach. It would be a very difficult thing to turn down. My background is like Bart Starr's. I've set up programs, worked hours and hours to make them succeed. I don't think you need all the money in the world. I can't imagine what a guy does with thirty million dollars. It's the pride of accomplishment that's my motivation.

"Sports gives you that. You don't even see if a guy is a black athlete or a white athlete. There had never been any black kids in my high school or college experiences, but I'll tell you . . . I came from an area in West Virginia where blacks worked in the mines with your fathers, but they didn't drink in the bars . . . they went to their own churches, their own schools. I never did think about segregation. I didn't know about prejudice until I started playing pro ball. We'd go to Dallas and they wouldn't let the black players stay in the same hotel. I mean, how could you not let a guy like Roosevelt Brown stay with you? Roosevelt Brown is one of my great friends. I don't care what color his skin is.

"In football, you take on a guy across the line, and you know if you defeat him you can win the game. It's basic. You know where you stand."

Sam Huff always knows where he stands. And he stands diametrically opposite the man who traded him away from his beloved Giants: Allie Sherman.

It was 1964, spring.

"He called my wife Mary and told her he had traded me to the Redskins. I just couldn't believe it. I was really shocked . . . crushed.

I remember walking around New York for two weeks, just destroyed. I couldn't think about anything else. I couldn't hold my head up. I never, never thought I'd be traded, not ever. And then, suddenly, I was gone."

It caused a storm of protest. Newspapers devoted space on editorial pages to criticize the move. The fans were in outraged revolt. Sherman's hold on the team, then tenuous at best, was totally destroyed. The most loved member of the once mighty defense, Sam Huff, had been shipped out, sent off to Washington for two journeymen players, Dick James and Andy Stynchula.

The Giants were dead.

"About two weeks later, I remember, Jack Mara asked me to come to the Giants' golf day and dinner. I told him I couldn't, that I wasn't a member of the team any more. He said he'd always consider me a Giant, and he'd take it as a personal favor if I'd go. Well, okay, I said I would. And I promised myself I wouldn't say a word to Sherman, no matter what.

"And I tried not to, really. I was just going to play golf and enjoy the day with my friends. I think it was up at Winged Foot, in Westchester County. Mara was a member, and, well, it was just a nice day out with the guys.

"But in the locker room, after the golf, Sherman comes up to me. And I don't say a word. And he says, 'I suppose you want me to say I'm sorry that I traded you, right?' And I don't say a thing. And he goes on, 'Well, I'm not going to. I did the right thing, and I don't care what you've been saying around town. I'm not sorry.'

"And he's right in my face, talking loud like that, and I'm trying so damned hard not to say anything, but he keeps after me. Finally, I couldn't stand it any more. I said, 'If you don't get away from me, I'm going to do something I don't want to do.' And I was getting very excited and I guess red in the face, and I started shaking. I think it was Alex [Webster] who came over and pulled me away. I don't understand that Sherman. I never did, I don't think I ever will. And he always acted like I was the wrong one, blaming him for something he shouldn't have done.

"Well, listen. I don't think he should have done it. I was still a top player. But it was his right. I didn't have to like it. I didn't. I hated it. I was just destroyed by it. But what the hell could I do about it? I was traded, gone. Just like that. But he made a whole lot of trades that hurt . . . me, Chandler, Grier, Modzelewski . . . what did it accomplish? Nothing, that's what. He traded away a team." Most of the veterans felt the same way. Most grumbled at the trades, at the dismantling of a championship team. Sherman, to his credit, was trying to rebuild, trying to replace the old heroes before they retired or were rendered incompetent by the years. But it created a rift that still is felt, an impasse between the players and the coach that led to a decade of disaster.

And Sam Huff's trade was the reason.

"I used to get great pleasure out of playing against the Giants when he was still coaching," Huff says. "I played harder . . . I played better. I had an incentive. And when those people gave me a standing ovation the first time I came back . . . well, it was great. It was like retribution, it was like they were telling me Sherman was wrong, Sherman had made a mistake.

"I remember walking off the field after that ovation, and Pete Previte, the clubhouse attendant who had been there for years, said, 'Sam, they only did that for DiMaggio.' That was beautiful."

Now Sam Huff is an executive. A prosperous executive. As a vice-president of Marriott Hotels, he works out of the corporate headquarters in suburban Washington. His office, complete with private secretary, is paneled in dark wood. The walls are hung with photographs: Sam with Vince Lombardi, for whom he played and coached with the Redskins; Sam with Joe DiMaggio; Sam with his family, with former Giants, with the Redskin coaching staff; Sam in his familiar number 70 uniform.

Sam's job is sales, really. He convinces teams to stay in Marriott Hotels, and at that he has been wildly successful. Most NFL teams stay in Marriotts across the country, from Washington to San Francisco, from Atlanta to Dallas.

"My idea wasn't new or novel," he says. "But I knew I had to come up with something different. I was working for a textile company in the off-season, sales, and I wasn't that happy. I realized the sales experience should be connected with my own field, sports. So I took my idea to the big man, J. Willard Marriott. I noticed that the Marriott hotels, like most, didn't do much weekend business. My idea was to fill the gap with the sports trade, the teams."

Innovative . . . driven . . . prodded by the scent of competition. Sam Huff has succeeded in an otherwise unrelated world because he has found the same motivations that exist in sports, has been able to put the unseen common denominators to work—to his benefit.

He also acts as color analyst for the Redskins' radio broadcasts on station WMAL for the full twenty-game schedule. On the scene, in fact, is one of Sam's greatest loves.

"I feel it's where I belong," he says. "I can feel it as soon as I get into a locker room. I don't think I'll ever get over being a football player. I enjoyed every minute of my thirteen NFL years. I didn't do it for the money, I did it because I was exhilarated by the game."

Huff learns from mistakes, too. In 1970, he ran for United States Congressman in West Virginia's First District. He ran unsuccessfully, and no longer harbors serious political aspirations.

There are people who do not like Sam Huff; they say he is self-centered, conceited, a braggart. But others respect his confidence, his drive, his ambition, his proficiency.

Somewhere in between is the real Sam Huff. He is not really the successful executive, with a country estate in Alexandria, Virginia. Nor is he the radio personality, because, simply, he hasn't the native ability for dealing with a microphone. But he is a man anxious to have friends, anxious to show people that he really can be decent, charming, the perfect host.

And maybe Sam wasn't the world's best middle linebacker, either. He wasn't as terribly, criminally wronged as he feels he was when Sherman traded him. He had begun to lose that step, to slow up for that vital fraction of a second before his instincts were able to be translated into movements.

But he was an outstanding athlete, and most of the reason was his pride and his drive.

He hit harder than anyone . . . filled holes faster than anyone . . . because they said he couldn't. He tackled . . . intercepted passes . . . blocked kicks . . . because they said Schmidt could do it better, George could do it better.

And he won. He was a winner on a winning team. Because he loved being part of a winner more than anything else.

His two favorite people were Lombardi and John F. Kennedy, whom he knew well.

"The President was a pat-on-the-back guy," he says. "He would have made a great football coach. He knew how to get results out of people, he knew how to motivate people. But both he and Lombardi could get rough when they had to, and you have to be that way." Explosive temper? Certainly. He almost came to blows with Weeb Ewbank, the Colts' head coach, during that 1958 game. It was said he played dirty. Jim Taylor, the great Packer fullback, accused him in public. Their battles, and Sam's running battle with the great Jim Brown, became legendary.

Sam seldom lost those battles. He didn't know how.

Gino Marchetti and Alan Ameche

... *Ameche* plus 2 to touchdown at 2:26
... *Ameche* plus 6 to 15 first down
... *Ameche* over RG for touchdown at 8:15 of sudden death

... Heinrich pass for Rote blocked by *Marchetti*
... Heinrich fumble on 45 recovered by *Marchetti*
... Gifford sweep right plus 3 to 43, short of first down by inches. Stop by *Marchetti* (Marchetti hurt, broken ankle)

"Except for Jim Brown, Horse was as good as any fullback then. And a damned sight better than any fullback playing today."—Gino Marchetti, on Alan Ameche

"Gino Marchetti was the best defensive end of his time . . . and today . . . and if there is pro football a hundred years from now he'd still be the best damned defensive end in the world."—Alan Ameche, on Gino Marchetti

GINO MARCHETTI CAME from Antioch, California. Alan Ameche came from Kenosha, Wisconsin. Both became All-American football players.

Together, they arrived in Baltimore, Maryland, where they achieved subsequent greatness in professional football. And in fast hamburgers. And little bags of French fries. And small, warm apple pies. And fried chicken and biscuits and fish fillets.

On the field, they became known as Death (Marchetti) and Destruction (Ameche). Off the field, they became known, corporately, as Gino's. Known to every schoolboy and on-the-road salesman and harried mother.

"We are," says Marchetti, "the two luckiest Italians in the world. We started with nothing. Now look. Just a couple of jocks who got lucky."

Did football do all this for these two men? Certainly. But thousands of men have played professional football. Perhaps only one in a thousand has made it this big.

"Everything worked out just right," says Ameche. "We had great friends, great timing, great advice. There just isn't another way to say it. We had great luck."

The San Francisco Restaurant, which is not in San Francisco at all but in Wayne, Pennsylvania, smack on the Mainline reaching into upper-crust Philadelphia, is owned by Marchetti.

It is a first-grade eatery. No quick hamburgers here, but steak and roast beef au jus and good wines. Big lunch trade. Big family dinner trade. It is decorated in posh-dark, deep-red walls, leather upholstery. The bar is always busy, and the tables seem more often occupied than not.

It is built like an old house. As a result, there is a second floor, for private parties, and it is in one of these rooms that the three of us are sitting.

Marchetti, always a great bear of a man as an All-Pro defensive end, is now paying the price of limited activity. He is much too heavy. Ungainly and huge, he is either well on his way to three hundred pounds or unsafely past it. He is wearing nondescript slacks and a flowery sport shirt, worn outside his belt, a predictable signal flashed by men who have become embarrassed by their girth.

"What do you weigh now, Gino? Two-what?"

"Too damned much," he says, grinning but not really amused. "It's tough to work out now. So I don't get much exercise."

Ameche is still trim. Playing weight, he says, which means two-ten, two-fifteen. Conservatively dressed. Gray suit, white shirt, tie. His hair is short, but Marchetti's flows back across his leonine head. Ameche smiles a lot, grins, even giggles. He is tight, nervous. Yet is by far the less emotive of the pair. He must warm to both his subject and his interviewer. But not Gino. He is loud and garrulous, totally at ease. Not quite coarse, but not far from it.

The subject is money.

"We opened the first Gino's in April of '59," Marchetti says, "right after the championship with the Giants. In fact, I used the winner's check to help start it. [Checks were in the amount of $4,674 to the winning Colts, not much of an investment to profit by millions.]

"Ameche, Joe Campanella and Lou Fischer had started what they called Ameche's Drive-In Restaurants. They had four at the time. And then they wanted to go into this Gino-type operation . . . they had served a fifty-five-cent hamburger, a Powerhouse, and they wanted to go into a cheaper-type menu. At that time, our hamburgers were fifteen cents. They didn't want to use Ameche's name for both of them. This was like a pilot model, and they didn't want the people in Baltimore to say, 'Gee, they're selling a fifty-five-cent hamburger here and the same thing for fifteen cents over there. They didn't want to connect the two, because people thought the fifteen was cheaper meat, which it wasn't.

"So that's when they brought me into the company to start Gino's."

Ameche, who has been nodding in agreement, interrupts. "We opened the first Ameche's in '57," he says. "In the summer, before that season started. There were three or four of them around Baltimore, but they aren't there any more. They've all been converted to Gino's. The company really started moving when Gino came in. I think we were the first of the chain-type fast-food operations . . . in the East, anyway. McDonald's started out in the West, but they didn't get here until we had already been established."

Talking business makes Marchetti impatient, so now he breaks in. "We'll have close to five hundred stores by the end of this year," he says. "They're all company-owned, too, not franchised. We have our own training, advertising, purchasing, the whole thing. We just hire managers for the stores."

One of the original partners, Campanella, is dead. He died of a heart attack while playing handball with Don Shula, then the Colts' head coach, at a YMCA in Towson, Maryland. He died just weeks after being named the team's general manager.

"That was his life's dream," says Marchetti. "He had two dreams . . . either own a football team or be a general manager of one. If he had stayed alive, there's no doubt in my mind that he'd have bought a team. Some team. No doubt about it."

Ameche now: "I'll tell you one thing, he'd have been one hell of a general manager. He knew football, and he was a smart business-man. But we don't want to buy a team. Oh, we talked about it, because Joe was always interested in one. But he was really the pusher in that thing. For one thing, I don't think there's any kind of a return on them now. They're priced so high."

Marchetti's face lights up. "I'll say this. If I owned a team now, or bought one, I'd kick some of those guys right in the ass."

Okay. From the business of money, we have come to the business of pride. Marchetti and Ameche, both old warriors, have come to view modern professional football with no small amount of distaste.

"I think it's terrible what they're doing," Gino continues, deadly serious, his face hardening into lines of determined outrage. "The showmanship . . . I think the Eagles got a thing going that turns my stomach. You ever see them, that thing like they're shooting crap in the end zone? After one of them scores a touchdown? And I think that's . . . geez . . . and three guys grabbing each other and swinging around . . . I think for a professional to do that is so goddamn bush. I think it's degrading to the game, to the sport. Why don't they stop that? Colleges stop it."

Ameche, warming now: "It's hot-dog, and it really shouldn't be allowed. You can see a coach's problem. When you've got a great player who's a hot-dog . . . well, you've got a problem. Like that baseball player, Richie Allen. I mean, potentially . . . your tongue is hanging out because the guy does so many things well. But his attitude is so crappy it hurts the team. I respect a guy like Yogi Berra. When Allen was available, he said, 'I'd love to have the guy, you know, for his bat, but as a player he'd ruin our team.' And that's just what's happening in football."

Marchetti again, really rolling, really hot: "I think the fans are getting tired of it, and it's going to hurt the league. It's getting worse all the time. How can you play like that? I see the Eagles a lot . . . and one game, [Bill] Bergey gets a cheer, right in the middle of the game, and he stops and waves to the fans."

Ameche: "You know, I saw him coming out of a game—and this is confidential, you know a lot of this is confidential—so he's coming out of a game with a football and he's passing it between his legs. Did you see that? Then when he got to the sideline he threw it up into the stands. I mean, you couldn't have had a bigger hot-dog. Did you see that, Gino?"

Gino had.

"I don't know how it happened," Ameche continues, "it's a phenomenon that's spreading like wildfire. And as I think back, I don't know what did it. Is it the fact that the Players' Association gave the guys more independence? They're not worried about the coach telling them not to do it any more? Whether it's the big money . . . whether it's the press . . . football, from the time we played, even from that '58 game, which was a big deal, has grown from there to the point where these guys think they're like gods. And you talk to guys now . . . hey, we were always a little cocky, I think good athletes have to have a certain amount of cockiness . . . the guy today is incredible.

"Look at the way they dress. They're wearing capes . . . crazy shirts . . . I bet they spend half the money they make on their cars and their clothes."

Marchetti: "When I was playing, they wouldn't even let you on the plane dressed like that. You had to wear ties, sport jackets. Big deal. But I can see a dumb lineman, he races for a touchdown, thirty yards, he's got to do something. He doesn't know what the hell to do. But now they make a first down and they thump the ball, right in the middle of a game. And it could be stopped so easily. All the league has to do, you know, is put out a policy statement . . . there'll be no more of this, this and that, or it's fifteen yards. That way it would get all the coaches off the spot, get everybody off the spot, and stop all that shit."

Ameche: "Funny, when we played, I don't remember anybody doing stuff like that. Do you, Gino?"

Marchetti: "I remember Chuck Bednarik throwing the ball in the stands against us once. You know, he had intercepted a pass and run forty yards for a touchdown. It was the first touchdown he ever scored. But you know what? He threw it in the stands, and the stands were empty. They were able to get the ball back."

Which brought us to money.

"Most I ever made," said Marchetti, the finest defensive lineman of his time or ours, "was a little over forty thousand. But that was my last year or two. You see, I was with the All-America Conference when it first started in Baltimore [1952] and up to '58, the guy who made ten, twelve thousand . . . well, that was a lot of money."

Ameche: "Hell, you made your biggest money after you peaked. If you had been paid what you were worth, as the best player in the country . . . well, today you'd be making two hundred grand. Easy."

Marchetti: "See, I don't know if money is the whole answer. It's other things now, like what they struck for last year [1974]. Freedom. No bed checks. Nothing. To me, football without discipline is nothing. You can't run a team. But the great coaches—your Shulas, your Lombardis—they're the strong coaches. They're great disciplinarians. They survive by working harder, by making their players work harder.

"Like I can remember something about Shula. Okay? With Weeb, it was five hundred dollars [fine for breaking curfew] the night before a ball game. Now every once in a while a guy decides to get out, have a couple of drinks, run around a little . . . you know, for five hundred bucks he might take a chance. But with Shula, it was an automatic suspension, no pay. He said, 'I'm asking you, one night a week, to sacrifice.' I don't know anybody who ever tested him. They were all scared of him. The night before the ball game, all the guys were in. The way Shula wanted it.

"So I don't think it's the money so much. It's like a revolution. The attitude . . . the union . . . the strikes . . . I don't know. I had to go testify in some court case, fourteen players were suing the league for being deprived of making a living.

"Poor guys, making seventy-five thousand a year, and that's being deprived of making a living. And John Mackey, he's one of them suing, he said the Colts loaned him fifty thousand dollars one year, tax-free, interest-free. I said, 'Where the hell else could you get a loan like that, tax-free?' That's really being deprived, isn't it? It hurts the system, but if they do away with it, I suppose the great ballplayers will make all the money, the average guys would make less. I don't know what the answer is. All I know is how guys like me and Horse here feel. We just don't understand it any more. What do they want? How much?"

This part of the conversation began with the creation and fruition of Gino's. Although they remain on the board of directors, Marchetti and Ameche sold their interest in the company in 1973. For a great deal of money.

How much? As it turned out, it was none of my business.

For the thirteen years Marchetti played professional football (all of them with Baltimore), he was considered the greatest defensive end in the history of the game.

But before that, he had been a vital member of one of the greatest college football teams in history, the 1951 University of San Francisco team. The coach was Joe Kuharich, who later coached Notre Dame and the Philadelphia Eagles.

On the roster were ten players drafted and signed by the professionals: Marchetti, halfback Ollie Matson, quarterback Ed Brown, tackle Bob St. Clair, linebacker Burl Toler, guard Red Stephens, tackle Merrill Peacock, halfback Scooter Scudero, receiver Ralph Thomas, guard Mike Mergen.

Even the team's young publicist was something of a budding hero. His name was Alvin "Pete" Rozelle, and he has made something of a name for himself in another area of professional football.

"You know, I look at teams now, and I remember our team then," says Marchetti, "and I'm convinced ours was better, better than any of them."

Matson and Marchetti, of course, are now safely bronzed, mounted and enshrined in the Pro Football Hall of Fame. They are the only two members of the Hall who played for the same college team at the same time.

Kuharich remembers Marchetti's ferocity and intense competitive drive. "For speed drills," he says, "we'd give Gino a five-yard sprinting start on Matson and goad him into not letting Ollie catch up. If Matson did, we'd up the margin to eight yards, and Gino would cuss and rave. It was fun."

Marchetti, dogged and stubborn, reiterates: "No one will ever convince me that our team that year wasn't the best. Ollie led the nation in scoring. We played our best in the toughest games. If we had been at Notre Dame, they'd still be writing books about us."

Ameche, the Horse, distantly related to comedian-actor Don Ameche, was Baltimore's number one draft choice in 1955 out of the University of Wisconsin, joining the team three years after Marchetti.

"One of the things that has happened in my football career," he reflects, "that has been most gratifying, is that on every team that I played with we were dead last and at some point we ended up winning a championship. When I went to high school, we scored one touchdown the whole season the first year I played. One touchdown. We lost all the games.

"But by my senior year we had won the championship, we were undefeated. Wisconsin was the same thing. And more dramatically with Baltimore. I don't want this to sound like I'm blowing my own horn or anything, but like Gino said, the reward is so much sweeter when you start at the bottom and you get the shit kicked into your face, then you see yourself climbing a little bit, and a little bit more. And when you make it, it's really a beautiful thing."

Then it was 1958, and the Colts won their first Conference championship ever. The game for the NFL title was to be played away from home, against the New York Giants at Yankee Stadium.

"The first thing I remember about that game," says Marchetti, "is a very simple thing to remember. Every time I walk, I remember that game. I broke my ankle, and something didn't heal right, so I've got a bit of a problem with my ankle, my whole leg.

"I broke it in the fourth quarter, the last defensive play of the regulation game. It was when Gifford tried to make the first down on that third-down carry. I tackled him. He didn't make the first down. Frank says he's sure he made the first down? Well, Frank doesn't know what he's talking about. From where I was laying, he didn't make it.

"Frank was funny. He was hollering. I guess he thought I was laying there, faking it, to get an additional time-out. He said, 'Get your damned butt off the ground, Gino, I was down, the play's over.' And I said, 'Frank, I can't get up. I can't.' Big Daddy fell over my leg, that's how the ankle got broken. Most guys in football get hurt by their own players."

So Gino Marchetti, the heart of the Baltimore defense, lay on the ground, shrieking with pain, begging for surcease, for a shot. Right? "Bullshit," he says. "I wanted to see the end of the game. I told them to put me down on the stretcher in the end zone. I did see Steve Myhra's field goal to tie it, and I saw the drive that John put together to get him there. And then, when it went into sudden death, they took me off. They were afraid that with one great play or something, the field would be crowded with spectators and they wouldn't be able to get me off.

"I was in a lot of pain. It was really hurting me. But still, I wanted to see the end, and they wouldn't let me. They took me down into the locker room, which was as quiet as this room is, and I couldn't hear a thing. I didn't know what was happening, who was winning. I didn't know a thing until one of the players—Ray Brown, I think it was—came bursting into the room yelling, 'We're the greatest!'

"Imagine being in a game like that and not seeing the end of it."

Ameche has no wounded leg to remind him of the game. So when he is asked to put his finger on the one moment that stands out, he wavers.

"I think of so many details in that game that a lot of people have probably forgotten about now," he says. "Not that I spend all my time thinking about the game. I don't want to mislead you. But there were so many dramatic events. For example, early in the game we had a chance to score a third touchdown in the first half. And we could have blown them out, but we didn't score from the one-yard line. Unfortunately, I was involved in three out of the four plays down there. Had we put it in there, I'm convinced it would have been a rout. It would have been twenty-one to three.

"And it was a fluke, the way they came back from there. It was a crazy play . . . a pass that was completed, a tackle, a fumble, a recovery and somebody running . . . and by the time it was over they were on our one. It was early in the third quarter. So instead of being twenty-one to three, it was fourteen to ten. And instead of us putting them away, we had to scramble from then on. "Then the dramatic play of Gino's injury, at a key time, you know, a key stop there. Stopping Gifford on that sweep was a key play. And Gino never gets hurt, and then to have that happen.

"Then Myhra, who was always a little shaky as a field goal kicker anyway, comes through in as clutch a field goal as he ever kicked in his life. He's a hell of a guy, don't misunderstand. But he was a nervous-type guy, pacing up and down, and then he goes in and puts the ball right through there. We couldn't tell if it was good or not. He kicked it from a funny angle, like from the hash mark away from us, kicking toward us. But it was a hell of a moment there on the sideline, with everybody standing still, watching, wondering if we'd tie it up or go home losers. Then he jumped up and down, and the holder—George Shaw, I think—began jumping around, so we knew it was good."

Trying to ascertain the players' thoughts as to the quality of the game, I pass on the information that the Giants' Andy Robustelli thought it was "a horseshit game."

"Sure, 'cause they lost," says Marchetti.

"I heard Gifford on an interview once," Ameche says, taking back the floor, "that he thought they could have very easily won the game. I really feel that we had a better team. If we had put in that third touchdown, it could have been the same rout it was the next year. But from a technical standpoint, I think it was a hell of a lot better game than any championship game I've seen lately."

Neither man, however, feels it was the most glorious game they ever played. Both opt for the game that clinched the Western Conference that year, against San Francisco.

"We were down at half time, like twenty-seven to seven," Marchetti says, "and we shut 'em out in the second half, and John and them scored four touchdowns and we won it, thirty-five to twenty-seven. That has to be the game that sticks out in my mind.

"Listen, I was with Baltimore when we used to get beat so bad that making a first down was a moral victory. And in 1955, when we got Alan and [Jack] Patera and Shaw and Ray Berry and George Preas —we had that fantastic draft, where I think we got eight guys who made the team big—it started turning around then. And winning the championship, after being so bad a few years ago that we'd be down forty-five to nothing at half time . . . well, it was just a big thrill, something we worked so damned hard to get."

To men as proud as these, the Giants themselves provided another incentive for winning the championship game.

"They had beaten us during the season," Marchetti growls. "It was a game when John was hurt and didn't even play. Shaw was the quarterback, and they only won like twenty-four to twenty-one. Then we got all the clippings from the New York *Times* and all the other papers where Frank and Conerly were saying, 'We outgutted them.' You know, talking about what a great job they did, so that made us want to beat them even more.

"And that championship game, I'd have to say that Weeb gave probably the best pep talk he's ever given, prior to the game. There's a lot of pep talks so shitty that, you know, you laugh at them. But he went down everyone on the roster, and he had something for them. For instance, Artie Donovan. He said, 'Dunny, the Cleveland Browns didn't want you, they cut you. And the New York Yankees cut you. Now you're here, show 'em how good you are.' And he had a thing about Alan and a thing about me. Everybody. I think that was the best pre-game speech he ever had. He's had some sickening ones, I'll tell you that."

"Once a game started," Ameche says, "John was in complete charge of the offense. You had to lock Weeb up at game time, I'll tell you that. Those two drives were as good as John ever made. He didn't miss a pass. Then you take a guy like Raymond. The beautiful thing about it was that this was like a culmination of everything for him, of all this guy's efforts. Because Raymond was a perfectionist.

"He and I came to the Colts the same year. I was the number one pick and he was like twelfth or fourteenth. And everybody wondered what the hell this guy was doing there. He had one leg shorter than the other, he wore contact lenses . . . he was barely a hundred and eighty-five pounds, he didn't have speed, wasn't particularly strong. But just from hard work, he made it.

"He'd drive John crazy keeping him out after practice. John called a masterful game, but it was really the perfection of Raymond as a player that made it work."

Marchetti is lavish in his praise of Berry, one man's man speaking of another. "I can remember one catch Raymond made against the

Forty-Niners in that game we had to win," he says. "It was a fourth-down play. It didn't look like much until you saw it in the movies. John had overthrown him. And Raymond had extended himself, but somehow, some way, he found a second effort up in the air. At the height of his jump he just sort of gathered himself and caught that ball. It made us a first down, and we went in and scored."

Now Ameche: "The amazing thing about Raymond is that these were not lucky things. He worked on these. He not only accentuated the things he could do well and tried to improve them, but he'd think of the exceptions . . . the ball that's thrown behind you, and the one that's too high, and the one that's down on the ground. He used to devise drills to work on those. Like he started one drill with his back to the quarterback, and the quarterback would throw the ball like from ten yards, and just as he released it he'd yell, 'Now!' And Raymond would have to turn around quickly and adjust to where that thing was. You do that a couple thousand times and you've got to get good at it, even the things that look impossible.

"It's the thing I always admired about Raymond. He never thought anything was impossible."

Both men feel that Berry was the best receiver they had ever seen, a feeling which has been bolstered even by watching today's superstar receivers.

But what of themselves?

"Are you the best defensive end you ever saw?" I ask Marchetti.

"I don't think I looked at it that way," he says. "But the guy I respected the most was a guy in Washington named Gene Brito. He was a light guy, a fast guy, a quick guy. Had a lot of moves. And Willie Davis of Green Bay, of course. And Deacon Jones. I'd have to say they were three of the best. Doug Atkins of the Bears was the biggest, and there were times when he was the best. But he wasn't steady, year after year, even game to game. When he wanted it, he was the best around. He was so damned big, too [six-eight, two-sixty]. And Robustelli was a great end, very quick. Very strong."

At this point, Ameche is giving his impression of a kid with his hand raised in school, in a fit to be called on for the correct answer.

"No question about it," he says. "I may be a little prejudiced, but I've looked at the game, then and lately, and I don't think there was anybody who played the position all the way, from a pass rush to defending against the run, the whole thing, better than Gino. I

wouldn't put anybody close to him. There are only a couple, three
guys, in my estimation, that I'd put up in the real high superstar
category. Gino happens to be one. Jim Brown happens to be another
one. And John Unitas.

"Then there are a lot of good players . . . but I don't think there's
anybody real close.

"Jim Brown and Jim Taylor were the best fullbacks. I'm down there
somewhere in the next level. I knew my limitations. I worked hard
and did things pretty well. Could I play today? Hell yes, I'm as good
as anybody playing today. And Gino? [Laughter here, derisive laughter for asking a stupid question.] That's a hell of a question. Gino
could play now or a hundred years from now and be the best at his
position. And Jim Brown. And Unitas.

"Larry Csonka? I hope this doesn't sound wrong, but I'm as good
as Csonka."

It's Marchetti's time to break in. "Listen, Csonka got with a coach
[Shula] who adapts his offensive plans around his personnel. Now,
Horse got into a situation in Baltimore, he comes off a great year, over
a thousand yards as a rookie in twelve games. Today they think a guy
who makes a thousand yards in fourteen games is a big hero. But we
used to say they made a third guard out of Alan, a blocking back.
When Unitas got here, they had such confidence in his passing that
it got so Alan would get the ball on third and one, third and two,
fourth and one. They were the only times he'd even touch the ball.
Sometimes he'd carry the ball six times a game, and before Unitas he
carried the ball twenty-five, thirty times a game."

Ameche's head bows. "I was bitter as hell when it happened," he
says, "but you can't argue with the success we had. I can't argue with
what they did. I got to be a better blocker, and after all, how many
times do you get a Unitas? But if I played with Green Bay or Cleveland or now with Shula in Miami, I could do as well as their fullbacks.
I put myself close to Jim Taylor and about even with Csonka.

"You know, I don't even like the way this sounds. It sounds like
I'm blowing my own horn, and I don't like it. But Shula is a fullback-
oriented coach. Maybe Csonka is Shula's Alan Ameche, maybe he
built it the way he learned it in Baltimore. You take Csonka and put
him on a team geared to pass, and he'd have a hell of a hard time
coming near to a thousand yards. He'd be working just as hard, but
he wouldn't be getting so many chances to run it."

. . .

Neither man has stayed close to football after retirement. Ameche, father of four sons, says it took a while to learn to be just a fan.

"I used to get angry at the mistakes that junior high school and high school coaches make," he says. "They're entitled to make them. They're learning. But when you've played pro ball, you don't think like that. Now I just watch games, like a fan. I still pull for the Colts."

Ameche never tried coaching, but Marchetti did and liked it. Once, at Shula's request, he tutored a young defensive end named Bubba Smith.

"I enjoyed working with kids," he says, "and if it wasn't for the Gino's business, if I didn't have anything to do, I'm sure I would have wound up coaching somewhere. But this is better . . . the business, this restaurant. I can be a fan."

It's time to eat.

And even at the San Francisco Restaurant, lunch for three is a hamburger, French fries and coffee.

But the hamburger is huge, not a Gino's special. And the French fries are long and plump. And the coffee is served in mugs, freshly brewed.

And then the two former athletes go back downstairs, to the bar, to visit with the men on lunch who remember the old days, the better days, the days of championships.

Millionaires? Maybe. But still football men. Purely and simply football men, trying hard not to let their money become a source of embarrassment to them or to their old friends.

Alex
Webster

. . . Conerly to Rote complete; Rote fumble on Baltimore
25; picked up by *Webster*, who goes to Baltimore 1.
Total 86 yards. First down.
. . . *Webster* plus 5 to New York 24
. . . *Webster* plus 3 to New York 13
. . . *Webster* on double reverse plus 4 to 43

*"We never lost a game. When the other team won, it was luck. When
we won, it was just the way it was supposed to be. We figured when we
lost the game just wasn't long enough."*

By winter, the New Jersey shore is both memory and promise. The perfect days of summer, unflawed and golden, are gone. Winter at the shore is a single word: shuttered. Summer homes are closed, their windows shuttered. Boardwalk restaurants and amusement stands are shut. Within, the smell of must, of no one. The buildings wait for the first door to open, the first window to be lifted, the first warmth of spring sunlight.

In winter, the wind slices across the dark ocean and cuts the shore-line with blind cruelty. The salt air is raw and chill. The ocean is black, somehow louder and more ominous than in summer. The streets are empty, deserted; you can walk their center lines unhurried, unthreatened. Mist is a nightly companion, obscuring road signs, turning street lights into prisms of fuzzy color. There is a clamminess to the air, sticky, damp, rank. The occasional stare of headlights is cause to wonder—who goes there and why?

But to those who call the shore their home, the shutters of winter are as normal as the delights of summer. Through the long winters and the summer carnival, shore people are at ease, strolling to an inner rhythm, not rushing. There is time for everything. It is a quiet, leisurely way of life.

Alex Webster is a shore person, accustomed to the slow rhythm of the seasons. He spends quiet days near the beach, has adopted the pattern of the locals, learned how to walk slowly and pass the time. But somehow it doesn't fit.

This man should be living as he did before, in the grimy gray of a North Jersey industrial town, with the smog hanging in a sky made all the wrong color, with the men who toil too long for too little and live with gloom and quiet desperation. Webster is a product of such a town, brawny and rough, crude and unpolished, most comfortable with beer and Scotch and belly laughs.

Nobody, really, escapes the dead-end towns. People move. They may find wealth and fame. But they remain the way life made them early on. Tough. Physically inclined. Quick to laugh, to anger, to forgive. School is tolerated as long as the law requires it. Then to work. College? An alien land. Reading? That's for others. They take care of their families, spend spare hours at the local bar, anxious to celebrate, for any reason or for no reason at all. They are addicted to sports. They worship macho.

There have been fights in Alex Webster's past, great bloody fights he recalls with a grin, fights become legendary among those who were there.

"The toughest man I ever knew," says Gino Marchetti, who is almost everyone else's choice for that singular distinction, "was Alex Webster. If me and Alex were out drinking some night, and if we got jumped by half a dozen guys, we'd walk away from it. And Alex would be the one to bust most of the heads."

Sam Huff, who was as violent as any who ever played for the New York Giants, alludes to a rift between the team's offensive and defensive units. "We didn't like some of the guys on the offense," says the middle linebacker, "we'd go after them in scrimmages. We'd try to get them out. They were the heroes. They got all the notice. They got protected. But we never fucked with Webster. He was one crazy son of a bitch. He should have played defense."

This brings a smile to Webster's craggy face, and the smile puts wrinkles at the eyes. "I remember once, back home in Kearny, we were in this tavern owned by a blind guy. Really nice guy, neighborhood guy. Anyway, he was blind, and he had the whole bar memorized. Man, he could work as fast as anybody, he knew where each different bottle was, where all the different glasses were, the whole bit. Only thing was, we had to tell him what kind of money we gave him. 'It's a ten, Joe,' or 'Make change for a twenty, Joe,' and nobody ever screwed him. He was our friend.

"Anyway, one night we're in the place, it's quiet, during the week, and a couple of strangers walk in. They order a beer and a shot each, and they pick up on Joe being blind. So they figure to do a little business. The first guy gives him a single and says it's a five. He made change. Then they order another round, and the other guy gives him a one and tells him it's a tenner. Poor Joe made the change. They were stealing him blind, you could say. So I walk up to the bigger one, you always go for the big one 'cause that scares the shit out of him and the little one, and I said, 'Hey, man, the guy is blind.' And he says, 'Yeah, so what? Mind your own fucking business.' I got angry. I was real close to him, talking and all, and our heads were like six inches apart.

"So I just slammed my forehead down on his head, knocked him right out, cold on the floor. His friend starts for the door, but I grabbed him and threw him through it. Then I took the money they had stolen from Joe and gave it back. They weren't local guys, or they wouldn't have tried that shit. And I knew right away they didn't know who I was, or they wouldn't have messed with me."

And now this same Alex Webster lives the gentle life of the Jersey shore, a life of dinner out, drinks before and after, golf on bright weekends, infrequent trips to the city in a big car. He was not born to it, but the people of Sea Girt love him.

Everybody loves Alex Webster. He is Everyman, elevated from nothing. He has a name. He drinks, smokes, and he's super fun. His friends include judges and senators, men who enjoy acting the way they want to act, not the way they must act. He is plain enough to offend no one, rugged enough to impress everyone, decent enough to inspire only friendship, never envy. He poses no threat. He is the catalyst when the more complicated men want to be natural. He is everyone's friend. Instantly.

In one respect, Alex Webster has remained true to his background. We are sitting in a bar—it is his bar, and it has become a restaurant, too, because of its popularity. It is called The Stadium and the walls offer glaring testimony to what brought him here, to what made it possible for him to flee the factories of Kearny. There are photographs of Webster in action, a fearless fullback whose lack of speed was compensated by great agility, great quickness and killer toughness. There are autographed pictures of his friends, men like Conerly and Rote, Gifford and Tittle. There is, in a special glass case, his blue and white jersey, number 29 on its back. There are other displays which house his helmet, a pair of his cleats.

It is a jock's place, and the jocks who have only dreamed of Webster's glory flock through the doors, hoping tonight will be one of those nights when Big Red is in his bar.

They are seldom disappointed.

We are seated at a table in the back, in the back but not set apart from the others, for that would not be Alex Webster's way. We are kept company by a bottle that started out full, but is rapidly going empty. It seems to help him remember.

"We didn't have much money, but it was okay," he says of his early years. "Kearny was a factory town with a bar on every corner and a lot of great people in it. There was Otis Elevator and the Kearny Shipyards and the DuPont plant, and I guess most of the people worked in one of those places. My father died of cancer when I was nine years old . . . my brother was five. He was only thirty-three, and that changed our lives a lot. My mother had to go out and work, and suddenly we didn't have a father. But my mother did a hell of a job just raising us . . . me and my brother were two S.O.B.'s, real tough to manage. We were tough kids, because it was a tough town and it was tough to grow up. We had jobs and like that all through school, and we had fights and we'd get drunk a lot."

Webster says most of his friends never found a way out at all, spending their lives in the beer-and-a-shot factory world. Many of them ended up in the slammer.

But some made it.

"In my case, it was football," he says. "I always loved football, I'd play it all year. It was tough, a man's game. So I played it. And because I was tough, you could say I was a man before my time. I did well. I made All-State in my senior year in high school, but my grades were lousy. I just figured I was never going to go anywhere, and I could care less. I never thought much about what I was going to do after.

"But all of a sudden the scouts started to come around, and after that I raised up my grades a little bit. I had a lot of scholarships offered to me, I don't know how many. I never counted.

"I went on a lot of those visits to the different campuses, and to be honest I was scared of most of them. Everywhere I went, the people were well-dressed, had cars and so on. I only had one sport coat in those days, because I never wore much more than dungarees and sweat shirts."

Ultimately, Webster chose North Carolina State.

"In those days it was an agriculture and engineering school, and I

felt most of the people there were like me. Relaxed. Poor. If I had to go to one of those fancy-ass schools, I probably would have stayed home. Fuck it, you know? I didn't need that aggravation."
Going to college meant only one thing to Webster: football. "I was happy that it was a single-wing team. I played single-wing in high school, and although the pros had gone to the T-formation and the spread formations, I figured out the wing was best for me. Number one, I knew it, so it would be easier to make the team right away. Number two, since I was a fullback it gave me four years of hitting the middle, getting the feel of that. Plus, I played both ways and I wanted to do that. I was a tailback and a safety. I wanted as much football as I could get. I didn't like platooning. My place was out there, hitting."

Despite a change in coaches and a switch to the T-formation in his senior year ("I didn't like that, or the new coach. His name was Horace Hendrick, and let's leave it at that. He's in business today, selling stone, and that's just fine with me."), Webster was drafted on the twelfth round by the Washington Redskins.

"I made the team as a safety. They cut down the roster to thirty-three guys and I was on it. Then, three days before the opener, Don Doll was cut by Detroit. The Redskins picked him up. Right, I got cut. It was my position, and he was a veteran and I was a rookie. So I had to leave."

And now, the first of the incredible breaks.

"I came home and that's when I went to work for Otis. I was a stock clerk. I enjoyed it. It was a good job and most of the guys I grew up with were working there. Then one night in Riley's Tavern, we were sitting around drinking beer, the guys decided I should give it another shot. So we all chipped in and sent a night letter to the Montreal Alouettes in the Canadian League. I didn't think nothing about it. I went home and went to sleep. It must have been a Friday night, because I was in bed, late, when my mother woke me up. She said there was some Southern gentleman on the phone, calling long distance, and he had a funny kind of name. It was no gentleman. It was Peahead Walker.

"He was the head coach at Montreal, and we had written to him because he used to be the coach at Wake Forest, so we figured he'd remember me. I got on the phone and he said, 'Webster, you must be a dumb son of a bitch. You send me a goddamn telegram and you don't put a damned telephone number or address in it. I been up half the night trying to find out where you live, you jackass.'

"That was Peahead. But he asked me if I could get up there that day. I said yeah, I could. So he told me there would be a practice at four-thirty and I better have my ass there on time or I wouldn't get a tryout at all.

"Well, we didn't have the money to get me there. Louise was eight months pregnant and we were living with my mother. I had quit college before I got my degree and I had been cut by the Redskins. We were about three thousand bucks in debt. So I went across the street to the guy who owned the candy store and borrowed it. He said I better make the damned team, because he wasn't going to loan me any more and he damned well wanted this back. It was about fifty bucks, I think. My mother gave me some money, too, so we got it together.

"I got to Montreal and went right to the ball park. That first practice is a real story. I'm playing fullback and they call a play in scrimmage, but I didn't know any of the plays. The quarterback told me where to be, it was a pass play and all I had to do was block. So the ball is snapped and this big defensive end comes roaring through. Sam, the quarterback, he gets rid of the ball and I relax and then *pow!* this end levels me with a forearm. I was so damned mad I asked Sam to call the same play. He grinned and said, 'Hey, rookie, that's a tough man,' and I said I didn't give a damn, nobody sucker-punches me like that.

"So he calls the play, grinning, and I swear to God I wound up an uppercut that started on the ground. I didn't give a damn about blocking, I just cold-conked the guy. There he was, laying on the ground, and Peahead walks over, a big shit-eating grin on his face, and he helps wake the guy up. Then he looks down on him and says, 'See, Canuck? You ain't supposed to fuck with us Americans. And he cuts the guy. I knew right then I made the team.

"I played the whole season, plus two playoff games, and I made thirty-five hundred bucks. But it was a job. And it was football."

Making the team was the least of it. Webster became a Canadian hero. The Alouettes played in the Grey Cup, Canada's Super Bowl, and Webster was the league's Most Valuable Player.

"By then, the NFL teams had started to contact me. I heard from Detroit, from the Redskins, and from the Giants. I didn't really want to leave, but I knew the other guys in the backfield were making a lot more money than I was. I asked them for a raise and they said no. I went to meet with the Detroit people . . . about the only thing I remember was getting on the team bus and there was big Les Bingaman sitting with a case of beer . . . but I still wanted to stay in Montreal. Louise and I loved it. We were thinking about settling up there.

"But Montreal still wouldn't give me more than eight thousand. I told the guy I could make more in the States, and he said he didn't think I was good enough to play in the States. So I told him to go to hell and came home and three days later I signed with the Giants. Then he came down, and offered me a lot, but I had already committed myself. Our quarterback up there went to the NFL, too. Sam Etcheverry. And the Montreal newspaper ran a big headline right on page one. It said, WEBSTER AND ETCHEVERRY JUMP—THE WAR IS ON!"

And the Giants had bought a fullback. Cheap. They had also bought a local hero, since Kearny was just across the river. The people of Newark, Jersey City and Bayonne as well as Kearny would consider Webster was one of their own.

And he hit the NFL with a right cross.

"Shit, fighting was my middle name in Kearny. I was a redhead and I got very excited and I was always popping somebody in the mouth.

"I was never really big until my sophomore year in high school, and it seemed the little guys always had to fight. I had a lot of fights. Sometimes I still do. Couple of years ago I had to throw some guys out of the bar. That was a wild one. The older I got, though, the less I fought. But in the NFL I had some good fights. I once had a thing with Big Daddy Lipscomb, but he was so-o-o fucking big I was smart enough not to swing a second time. But the worst I ever had was with Johnny Sample of the Colts.

"We were playing this game, and I got tackled, and that little bastard, he was a cornerback, he ran over and kicked me in the ribs, hard. Then he jumped up and down yelling, 'I got him, I got him!' Well, I staggered back to the huddle and I couldn't catch my breath. But when I did, I asked Charlie Conerly to call the same play. It was third and two, and it was an off-tackle slant, so it probably would have been a good call anyway.

"I was supposed to carry the ball, but when we lined up I told Phil

King, the halfback, to switch positions. That meant he'd carry, and I took his job, which was to block out the linebacker. I knew Sample would be up, close to the line. I wanted him. So I ran right past the linebacker to get a good shot at Sample. He saw me coming and turned and ran. I chased him halfway down the field, but I got him. Then I looked back. The linebacker I ran past had just wiped out Phil. I learned a lesson there."

Webster's reputation spread throughout the league, and those with similar inclinations congregated to his side. Marchetti, for one. Ernie Stautner and Bobby Layne. The only criteria for membership in this fraternity were toughness and a taste for the free, spirit-spiced life. Webster passed with flying colors.

"One time we were in Los Angeles for a Pro Bowl, and Stautner, Layne and me were sitting in a restaurant about three A.M., having breakfast. There were these four Marines in there, real nice kids, clean, with crew cuts and all. Then about seven or eight guys walked in, tough-looking, dirty. They started to pick on the Marines, real nasty-like. Anyway, Stautner stood up and he started to cuss out the Marines, too, to bring these creeps over to us. Well, it worked. They came over and Ernie turned around and belted one and we took them all on. It was a pretty good free-for-all, but it was no contest with Ernie. He was stone crazy. He loved scenes like that."

Webster's addition to the Giants of the middle 1950's was another of those unplanned fortunate moves. He fit right in. The team had a character all its own, a collective psyche that demanded victory and fame, that promoted arrogance.

"We never lost a game," Webster says. "When the other team won, it was luck. When we won, it was just the way it was supposed to be. We figured when we lost the game just wasn't long enough.

"I remember one time when Phil King was a rookie. We played Green Bay in Milwaukee and we were losing, but we came back and won it with a field goal with just a few seconds left. Phil turned to Gifford and said, 'Boy, were we lucky to get that one.' Giff gave him a cold look. 'Listen, rookie, we knew we'd win,' he said. 'Luck had nothing to do with it. That's the kind of team we are.' "

Webster was the perfect complement to the fancy, elusive Gifford. He was Earthman, down in the dirt, scratching and plowing with his body for yardage.

He came up as a tailback . . . a halfback in the T . . . when the NFL teams used three running backs and the quarterback in their back-fields. But he was always more of a fullback, and for the bulk of his career fullback was where he played.

"Nobody was ever more reliable on third and short," says Jim Lee Howell, who for the most part was Webster's only pro coach. "That man knew it would be tough. He knew they were waiting for him. He knew it was going to hurt. But he just threw his body in the hole and he fought for the yardage. And he never complained about injuries. He was one tough bastard."

It was the Kearny way. In Kearny, that's not tough. That's a way of life.

Webster joined the Giants in 1955. In 1956, the team won the NFL championship with a brutal 47–7 victory over the Chicago Bears. In 1957, the Giants finished second to the arch-rival Cleveland Browns.

And then it was 1958.

"We knew we were good," Webster says. "But hell, we always knew that. It was no surprise when we won our conference. We had to beat Cleveland in a playoff game, and it was tough [10–0] but we knew we would. And when we were ready to play Baltimore for the champion-ship, we knew we'd win it. We liked to play the Colts. They were tough, but we could beat them. We had beaten them in '55, and we beat them three games before the title game. We knew we'd win it."

But they didn't. And none of the Giants, who had always prided themselves on their ability to win the big ones, would have admitted to the possibility of losing such an enormously big one.

"It sticks in my mind," Webster says, "because it was the first championship game that went overtime. But I remember a lot of games. It seems like you remember mistakes, even more than great games. Even today, I get mad at myself when I remember a fumble or a dropped pass twenty years ago. Like in '58, we beat Cleveland on a fifty-yard field goal by Pat Summerall. I always told him I made him a hero, because the play before I told Charlie I could beat the cornerback deep. Now, I never had speed, but I just knew I would beat him. And Charlie, bless his soul, he just looked up and nodded and called the play. And damned if I didn't beat my man. I was so damned surprised when the ball fell into my hands that I took my eyes off it and it hit my shoulder pads and I lost it. So Pat had to kick that big field goal. We won, thirteen to ten. But I still get mad when I remember it.

"Anyway, the morning of that game wasn't anything special. We got the baby-sitter about nine-thirty, and Louise and I drove up the Jersey Turnpike to the stadium. We were living in East Brunswick then, and I guess it was a drive of about an hour or so. I do remember one thing, we didn't talk at all, the whole time. I was real quiet, and she let me be. I never felt any tension. We were all relaxed. Sometimes I'd go out and have a few drinks before a game, but I was never nervous, never tight. I drove to the stadium and I got out and Louise took the car up to the Concourse Plaza Hotel, where we all met after the game. Always. I got in about ten-thirty, went down to the locker room, stripped and sat around.

"Nobody said anything special. We just got suited up when the time came and went out to play it. We knew we'd win. We got very pissed off when it was over and we had lost."

Even now, Webster is reluctant to give the Colts full credit. As with all the Giants, the loss was a blow to his pride, his pride in himself and in his team.

"I always said that game made the Baltimore Colts. They played better than they thought they could. They hadn't won anything up to then. They were good, but we should have won the game. Easy. They weren't that big, either. They did have a big front four . . . who was it, Marchetti, Big Daddy, Ordell Braase, Art Donovan . . . and they had good linebackers. But they just weren't that big. I thought we should have been able to move the ball better. It was a good physical game. A lot of people said we weren't that good offensively, but we were playing a team that was better than we thought they were.

"But look. Unitas hadn't done anything very much in the league until then, until that game. A guy like Raymond Berry, he just wouldn't have been drafted today. He wasn't quick enough, he wasn't big enough."

The pride in Webster comes through when he remembers one play in that game, perhaps the most critical play of the day. It was late in the fourth quarter. The Giants had come back from a 14–3 half-time deficit. They were leading, 17–14. Two minutes remained, separating them from a second league championship in three years.

"We went out and made a first down or two," he says. "It's our game. The clock is with us and we cannot lose. Then it's third down and four to go. Gifford got the call. That's the only time I can look back and say I wish I had carried the football. A lot of guys on the club . . . and in my own mind . . . we all figured I could have made it.

"I know I could have. But the call came off the bench, and it was a good play. It was called 'Shoot-25 Trap' . . . it was off-tackle, to the strong side, off what we called a 'Brown' formation . . . and normally I would carry that ball off the left side. We figured they would overshift, which they did. Everything fell right into plan, but somebody missed a block.

"That was the play when Marchetti broke his leg, and in all the confusion the ball got moved around before the referee spotted it. A lot of us on the field knew it was good. Jack Stroud nearly went crazy. He said the guy marked the ball with his right foot, reached down and put it by his left foot. Anyway, it was short. We wanted to go for it on fourth down. Players always want that. But the coach called for a punt, and it was a hell of a punt.

"And then we couldn't stop that damned Unitas. He moved them from the Baltimore fourteen to our thirteen in seven plays, which included two incomplete passes. So in five plays he gained seventy-three yards, and they kicked the field goal just as time was running out and damned if we weren't in an overtime game."

The Giants ran three plays and had to punt. Thirteen plays later, the game was over.

"In all my years, that was the toughest thing I ever had to do. I mean to just stand and watch when Unitas and Berry went to work. We double-teamed Berry, but he kept making the damnedest catches you ever saw, and they just kept coming down the field. We just stood there, and we kept waiting for them to cough up the ball. They were passing a lot, gambling. I felt sure they'd give up an interception."

And when the Giants lost:

"We just came in and sat in front of our lockers. I've never been in a quieter locker room. Nobody made a move to dress, or shower. Nobody talked. It was like a tomb. It was the end of the season and we had no place to go, no chance to make it up the next week. We were losers, in the greatest game ever played."

But even for the Giants, the game proved to be of much benefit.

"The first five years I played, nobody knew who I was. I could walk down the street unnoticed. But right after that game, none of us could go anywhere without being stopped. Restaurants . . . movies . . . bowling alleys . . . everywhere. We were in demand to make public appearances, to speak at banquets. One guy once stopped me in the street just to say thank you. He said watching that game had been his greatest moment.

"Financially, it really helped us. We got more money from appearances, we got bigger salaries, the teams all started to make more money. I think it's being felt even now. I think it helped expansion, television contracts, all of that. And I think that game even pulled us more together. We won in '59, and then again in '61, '62 and '63. I think that game made us a powerhouse. The fan reaction was so great it became like plus-points for us to play in Yankee Stadium."

Big Red played through the 1964 season, when the ferocious pounding finally took its toll. And perhaps the 1961 season was his best, not simply statistically but because no one had even counted on him to make the squad.

Jim Lee Howell retired after the 1960 season, and the Mara family, after failing to lure Vince Lombardi back from Green Bay, surprised most people by naming Allie Sherman, a one-time assistant coach in New York, a left-handed Jewish kid who had played quarterback for Brooklyn College and the Philadelphia Eagles.

Sherman was a rookie head coach in '61. Webster was a slow, plodding, aging and injured fullback.

"He didn't even list me on the three-deep chart," Webster says, his anger rising. "I told him I was coming to camp and that I'd win the job. He said I could come, but he doubted I'd stay. Man, did I work my ass off that summer."

It paid off in a 928-yard season in 1961, Webster's career rushing high.

"It was the most satisfying year I've ever had," he says. "Nobody thought I could do it any more, except me. I had a lot to prove."

Sherman's first three seasons were successes. Y.A. Tittle had replaced Conerly as the quarterback early in the '61 campaign, and he led the Giants to three memorable championship games. But the fine old team was crumbling. Several disastrous trades brought ruin and resentment, and by 1964 it was gone. When Tittle retired that year, after fourteen years in football, he made one of the most poignant statements ever made by a professional athlete:

"I just figured it would never end," he said. "I figured Webster and King would always be there to pick up the linebackers and Shofner would be flying way downfield somewhere and Gifford would be faking out a back and be standing there open and Walton would somehow get free for the third-down pass. I never thought we'd get old. And when we did, when we got to be old guys and washed-up athletes, I couldn't handle it. When something was not in its right place, I was mediocre, a loser. That's when I realized it was time to retire."

It was, indeed, time for many of them to retire. Including Alex Webster.

For Webster as for so many others, it was not to be a time of ease and success. Thrust into the business world, forced to earn without football, he went through a succession of employments.

"I had a radio job for a year, doing the color on a small network that fed the Giant games into upstate New York towns. Then I got a job as a salesman, selling paper, high-grade stock for printing companies. On the side, I did a little scouting for the Giants. It was tough, but I caught on, and pretty soon I was starting to come on as a salesman.

"Then I got called into the Giant office in '67. Wellington Mara offered me the backfield coaching job with the team. In all the years I've been married, that was probably the closest I ever came to getting divorced, because I took a pretty good pay cut. But I had to get back into football. It was my life. I missed it, and I didn't like sales. I was out every night, taking clients to dinner, drinking too much.

"I was the backfield coach for '67 and '68, and the summer schedule in '69. We played our last exhibition game on a Thursday. When we got home that night, we had the following day off.

"The fans were really getting on Allie's ass, but they always do when you lose. I thought everything would straighten out. We got home about four in the morning, and at nine Timmy Mara called. He asked me to come in to the office in New York, right away. He said he wanted me there by ten-thirty."

This time, Alex Webster did not have to touch the candy store man for traveling money. He drove into Manhattan.

"I thought I had gotten fired. I was in my golf clothes, so I changed into a suit. I walked in and the first thing was that I never saw an office jumping like that. They were knocking the doors down, everybody was hustling and bustling, and they took me right into Wellington Mara's office and closed the door.

"I knew something was wrong. It looked like he had never slept. He said he had fired Sherman, and it was the toughest thing he ever had to do. It really shocked me. I didn't think it was much Allie's fault, considering the kind of players we had at the time. So I finally asked Mara what did this mean to me.

"He looked right at me and said, 'I would like you to be the head coach of the New York Giants.' We were on the eighteenth floor of the Coliseum, and I must have hit the basement before I realized what he said. My first question was, did he think I was qualified? He told me I'd have all the help I needed. I was still uncertain until he mentioned my contract. It was one hell of a jump for me, so I said, what the hell, I've never quit on anything in my life, why not try it."

Webster tried it. For five years. Year by year, he grew into the job. He went from a stumbling, nearly inarticulate interview into a poised yet still blunt subject. His knowledge of the game had never been faulted, nor his rapport with players.

He turned to his one great asset: hard work. He drove himself, drinking too much, sleeping not enough. Smoking too much, resting not enough.

And then, after a six-game sweep of the exhibition schedule in 1973, following a strong, improving 8-6 finish in 1972, it all crumbled. The proud New York Giants, who felt the horrors of Sherman's tenure were behind them, died for Alex Webster. Their season record was two wins, eleven losses and a tie, but before the final game of the season Big Red announced his resignation.

"The pressure grew as we lost," he says. "Television people were tough, newspaper people were tough. It got to the point where I was really scared. People would throw things at the bus, and at the Yale Bowl [where the Giants played home games in 1973 and 1974] the fans yelled things at me I just can't repeat. Hell, if one guy says those things to me, to my face, I put the guy up against the wall and cripple him. But how can I take on fifty thousand of them? We needed extra police, just to protect me. I decided, who the hell needs this? It was affecting my whole life.

"It seemed in the last couple of years odd things happened. I could always get along with the players, but in my last year I almost had a fight with one of them, Charley Evans. He was on the payroll, the Giants were paying him, and he made a whole series of speeches knocking the Giants. We got phone calls. I got a lot of them. I got a letter from an eleven-year-old boy who said he was very sad that a player could say those kind of things about his team, that his Little League coach said it was the worst thing an athlete could do. It all got to me. I confronted Evans and he denied it.

"I got more calls, and it really aggravated me. He wasn't playing and he wasn't happy because he wasn't playing. And he wasn't playing because he was too fat. He came into camp twenty, twenty-five pounds overweight. Well, at practice one day it all broke. Charley is a strong blocker, a good player. Nobody could block better than Charley. But he was just immature. Well, I confronted him again and he said something I didn't like and I exploded. I started for him, challenged him to fight me, and then I suddenly realized what I was doing. But that was all the pressure, all the tension. It got to me, and that's dangerous."

Webster quit. One of his best friends in football, a quarterback-turned-executive named Ralph Guglielmi, set up an office in New Jersey for his buddy to run. Computer-leasing, time-sharing, selling again. That, plus the income from The Stadium, has allowed Alex Webster to stay in Sea Girt, to stay away from Kearny.

So it is in Sea Girt that we sit, talking about Kearny. Fondly. Alex Webster loves Kearny and the people and the boyhood he spent there.

"My grandmother," he says, "What a super woman she was. Next-door we had a Lithuanian family . . . and they'd speak English and the whole bit, but as soon as my grandmother went out in the yard, they'd start speaking Lithuanian. And my grandmother used to get upset . . . she'd say, 'Damn foreigners, would you speak English?' And she only stepped off the boat like a few years before."

Sea Girt is a long way from Kearny, but not long enough to stop the visitors from Webster's hometown. They come, and they drink, and they talk with him about the old names, the old places, the girls they pinched, the bars they wrecked.

And when Webster shows up in Madison Square Garden for the Ranger hockey games he loves, he still gets applause.

"It's damned embarrassing sometimes," he says. "I go there with clients to show them a good time and the people don't leave me alone. It makes me feel good, but it's embarrassing. Usually, my customers are more impressed than I am.

"But it's a good life now. Louise and I have been married almost twenty-five years, and we're closer than we ever were. The kids are gone . . . one's married, the other one's in college. Sometimes I wish I was here, doing what I'm doing, when they were growing up. I'd be able to spend more time with them, instead of being a football player off on the road someplace."

Then he pauses. A long, deep, introspective pause.

"No, that's not right. I wouldn't give up anything I did. I enjoyed the hell out of my life, and football did it all for me. What the hell would I have been without football?"

Johnny Sample

... Conerly long to Gifford incomplete (broken up by *Sample*)

... Conerly to Rote incomplete (broken up by *Sample*)

... Conerly to Gifford complete on left sidelines (Gifford hit by *Sample*, fumble, ball recovered by Lipscomb on NY 20)

"Handcuffs. I don't think there's anything more humiliating. I just couldn't believe it was me, man. Not John Sample."

THERE IS NOTHING in the store except a desk and a telephone and one chair. So you have to sit on the edge of the desk.

On the window, a hand-painted sign proclaims the splendor which is soon to come: JOHN SAMPLE'S END ZONE . . . BUY YOUR SPORTING GOODS FROM A REAL PRO.

And inside, on South Fortieth Street in Philadelphia, across the street from the University of Pennsylvania's main campus, sits John Sample himself. Black. Lean. Fit. Wearing a tank top and white cotton slacks. Confident and arrogant and bubbling over with false optimism.

If he were white, he'd have a prison pallor. But he is black. The pallor is on his psyche.

This is July of 1975. Three months before, John Sample was released from prison. A year and a day, three hundred and sixty-six days in three different jails. He will never forget, of course, and he still boils and seethes about his confinement.

He talks too loudly, too jovially, putting up defenses against the shame within, against the mark he will always carry with him. And, predictably, he says there is nothing he won't talk about. Not even his prison record. He says it with a hearty, man-to-man directness.

"You just ask me the questions," he says. "I'll answer anything. I'll talk about anything. There's no sense in hiding it. I was in jail. I'm out. And I'll straighten out this mess yet. Go ahead. Ask."

But his eyes never meet your eyes. And his hands, clenched, work at a myriad of meaningless exercises. He punches buttons on the telephone console. He fidgets with his thumbs. He opens the top drawer of the desk. Closes it. Opens it. Closes it.

And he talks compulsively, the words gushing forth in a torrent of self-justification. It is an uncomfortable moment, one better passed up, ignored, glossed over.

But it is important to him.

"When I retired from football," he says, "I had a ticket agency. Johnny Sample's Ticket Agency. Theater tickets, sports, things like that. I opened it the beginning of '67, maybe the last part of '66. And I was doing fairly well at the time. I was making a decent living. Then I got arrested for cashing federal checks. That was the charge. I did not do it. I did not cash federal checks. I had a trial. And I was convicted. I was convicted and put on probation.

"The people at the bank, two tellers at the bank . . . I had an account there, the Providence National Bank . . . the two tellers said the person who cashed the checks there looked like me. They testified to it. But the handwriting expert for the United States Government, whoever it was, he testified that it was not my signature on any of the checks.

"And the checks were not put in my account. I had an account there. They were not deposited. They were cashed by someone, and the tellers said it looked like me. So the jury came back . . . they convicted me. The judge, he's sentencing me, he says, 'I'm giving you the benefit of the doubt, that's why I'm putting you on probation.' And he did. He put me on three years' probation.

"That was March of '72. After that, I lost some of my business. I guess about fifty-five percent of the business. I lost it. As a result, the business went bad and I went into bankruptcy. I think it was the latter part of '73 that I went out of business.

"And then on February 27 of 1974 the Secret Service came and arrested me at my home and took me down to the judge that gave me probation. He said I had violated my probation by fencing federal checks. They said a fella had brought 'em to me and I was fencing them. Before this, they had taken all the information to a grand jury and tried to get me indicted. The grand jury refused to indict me. I had no new indictment, that's what a lot of people don't realize about my incarceration. I had no indictment . . . I was not arrested . . . I had no new case or charges. I had no new arrest. I was called a violation of probation. I was not arrested for some ot' ·r crime.

"It was not true. I never saw a federal check, I never touched one. There was no new trial, just a hearing with the judge. No jury. They had a witness to come in . . .

"Did I know him? Yes, I did. He was in my ticket agency several times. He testified that he had sold me some federal checks. But he never did. He never sold me anything whatsoever. He came in and testified, and the judge took his word against mine.

"They alleged that on January 21, in '74, Melvin Grover came by my house and we talked about these federal checks. Well, on January 21, 1974, I was at the Spectrum from eight o'clock in the morning until eleven o'clock at night. And I had eight witnesses come in to testify that I was there watching the pro tennis matches. These people had never been arrested for a traffic ticket. They had no reason to lie. Even the parking lot attendant at the Spectrum testified that my car was there . . . he said my car was there from a quarter to eight in the morning till he got off at five.

"And this conversation at my house was supposed to have taken place at four in the afternoon. No doubt about it, I got set up. And the judge refused to believe my witnesses and me, to believe this fella. As a result, I was incarcerated. He voided my probation and sentenced me to three years' incarceration. They took me up to Danbury Federal Penitentiary in Connecticut and I was there for two weeks.

"Then they took me to Allenwood [in Pennsylvania], where I spent the rest of my time. I was in twelve months and a day. Allenwood was where the Watergate people were. I met Magruder and them. I'm appealing my case. I just want to clear my name. I know they can't give me my twelve months and a day back. If they gave me ten million dollars I couldn't get that back. I just want to clear my name. I want to prove . . . well, I don't have to prove it to my family . . . my son was with me at the Spectrum that day, and my wife knew I wasn't home, because she came down [to the Spectrum] to meet me, and my little girl, it was her birthday, January 21, she was at a friend's house . . . and they had said my daughter was also home when I met with Grover. I never fenced any federal checks. I want to clear my name in the record books of the United States Government. I never cashed any federal checks and I never fenced any federal checks. Those two things I've never done.

"The United States Government, it's been proven in the last two, three years, they do what they want to do. See, they don't look for justice. They just want convictions, when they should be looking for the right people, to do the right thing."

And so Johnny Sample—three-time member of an NFL championship team, consummate professional athlete—went to jail.

"Before I was convicted, I spent four and a half months at the Philadelphia Detention Center. And man, that's like total war. There was fights in there . . . everybody's got a knife. The food is horrible. The judge, Daniel H. Hewitt III, he kept me at Philadelphia Detention, without bail, with no new case, until he decided whether he was going to violate me or not. The whole time I was there I was fighting my case . . . going to hearings, writing writs . . . but he would not give me bail.

"Hey, guys were in there for murder and they got out on bail. I had no priors, no new case, nothing. And he held me there all that time without bail.

"Anyway, I was in a cell for a while by myself, then they put me in a dormitory room, like, with twenty guys. In the summertime the heat was unbearable. I was there from February to June 29, when I left to go to Danbury. The food particularly, you just can't imagine how bad it smelled . . . roaches in the food, all kind of rodents in the food. Guys working in the kitchens that were junkies, had syphilis, clap, all that kind of stuff. Hair was in the food, dirt, greasy. They took the cups you drank out of and dumped them in garbage cans. They would feed you with plastic spoons and forks that would melt if you washed them in hot water, in a dishwasher. And the guards were just ignorant, no other way I can put it. They'd hit people, curse, tease us.

"And dig. I saw guys get stabbed. I saw guys get raped. You know, by twenty different guys at the same time. And that was the only place I've ever been where a white man was at a disadvantage. Every time they brought a white guy up there, the black guys just raped him. Not one time, several times. I tried to tell some of them they shouldn't do that, but you try to stop 'em, they gonna stick a knife in you.

"They knew who I was. I was like a hero. I'd say most of the guys there were young . . . they looked up to me, wanted to talk to me. I had no fights there, none whatsoever, they couldn't have been any nicer to me. The inmates, I mean. The guards were a little pissed off at me.

"They figured I was a guy who had made a lot of money, had some money, because I had two, three lawyers coming up to see me every day . . . I had a lot of money on my commissary account where I could get anything I wanted . . . well, a few of the guards were envious. I played basketball there, on the basketball team . . . I was in D dorm. And we won the championship.

"Then I got moved out, and up to Danbury. And going to Danbury was like going to the Waldorf-Astoria. I was there only two weeks . . . I didn't even get assigned to a dormitory or anything. Then one day the warden tells me I'm going to Allenwood. What am I going to say, no? You don't have any choice. So they put me on a bus . . . there was thirty-five of us on the bus . . . and I was the only one on the bus that wasn't in handcuffs. But I had had handcuffs on. I got handcuffed when the marshals took me back and forth from the Philly Detention Center to the courthouse. And when I went up to Danbury in a car, a fella named Vic and I were handcuffed together. Handcuffs. I don't think there's anything more humiliating. I just couldn't believe it was me, man. Not John Sample."

The desperation of men in prison—the frustration, the hopelessness —brought John Sample to a conclusion.

"At night I'd lie there and tears would come to my eyes. I missed my family, and they knew I didn't do anything, so I knew it was killing them, too. But I knew I'd be there for just a year. If my sentence would have been twenty years, or twenty-five years, you'd have to think about breaking out."

And on March 3, 1975, John Sample was released on parole.

Is this all convincing? Is Johnny Sample the victim of misguided justice? Stacked justice? Harried, overworked and overburdened justice?

The fact remains that he was sent to prison. That he was judged to be somehow, someway involved in something illegal. He protests, with cause and justification. But what convicted man does not protest?

Is he believable? Perhaps the critical answers lie in the kind of man he is.

Some years ago, Sample co-authored his biography. It was titled *Confessions of a Dirty Football Player.* He says he didn't want to name it that, "but if they felt it would sell books, fine, go ahead and use it."

And though he denies having been a dirty player, there are many other athletes who swear to it.

"I played the game as tough as I possibly could," he says. "If you're out there and not playing tough, and not really trying to hurt the other guy, then you're gonna get hurt. Right. I tried to hurt other players.

Now look, I knew a lot of dirty football players. To me, Bill Pellington [one of Baltimore's linebackers in the 1958 championship game] was the dirtiest football player I've ever seen. He just would punch a guy for no reason at all. He would punch and kick . . . he didn't care who it was.

"Yes, I would try to hurt another guy, but legally. Like when I'm going to make a tackle, I'm not going to take the guy and just hold him up and just dump him down easy. I'm going to knock him down as hard as I possibly can. If he's got his back turned catching a pass, I'm gonna hit him in the small of his back, hard. And if I knock him out of the game, that's all well and good, 'cause the guy sitting in the bench can't be as good as he is. That's gonna help me.

"When Shofner was with the Giants, he caught a pass once, a little out pass . . . I was covering him . . . and it was maybe three, four yards . . . I was with the Redskins then . . . and after he caught it he fell down. Now, a guy who's down can get up and run again, and I could have gone over and just put my hand on him, and he'd have been down officially. But I went over and jumped on him, using all elbows and knees, and I really hurt him, broke a couple of ribs. And that's what I was trying to do, 'cause I didn't really like him. He tried to clip me a couple of times, so I really tried to hurt him. And that's what I did. And when I got up off the ground, I said, 'You won't get up this time,' and I wasn't sorry that I did it to him. He tried to clip me from behind, and that could end my career.

"If I would have killed him, it wouldn't have bothered me one bit. And that's the way I felt about it."

Shivers start, small warnings that John Sample was, indeed, a dirty football player. Would he really have felt no remorse for killing a man? Shall we send our sons out to play a boy's game against men such as these?

"Listen, there were a lot of guys I played against who I really didn't like. A lot of them. I didn't like Gifford very much, because first of all I didn't think he was as good as the New York media tried to make him. And then he said a lot of things about me being a dirty ballplayer the first couple of times I played against him, and I didn't play dirty against him. I called him 'Pretty Boy' . . . and I told him he couldn't play . . . trying to get him annoyed. But I never did anything to him dirty. But he told the news media I was a dirty player, the dirtiest player he'd ever seen, and all. So after that I tried to get to him.

"But, you know, I have no bad feelings against him now. He has against me. On that program they do, he does the best job. I think he's a great announcer. Cosell is awful. He knows nothing about football whatsoever. Gifford does a great job. I did a couple of TV shows, and I told the people he does a great job. Not that I'm crazy about him personally. But he does a great job, regardless of how I feel about him.

"But I didn't like him very much, and Webster I didn't like very much. He tried to clothesline Big Daddy once . . . and he tried to kick him, too. As a result, I didn't like him, and I tried to get him. And Shofner I never liked very much.

"And there were a couple of players in the American Football League . . . I don't remember their names now . . . but mostly, I didn't like anybody with a different color jersey. They was trying to take the bread out of my mouth. But once the game was over, those things were forgotten about. But some of the players just never forgot them."

There were problems with head coaches, too. Otto Graham. Buddy Parker. Weeb Ewbank. In fact, Sample played with four teams— Baltimore (1958–60), Pittsburgh (1961–62), Washington (1963–64) and the New York Jets (1965–69)—and those three men were the only head coaches he played under.

Why the problems?

"In '58, when I played in the College All-Star game right out of college, Otto Graham was the coach of the team. Weeb Ewbank had already told me that he wanted me to be a defensive back with the Colts. So I went to the All-Star game and Otto wanted me to be an offensive back. I told him he was hurting my chances of making the Colts if he made me play offense. He said I didn't want to help the team, but I told him I was looking forward to what I'm going to do for a livelihood. I'll be here only three weeks, but I'm going to play football for maybe ten, twelve years.

"I tried to explain it to him but he couldn't understand it. He said, 'Well, if you ain't gonna do what I want you to do, I ain't gonna let you play.' I said, 'Fine, do what you want to do, just let me practice with the defense. If you don't let me play, I don't care.' Well, he didn't let me play. I played only about a minute in the last part of the game. We beat Detroit. And I didn't like him very much for doing it.

"I told him that after the game. He was going around shaking people's hands. I told him, 'Don't shake my hand, you ain't no friend of mine, because you didn't let me play and I think I was a lot better than some of the guys you let play.'

"And he said, 'Well, you didn't want to help the team.' So we had some words, and I cussed him first and he cussed me back. We didn't like each other very much. Well, the next year he was the All-Star coach again and we went to play them, 'cause we was the NFL champions, and during the game I hit a couple of his guys near their bench, knocked them out of bounds, and I told him, 'I wish it was you.'

"Then, when he came to the Redskins and I was playing for them, he told me he thought I was making too much money for a defensive back, so I told him I thought he was making too much money for a coach. That was the beginning of the '66 season, and he traded me to the Chicago Bears. But I didn't sign with them, and they sent me a telegram saying I was a free agent.

"And then Weeb called me, asked if I wanted to play for the Jets. I had played for Weeb in Baltimore, and I told him I did, so I went up there and we agreed to terms."

Sample had joined the American Football League. He was black-balled, he says, by the National Football League teams, and that belief led to a festering resentment.

"When we got to the Super Bowl after the '68 season, it was a high point for me. We were playing Baltimore, but I didn't care which NFL team we played. But it made it a lot sweeter, it being the Colts. There were still a lot of guys on the Colts who I had played with . . . that made it better, us beating them."

There is a sensitivity to color in John Sample's mind, too, that was far more pronounced when he was playing.

"There were guys I played with who were bigots," he says. "When I got to the Redskins, there was a guy . . . we were sitting down to the table in a hotel restaurant . . . and we were just talking about things in general and he said something and then he said 'nigger' and I jumped up and popped him in his mouth and we were fighting all over the table. But, you know, he grew up in that atmosphere . . . that's what he was used to all his life, talking that way without thinking about it. He was a receiver, too. I was able to get him in practice.

"And a lot of the white guys, they were always telling jokes about niggers and such, but they never told them around me. They'd stop when I came around. They knew I didn't like that shit. I was gonna pick up a board and we were gonna have to fight.

"Guys with Baltimore, too . . . like Billy Ray Smith . . . very prejudiced. And for all these years, there's no excuse for not having a black head coach. Look at the guys they give jobs to . . . like Otto Graham, a great player who knows nothing about football. They just play musical chairs with the same dudes. Take a guy like Emlen Tunnell, the guy who just died. He was a great player with the Giants, but he was just there. He had no authority, no say-so, nuthin'. Wellington Mara, the owner of the Giants, it's like he said, 'Don't worry, Emlen, you have a job for the rest of your life.' Who wants just a job for the rest of their life? That's no big favor. He knew a lot about football, but they just took the man's pride by giving him a job, giving him a pay check and no authority. That's a shame. They couldn't give me a job under those circumstances. If I was hungry, or if my kids were hungry. Just don't give me a check for nothing. That's degrading. And that's what the establishment of pro football is doing to a lot of black people, degrading them."

This is Johnny Sample, then. He discounts those experiences which are less than flattering. He prefers to remember the good times, the good games. He colors things, too, with a broad stroke of ego and exaggeration.

But others remember other times, sick times.

Ordell Braase, a defensive end on the Colts for twelve years, from 1957 to 1968, tells about Johnny Sample and the Missing Money.

"Someone was taking money," he told Paul Zimmerman in *The Last Season of Weeb Ewbank.* "We thought it was a groundskeeper or somebody. Once at a meeting Weeb said, 'Leave your money with Freddy.' That was Fred Schubach, the equipment manager, so we did, and they locked the door, but the money was still disappearing. Once Weeb even came up missing thirty bucks. He told us he went to a barbershop, and he said he knew he had thirty-five dollars in his pocket, and when he got there he only had five. And you know how Weeb is on money. Anyway, how Sample did it was we'd all be watching movies, and the room would be dark, and he'd have his chair at the back of the room, near all the lockers. He'd have one hand here and one hand there, and he'd just reach into the lockers and take the money out of the wallets.

"Well, we found out, and we set up a trap for him before a game. All the players watched him. It's funny, everybody knew about it except me. I remember thinking, 'Gee, they don't take this game very seriously.' They were all giggling and saying, 'Look now. Look now.'

"And then he got caught, and Carroll Rosenbloom [then the Colts' owner] protected him. What's more, John started that ball game. He started ahead of Ray Brown at the cornerback, and I remember Ray saying, 'First he takes my money, then he takes my job.' "

"He wouldn't clean out a guy," Ewbank remembers. "Say a guy had sixty . . . John would take twenty and leave the rest."

The players, led by Gino Marchetti, wanted to take care of it themselves. ("I think they wanted to kill him," Ewbank says.) But Rosenbloom wouldn't let it happen, and Sample played the rest of the year before being traded to the Pittsburgh Steelers.

There were outbreaks of violence, too. And not the kind that erupts on a football field in the heat of battle, not even the sort of incident in which Sample tried to "get somebody" with less than legal tactics.

His festering feud with Otto Graham, for instance, flared up in the summer of 1969 when the New York Jets, as the Super Bowl champions, were playing the College All-Stars in Chicago. Otto was the coach of the All-Star team.

Sample ran to the sidelines on a pass play and yelled something when he saw Otto there. Otto yelled back. They began shoving. And Sample, losing control, brought the face bar of his helmet down across Otto's nose, cutting it.

Sample spent twelve years in pro football, with four teams. Each time, there were problems. Arguments with the coach . . . incidents with the players . . . unauthorized charges to the team . . . difficulties with the press.

It finally ended in 1969.

"I hurt my back in that All-Star game," Sample says. "They put me in the hospital as a result. And I stayed there ten days, in traction. They let me out, and it wasn't any better. So I saw my doctor here [in Philadelphia], Robert Bass. He advised me not to play. Then I went to see a fellow named Nixon, who was the Eagles' doctor at the time, to get another opinion. He told me the same thing; that I shouldn't try to play any more because I could get some permanent damage done to my back. So Weeb and them tried to get me to play, tried to get me to come back, but I told them my back hurt. They thought maybe I was telling them this because I just didn't want to play. So they refused to pay me, and as a result I had to sue them for the two years remaining on my contract. "They thought I was jiving them, which I wasn't. I went to Dr. Nixon, I went to another man, George Resta, who at that time was the Washington Redskins' team doctor. It wasn't only my own family doctor, it was doctors who were connected with football who gave me that advice.

"It left a bad taste in my mouth because Weeb and them thought I was jiving, thought I didn't want to play. They thought I just wanted to get paid for nothing, and that made me mad because Weeb and I were together a long time. We were with the Colts when we won the championships in '58 and '59, and with the Jets. I'm the only player to play on championship teams in the National Football League and in the American Football League. Weeb is the only coach to do it. Nobody can do it again, because they merged. We're the only two men. And Weeb was the only guy to give me a job after the National League blackballed me."

Ewbank recalls that Sample's wife sent him a letter: You're the coach John had the most respect for, she said. Give him a chance. It's his one chance. He'll do his best. Please take a chance. Football's his only thing.

Weeb took the letter to David A. "Sonny" Werblin, then the Jets' president.

"He'll wind up suing you," he told Werblin, "and he'll cause you a hell of a lot of trouble, but he's better than what we've got."

Werblin approved. Sample was signed.

Four years later, after causing a hell of a lot of trouble, he sued the Jets for back salary. And in 1975 he won his suit.

Did Sample's back hurt? Was it serious enough to force him out of football?

"He doesn't say 'ouch' at the right time," said James Nicholas, the Jets' orthopedic surgeon, and a leading expert on football injuries.

But as a football player—purely and simply—John Sample was truly professional caliber. He was vicious and violent, cocky and arrogant, just the sort of man who makes an ideal cornerback.

Dr. Arnold M. Mandell characterized the personality traits of a defensive back in the *Saturday Review—World* on October 5, 1974:

". . . in the defensive backfield, the aggression gets buried under more and more inhibition and discipline. These men are like long-distance runners; they are loners, but they are nowhere near as hungry for glory as are the wide receivers. In place of the vanity and fantasies of the wide receivers, the defensive backs experience depression and rage. They have traits that can be found in offensive linemen, linebackers and wide receivers. They are tenacious. They must learn . . . pass-defense patterns that require incredible self-discipline in the furor of battle . . .

"So they need controlled and timed brutality and anger. In my research team's recent study of more than six hundred potential NFL draft choices, six men were found to be almost suicidally depressed; all of them were defensive backs. The depression of a cornerback who has been beaten on a pass play may last for days, though the great ones shake it somehow. The depression resulting from the inhibition of so much aggression can put such men in danger of self-destruction."

Depression and rage . . . controlled brutality . . . in danger of self-destruction . . .

Is this not Johnny Sample?

There was no overt childhood deprivation. Though black, of course, and though born in the South (Cape Charles, Virginia), Sample did not suffer apparent scars.

"It was very prejudiced down there at that time," Sample says. "My father was a barber. He worked for himself. He didn't have any bosses, and he didn't have to depend on the white man down there for any crumbs or any throw-outs or anything. So we were pretty independent. We didn't have a lot of money, but we weren't poor by any stretch of the imagination. We always had food on the table. We always had our own home . . . very comfortable . . . it wasn't lavish, but it was comfortable . . . we had enough clothes and shoes . . . the home was always heated.

"I was an only child, and I got pretty much what I wanted. I didn't want too much, 'cause I didn't know about too many things to ask for, but what I asked my mother and father for, I got.

"I went to Cape Charles Elementary School and North Hampton County High School. I played football there, and basketball and baseball, and I ran track. I was captain of all four sports my last two years in high school. My mother and father split up when I was a senior in high school, and my mother came up to Philadelphia to live. When I graduated, I lived with her. And when I went to college . . . to Maryland State . . . I commuted. Sometimes I'd live with her, sometimes I went to the barbershop and lived with my father."

Sample was a highly recruited athlete. There were more than fifty athletic scholarships offered, many by the high-powered so-called "football factories."

"I went to Notre Dame's campus . . . and Ohio State . . . and the University of Pittsburgh . . . but none of them could promise me I'd play right away. They had that rule then that freshmen couldn't play [on the varsity] and I didn't like that rule. But the man from Maryland State, Verlon McCain, who was the athletic director and the head football coach there at the time, came down and talked to me. Then I went to see the campus, and I liked it. But what I liked best was when he said I could play right away."

He did play right away and he played exceptionally well. And from the tiny campus of Maryland State, which in the 1950's did not attract many scouts, he joined the Baltimore Colts.

"I was their seventh-round draft choice," he remembers, "and I signed for a thousand-dollar bonus and an eight-thousand-dollar contract. That was January of '58."

And less than twelve months later, Sample was in an overtime period, sudden death for the National Football League championship.

"The first thing that comes into my mind is the excitement of playing in a championship game," he says. "It was my rookie year, and playing in a game like that, and in Yankee Stadium, the mecca of all sports . . . well, it frightened me more than anything else. Saturday, the day before the game, we went into Yankee Stadium to work out and I just walked around and looked at it.

"The game didn't scare me. Once it started, it was just like I was playing on an empty field, like when I was a kid in Virginia. All the people . . . the television . . . that didn't faze me at all. Just Yankee Stadium, that rattled me some."

The Colts tied the score in those incredible last two minutes. And the game was headed, historically, into a sudden-death period.

"I didn't even realize they would do that," Sample says. "I really didn't know. Once we started going down for the tie, I figured, well, if we tie it up, that's that. I didn't even have any thoughts of an overtime. And just to tie it was shaky. Steve Myhra, our place-kicker at the time, was extremely nervous on the sidelines. Unitas was making the drive, and Raymond and Lenny were making great catches all over the field, and when we got into position for the field goal, Steve was . . . perspiration was just popping off of him. And he wasn't the world's best kicker. He didn't even have a good year . . . not by any stretch of the imagination did he have a good year.

"But he kicked the field goal, and I'm sitting on the bench with Leonard Lyles, who was also a rookie, and we just figured they'd split the money.

"Then somebody whispered something about overtime and sudden death, and I didn't know what the hell they were talking about. There had never been one before. So the game ended in a tie and they went out for the flip of the coin and I was surprised as hell. I guess eighty percent of the guys on the team didn't know what was going on, either.

"So Weeb got us together in a huddle, just like the start of a game, and explained to us what was going to happen, that the first team to score, regardless from where or how, was the winner. Field goal, safety, what have you . . . it wins the ball game. And we lost the toss, too.

"I was covering Gifford, he was the flanker, and I think on the second play Conerly threw the ball maybe sixty yards, and as I'm running six million thoughts went through my head. You know, 'If this guy catches the ball, I'm going to be the goat' . . . 'Everybody on TV is looking at me' . . . 'My mother and father are up in the stands' . . . 'My teammates are going to be mad with me' . . . I was scared to death. But fortunately for both of us, the ball went over our heads. I didn't get a chance to knock it down, he didn't get a chance to catch it."

Sample's memory fails him. The only pass Conerly threw in the sudden-death period was to tight end Bob Schnelker. It was incomplete.

"Gifford didn't catch a touchdown pass on me that day," Sample says, although Frank did score the Giants' go-ahead TD on the second play of the fourth quarter, a fifteen-yarder from Conerly. "It wasn't on me, it was on a guy named Milt Davis. It wasn't my side."

Memory fumbles again. It was Sample's side.

"I remember that key play in the fourth quarter for the Giants," he says, and this time his memory is accurate. "They had a fourth down, maybe only three inches to go, and I remember Roosevelt Brown was standing there when their coach said to kick. And he said something like 'No, no, we don't wanna kick, we can make it, we can make it.' If I was the coach, I would have punted, too. They got a great punt out of it. John just did a great job of getting the ball down the field.

"When we got closer, the Giants went into a prevent defense. But we were in field goal range anyway, so why prevent anything? Try to get the ball back.

"And in the overtime period, when we were driving again for the winning touchdown, I was standing right beside Weeb, and everybody was up on their feet, naturally, and I was thinking to myself, I even said it out loud, 'Well, couple more first downs and we'll be in field goal range, we'll be in good shape.' And Weeb said, 'You're right.' That's all he said.

"Then we got down to about the twenty-four, and the phone rings. I don't know who was calling, but somebody called Weeb over to the phone. Then he came back and walked away from me and Myhra, and walked down to the end, where the ball was. I know that after the phone call a field goal never crossed his mind. I don't know who called. I asked Weeb about it a couple of times after I got to the Jets, but he never told me. He never said who the hell called him. Look, he had coaches in the press box, and it could have been one of them. But it could have been anybody. But it never got to fourth down, so he never had to make that decision. But I know before that, he was thinking field goal a lot. I know he was telling Steve on the sideline, you know, 'You gotta think, you gotta relax . . .' But he never talked to Steve again after the phone call.

"It was not the most memorable game of my career," Sample says. "And playing on the Jets when we beat Baltimore in that Super Bowl wasn't, either. It was a game I played against the Eagles, in Philadelphia, when I was with the Steelers. It gave me more satisfaction than anything else. It was the first time I played a regular-season game in Philadelphia, where I was living at the time. I had all my friends down, and everything. I guess it was '61, because the Eagles were champions in '60.

"And Tommy McDonald was probably the best flanker in all of football at the time. I played him, and he caught two passes and I intercepted two and knocked about twelve down. I think that's the best football game I ever played. That sticks in my mind as the game that made me the happiest."

It was personally rewarding, personally spectacular. It is not surprising that it remains Johnny Sample's biggest thrill.

As I was leaving, the talk turned back to prison.

"Hey, when I was at Allenwood, I even got some pictures I wasn't supposed to take," he offered as a farewell shot.

Pictures of what?

"Of cells . . . the dishes there . . . the way food was prepared. I even got a picture of a roach crawling out of some rice. Things like that. Maybe we can sit down and talk sometime, all right?"

The words come back. The warnings are out.

Johnny Sample is intelligent. Articulate. Charming. He smiles a lot, laughs, has friends. But there is something lurking there behind those eyes. Something cold. Something mindless. Something that cautions, constantly. Something that tells of sudden anger, of possible rage, violence, destruction.

Johnny Sample is still controlled by an inner fire. A rage to be unique, to be noticed, to stand in the spotlight of attention.

"You have the number here, don't you? Give me a call sometime. We can get together."

Rosey Grier

... Moore minus 3 to 27 (*Grier*, Karilivacz tackle)
... "I had hurt my knee the week before, and after a
while, when it got really tough ... I wasn't able to
move. So I asked to be taken out."

*"Wherever we were, I saw the hope, people reaching out for his dreams,
black people, white, young, old. They were all there, man. They were
reaching out for him."* —Rosey Grier, on Robert Kennedy

ROSEY GRIER IS a lousy tennis player. Embarrassingly lousy. Flat-out, stone-cold lousy.

But who's going to tell him?

Rosey Grier is also gigantic. Not just tall. Not just heavy. Colossal. Large enough to block out light, large enough to crowd a ballroom. He is six-feet-five. He looks taller. He weighs . . . well, let's see. He'll admit to three hundred pounds, but when he says it he smirks. What he really sees when he steps on a scale is his business, his secret.

He wears small eyeglasses, though one supposes that pilot's goggles, perched way up there, precariously atop his head, would look small, too. He wears a goatee and a mustache, and they look small.

He is soft, plump, marshmallowy. But do not satisfy some deeply rooted urge by telling him that, for beneath the soft layers is a man of incredible brute strength, with arms like oaks, legs like redwoods, a girth like that of the great white shark.

Happily, especially so for saloon stalwarts and sidewalk warriors, Rosey Grier has the temperament of a bashful teddy bear. He has a high-pitched, almost-squeaky voice, so incongruous as to provoke behind-the-hand chuckles. But be strong, heart, do not succumb to the temptation. Rosey Grier is capable of some certifiably awesome feats of strength, such as picking people up and throwing them far, far away.

Indeed, Rosey Grier did not simply tackle other men when he played the defensive line for the New York Giants. He enveloped them, surrounded them and crushed the ball from their grasp. Then he probably smiled and apologized.

But as you listen to him talk, something else happens. To the stranger, it is nearly as incongruous as the tiny voice trapped inside the massive body. Rosey Grier thinks. And articulates. He is highly emotive, socially aware, politically alert and attuned. He knows where he's at, and he knows where most other people are at, and he has learned to accept or reject all of them with confidence.

At the moment, he and I are at Caesars Palace Hotel, in Las Vegas, Nevada, America's answer to bored adults looking for their own kind of Disneyland, where Mickey Mouse and Main Street, U.S.A., have been transmuted into roulette, blackjack, and perhaps somebody named Cindee or Candee or Tanjee.

Why is larger-than-life Rosey Grier here at Caesars Palace? It's the big time, baby. He is here to play in the celebrity segment of the Alan King Tennis Classic, that's why, right up there with other folk heroes such as Hugh O'Brian, Sidney Poitier, Buddy Hackett, Johnny Carson, Lee Majors and Ross Martin. This event is always concluded with a Grand Masquerade Ball, in which most of the men are disguised as knights in armor and most of the women are disguised as nudes.

So here is Rosey Grier, teaming with a pro, Harold Solomon.

Let us analyze Rosey's tennis game. He cannot serve. He doesn't have the faintest idea of a forehand or a backhand. He cannot move.

But he's having a wonderful time, because he knows why he's here and why he's been invited, and he's just happy to be around. A name. A celebrity. It's good for business. One might meet an agent or a producer or a director. And—perhaps the largest incongruity of them all—Rosey Grier is in show business. He has a string of credits that date back ten years. He's appeared on *Daniel Boone* and *Movin' On*. He's been in the movies. He even did an awful thing with Ray Milland —*The Beast with Two Heads*—in which Milland (who portrayed a bigot) had his life saved by transplanting his head onto Rosey Grier's body.

Or was it Rosey's head onto Ray Milland's body?

Rosey also sings professionally. He does guest appearances on other people's shows and grins with a helpless mirth when they make bad jokes about his size. He has written a book on needlepoint, and he practices needlepoint during his quiet hours. Incongruous? You tell him.

But this façade of jovial giant hides from most people the sadness which lives inside Rosey Grier. He lost one of his truly close friends, a man named Robert F. Kennedy.

Where were you the night of June 5, 1968? Rosey Grier knows where he was.

Robert F. Kennedy had just won the California State Democratic Primary, the most prestigious, the most critical, in the nation. He knew where he was going. He was on his way, from California to the White House. To the Presidency. He was guaranteed his party's nomination as its choice for President of the United States.

Rosey Grier was walking behind the Senator through the kitchen of the Ambassador Hotel in Los Angeles after he had accepted the adulation of his adoring public in the ballroom.

A shot rang out.

Chaos erupted. But Rosey Grier, acting as Bobby's bodyguard, reacted with the instinct of an athlete. He found the arm that held the pistol. He wrenched it up and away from more destruction. He threw the body to the floor. He pinned the assassin down until authorities came to take him away.

"I don't want to go into what I saw and what I felt," he says. "I don't want to go into I saw this guy doing that, and that guy doing this. We all know that. That's in the records. You can go read my statements in the courts, they'll tell you what I saw there. But they will not tell you my feelings . . . so I would rather deal with that, not with the specifics. It was the most tragic moment of my life, and it made me make the most important commitment of my life."

"It has only been the last eighteen months or so," says his second wife, Marge, "that he's slept through the night without waking up, yelling and screaming. He doesn't like to talk about it."

Rosey, who is a grandfather at the age of forty-three, also has a four-year-old son. The son's name is Roosevelt Kennedy Grier. Rosey calls him "Li'l Ro."

"For me to say exactly what I heard . . . what I saw . . . how I reacted . . . to me, that is exploiting it," Rosey says. "From my point of view, that's exploiting it. So I won't do that.

"But I can tell you how it was so confused, how Bobby got so far away from me by himself. It was simply because we had decided to go one way, then someone came up and said let's go back another way.

"I was with Ethel, who was pregnant, and Bill Barry [one of Kennedy's aides] helped me to take Ethel down, and another guy walked down with Bobby, because Bobby jumped down one end of the stage while we were making a decision which way to take him. Imagine if we went the other way. It would have been a different day today. It was a choice. We had two choices. We made the wrong one."

Rosey stares, at nothing . . . at everything. "I was not in command. We wanted to go the other way, we had cleared it, we had it all cleared. We had men standing all along the way. And I told him, I said, 'Bobby, when you finish your speech, let's go this way.' And he said, 'Okay, Rosey.'

"Bobby was the kind of man who made you get involved," Rosey says, pausing now at the tennis courts, with the heat of Las Vegas' nine-month summer drenching his shirt. "I met him, and I immediately liked him. I liked his style . . . which meant you never felt like you were an outsider. You never felt color . . . you never felt anything other than just being warm around the whole family.

"I met him when I went to do a telethon, with so many celebrities. At first, you know, I didn't want to go. My manager said, 'Why don't you go down there?' and I said, 'Well . . . I just don't know.' What really worried me was the flight. I don't like to fly, you know. But then I figured if God wanted to take somebody he wouldn't take Eddie Fisher and Connie Stevens and a lot of other people who were on the flight. We were flying from Los Angeles to Washington in a little plane. But I went. I didn't think God wanted me bad enough to take all those other people.

"And we had one tremendous telethon. We raised a lot of money for kids, you know, and it was cool. But when I first got there, the Kennedys invited me over to the house . . . in fact, they had a car waiting and took me straight to the house. And the first thing that happened there was Bobby Kennedy punched me in the stomach.

"And we were at each other like that from then on. Everywhere he went, he and Ethel took me. No big thing. Just like 'C'mon, Ro, let's go.' We just became friends. We did everything together. Where Bobby went, I went. I was sitting right between them or right beside them all the time. When Bobby got ready to go for a walk, he'd holler, 'C'mon, Rose,' and it was just one of those things. We went around like that, always together, or we'd just be in the house, you know, talking together. I really liked the guy. I got to know him very well.

"When I got back to Los Angeles after that telethon, you see, I sent back a thank-you note to them and they returned a note to me. Their friends would get out to Los Angeles and call me to say hello from Bobby. Then we got to calling each other. Then every time I got to

Washington, I'd be over to the house, and we'd talk and have a good time. When they were out here, I'd meet them wherever they were at and, well, basically we just got to be good friends.

"We talked about everything, Bobby and me. You know, we talked about everything you could think of . . . people and politics and sports and just everything. One time he asked me about my momma and I told him everything I knew about her. He was like that. He made you want to tell him everything, open up your heart.

"So it was the kind of thing where you just feel for a guy, that you felt a concern for what he was concerned about. That's what I liked about him.

"I saw little girls, old women, and they cried when they saw him. And I couldn't understand it. Why are they crying? Why are they crying? But you know what it was? There, among them, walking among them, they saw a hope for the future . . . a tiny, tiny ripple of hope. Each time a man stands up for an idea, or acts to improve the lot of others, or strikes out against the injustice of others, he sends forth a tiny ripple of hope, and crossing each other from a million centers of energy and daring, those ripples build a current that can wash down the mightiest walls of oppression and resistance . . . Words often used by Bobby Kennedy that was a quote from a French philosopher.

"I got so attuned to him that I began to read what Bobby had said, and I began to understand the man.

"Sometimes he'd get off a truck or a car and just start walking. And I'd get off, too. I wouldn't say anything to him, just get off and be with him, protect him. And he always looked over and he always saw me. He never told me . . . he just looked for me, and man, I'd always be there. Whatever needed doing, I'd do it.

"Like when we were in Watts, in a car parade. A kid jumped on the front of the car, straddling it. And whoever told him to get off, the kid would cuss 'em out. So they called Rosey, and I went to the kid and I said, 'Hey my man, what you doing, man?' And the kid sees me, and jumps off the car and hugs me and kisses me, and the car drives away and then Bobby tells them to wait. He said, 'We're not gonna leave Rosey.' And that's the way it was with us, just close friends.

"So you can see . . . this friend, who I loved so much . . . and the hope I saw in all people . . . wherever we were, I saw the hope, people reaching out for his dreams, black people, white, young, old. They were all there, man. They were reaching out for him."

Kennedy's life and death taught Rosey about commitments, and in the winter of 1968, the horror still fresh, the wound still new, Rosey Grier took the first step toward following his own.

"I had been entertaining at a Red Cross Fund show in the Anaheim Stadium," he says. "It was a Bob Hope thing, and when he saw how all the people reacted to me, he asked me to go to Vietnam for his Christmas show tour.

"I went because I wanted our soldiers, who were there because we sent them there, to see that we felt we owed them our respect. They were serving our country at the request of our government. And how could we, as people, feel anything toward them other than that they did what they were told? So I went for that reason. I'm terrified of flying, and when he asked me, I asked if we could take the subway. But I went.

"We got fired on in Da Nang, rocket fire at the airport. So we start running for the plane and a colonel yells for me to come with him. Damn if it isn't a guy I went to Penn State with, and he takes me up in a fighter 'copter, and they're shooting at it, and I'm saying, 'Damn, if it isn't my luck to get my black butt shot down and I don't have no business up here in the first place.' All these tracers are flying past, and I keep ducking, because I was in the Army and I knew enough to realize that there's all these bullets between the tracers.

"And another time we landed somewhere and Marines came to pick me up. All the others went on a 'copter, and here I am in a jeep with this loud yellow shirt, and there's snipers firing at us, and I'm thinking, 'Here I am, with a bright yellow shirt, a big damned target, right on the back of this jeep.'

"We went into where the soldiers were and I talked to them, man. Blacks and whites, they all liked me, and that felt good. I found camaraderie, man. They were beautiful miles I covered. And we went to all these places, and I saw all this brotherhood, and then we went on a battleship called the *Hancock*, and the soldiers were so beautiful. Then we went on the U.S.S. *New Jersey*, the only gun ship they had in Vietnam. There, I found a difference.

"There was no brotherhood at all between black and white. A couple of black soldiers helped me put my bags into my room, and an officer comes over and says to them, 'What are you all doing in here?' And I said, 'They're my guests, man,' but he said to them, 'You know you're not supposed to be in here.'

"So I says, 'What is this, man?' and they said, 'Man, you don't know. They treat us like we are dirt, garbage. We are the cooks and the washers . . . it's not the commander, it's those who are in between. They won't let us get through, to submit our grievances.' So I said, 'Okay, if you guys really feel that way, get together, sign whatever you want to sign, and give it to me. I'll call somebody in Washington.' But I never heard from them again.

"Then, when we were coming back, I was telling Bob Hope about this. I said something ought to be done about it. And he said, 'Well, why don't we just forget it . . . we came over here to entertain 'em, not to come back with the sad part about it.' I thought, hey, I don't feel that way. I understood what he was saying, but I found something that needed to be changed, and that's what I felt. I told him whether he did something about it or not, I was going to do something.

"When we landed back in the States, Governor Reagan was there to meet us. And I wondered, what's he doing here? So I wouldn't get up on the platform, I wouldn't let them politicize what I had done. But Bob called me up to be in the group picture, so I did."

Now, months after Las Vegas, we are sitting in Rosey Grier's office in the Los Angeles City Hall building. The twenty-first floor. One wall is occupied by a chart, a chart that contains Rosey's dream.

The dream is called Rosey Grier's Giant Step, a blueprint for a self-help project for Watts, all of south central Los Angeles. It is a renovation, a reconstruction, a rejuvenation of this blighted area torn by race riots in 1966, stripped of all pride and economic capabilities, of educational facilities, of medical centers.

Rosey was in the midst of preparing a plan. And the only way he thinks it can be done is to get the people involved in owning a piece of their community through entrepreneurships. And he thinks the federal government should be involved if it takes $150 million.

"He has been giving it all his time, day and night," says Marge. "It's his life, his dream. He will get together a board of directors, form a nonprofit corporation, and build. He wants to change things, to give people the chance to help themselves. I mean it, he's given his time from his family, from his acting career, to get this started."

Rosey talks at length about Giant Step, and calls it an outgrowth of what he learned from Bobby Kennedy. Some who have seen the plans call Giant Step an outlandish, but realistic dream.

Rosey also works for the City of Los Angeles, as a consultant to Mayor Tom Bradley of Los Angeles on youth gangs. He roams the streets, and he has tamed the terrors of Watts.

"He has a great rapport with those kids," says his assistant, Roberta Ernisse. "He just walks through there, and he tells the tough ones, 'Don't trust me, watch me. See what I do, how I do. Then make your decision.' He is a totally committed, most remarkable man. I've been with him a long time, and I believe all the things he believes. He has taught me."

Meanwhile, Grier lives "modestly," according to his own estimate, in a two-bedroom apartment in Brentwood, a fashionable section of Los Angeles near Beverly Hills. He drives two leased cars—a Firebird and a Mercedes. He likes traveling, especially the drive to Vegas.

But, he says, "I am not a greed merchant. I would like security for my family, but that's all. I would like to know that my son can go to college."

Grier's wife is white. He met her when she came to him for help in getting some black kids into a school.

"We're married five years now," he says, "and we're growing together. She's white, I'm black, but it doesn't make any difference. It never does. My friends are not numbered that way."

It has been a long trip for Roosevelt Grier, born in Georgia in 1932. He was one of eleven children, the seventh child.

"In terms of finance," he says, "yes, we were poor. We lived on a farm, so we had food. We didn't have money . . . we didn't have all kinds of clothing . . . but we made clothing."

Rosey's family moved to Roselle, New Jersey, when he was eleven. Later, they moved to Linden, New Jersey, where Rosey played football and threw the shot. He went to Penn State on an athletic scholarship, and there he struck up an enduring friendship with Lenny Moore.

"I was always the oddball in the family, I guess. I loved education. I always pushed to go to school . . . I fought to go to school . . . I worked to go to school. My brothers and sisters . . . I guess they liked

school, too, but, you know, like in the South it was the big family
. . . they stayed home to work on the farm.

"But I never planned on going to college. I had no idea I could go
to college. When I finally did get into college, I became another
person. In other words, I wasn't looking at Rosey Grier, I was looking
at another guy. It wasn't really me, it was somebody else.

"I guess even now I look at that 'other guy' and I say, 'Who is he,
man? How is he able to do all the things he does?' You know, how
did I get so lucky to be able to do the things I do?

"But I know that I made a commitment in '68, after Robert Kennedy was killed. I made a commitment that I was going to be a strong
servant for my fellow man. There were things I could do, with power,
that perhaps other people couldn't do. I know lots and lots of people.
I try, with all my might, to encourage people to get involved, to not
stand on the sideline but get into things.

"You see, I categorize people . . . politicians . . . in groups. There
is the dove, and the hawk. And the fox. The fox runs with any group
so long as he gets what he wants. Then there's the ostrich. The ostrich
sticks his head in the sand, he don't care what happens . . . he says,
'I hope you all go away pretty soon.' Then there is the pigeon. That's
us. Everybody feeds on us, and we don't have the strength to fight
them off. That's what we have to do, stop being pigeons or become
damned tough ones."

This is clearly the teaching of Bobby Kennedy, and Rosey Grier
was an apt, rapt pupil. Bobby got to Rosey Grier in a way that few
things had ever gotten to Rosey Grier before.

As a football player, Rosey Grier was lazy. A laziness, it should be
said, almost natural in one so big, so strong, so noticeable. Things
physical came easily to Rosey. Perhaps too easily. What need was
there for strain when the offensive linemen opposite on the line of
scrimmage weighed two-twenty and Rosey weighed three hundred?
What need for extra effort? What need to prove himself? They all
knew him, the giant, the mountain. They all knew it was impossible
to move him. They knew the incredible length of his arms, the power
that existed in that bulging body.

He did things the easy way, and still he excelled.

Andy Robustelli has said Rosey was subject to "some mental
lapses." That means, translated from football-ese, that Rosey didn't

play hard every down. But then football was part of Rosey's life, not all of it. There were other things, more important.

"That sudden-death game," he says, "what I remember first is the game before . . . We were playing the Cleveland Browns in the playoff, and I was chasing Milt Plum and I got my knee hurt. So when we played in that championship game, it was advertised all week that I had a bad knee. And so what Baltimore did, they came out and first thing they did was they ran . . . like they lined up right fast and put all the guys on my side and used a quick pitch . . . but it didn't get anywhere because we had what we called 'automatic defenses.' Something like that was always covered.

"And, so, I just played my position so it didn't affect my knee, but later on in the game, when it got really tough and I wasn't able to move, I asked to be taken out.

"We had a guy named Charley Janerette, and he came in for me." (It was not Janerette. He didn't come to the Giants until 1961. Frank Youso, an offensive tackle who doubled on defense, came in for Grier.)

"But it was a very exciting game, one of those games that you wanted to be up to your top, and it was probably one of the saddest moments I had in playing football that I wasn't able to do the thing that I could do best, get off on the ball and really move. It was the kind of game you really wanted to get into.

"It's the game I remember most about my career, even though we lost, because it was the year that the defensive team began to become very well-known. We had stars who were made from our defense . . . Sam Huff was made, Jim Patton was made, I was, Andy Robustelli, Jim Katcavage, and Lil' Mo. It was our style. We dictated to the offensive teams.

"Unfortunately, in this game Unitas was so great that even with our style of play we were not able to stop them when he and Raymond Berry got really going. So the thing I remember is that this was the game that really popped football. It became the exciting game that it is today . . . I mean, it kinda like broke it open, it was the most exciting game that was ever played, in terms of strength, in terms of determination and teamwork, and in terms of two teams giving all out to win.

"This was the turning point, I think, in pro football. It was two really top teams, throwing everything into wanting to win."

But the loss, the crushing overtime defeat, didn't stick with Rosey.

"Yeah, everyone talked to me about it, the first few weeks and months after it was over. But I'm the kind of guy that ... well, that was just one Sunday during the football season. That was only a game. To me, life is lived year-round. So that was only a moment in the history of my life. It didn't mean that much, significantly, to me, other than the fact that it was an important game, that it did something for football. But as far as it meaning so much to me as an individual, because we had played in a sudden-death overtime ... well, we had lost the game. And now ... who did the Baltimore Colts play when they played that sudden-death overtime game? We were those 'other guys' in the game.

"But it doesn't become a bad game because you lost. It's a bad game when you didn't try. To me, living is giving it all you got. No matter whatever condition you're under, you have to give it all you got. If you lose, so what? You didn't lose your life. You only lost a game, or a fight."

So what ... That marked much of Rosey Grier's time with the Giants, from his rookie year of 1955 until he was traded to the Los Angeles Rams in 1963.

"I remember once," said Ed Kolman, then a line coach with the Giants. "It was during one of those times when I was always needling Rosey about his weight. I mean, he was just too heavy. I think we listed him as two-ninety, but he was much, much heavier. So it was near the end of the season, and I made him promise to me he'd go on a diet over the winter and get down to two-seventy, two-eighty. He promised.

"Well, the next summer, there he was, big as ever. I walked over and said, 'Rosey, you lied to me, you didn't even try.' And he got all upset and he said, 'I did so, Coach, I really did. I tried to diet. I even went on one of those Metrecal diets, and I got to like it so much I drank a can with every meal.' Metrecal was a high-protein drink, something you had *instead* of a meal. But you just couldn't stay angry at Rosey. He was like a big, friendly kid. And he was a hell of a football player. He really was."

But he was overweight, disastrously so. Finally, as part of Allie Sherman's housecleaning that in fact brought about the fall of the house of the Giants, Rosey was traded away, even-up for another defensive tackle, John Lovetere of the Rams.

"When Sherman traded away Huff, Mo and Ro," says Kyle Rote,

"he took out the heart of the defense. Ro and Mo were the two tackles, Sam was the middle linebacker. You just can't do that easily." Rosey played another four years with the Rams, retiring in 1968 after a serious Achilles heel injury. By then his acting and singing interests began to take a turn upwards, and he astounded many by gaining success in those shark-infested waters.

Rosey Grier is many people. To those who know him only as a figure on a screen, he is glamorous: a giant of a man, who sings and acts and walks and talks just like real people. To those who know him well, he is a gentle friend: big because he is big, but not nearly as big as the friendship he brings.

And to himself, alone, private, unseen, he aches to remain Bobby Kennedy's comrade. He mourns his loss. He is dedicated to somehow taking up the slack, filling the void. He feels the void is in all of us. But the void he feels most is in himself.

Jack
Stroud

... Webster plus 3 to 13, *Stroud* block
... Gifford plus 5 to 10, *Stroud* block
... King plus 4 to 24, *Stroud* block
... Triplett slant left for TD, *Stroud* block

"Football isn't like any other job, and I refuse to ever again feel the way I felt then . . . You put your blood and gristle and everything into it . . . Teeth, knees—you give up a lot . . . You can get that dedicated only once."

"THAT WAS THE darkest day of my life," said Jack Stroud, staring out at the George Washington Bridge far below his fifteenth-floor apartment in Fort Lee, New Jersey.

He did not mean The Game.

It was a humid, rainy night. The glare of hurrying automobiles was only partially visible, sending up uneven shafts of light through the mist.

Jack Stroud is a success. He is a respected, highly paid institutional research salesman for a Wall Street brokerage firm. Twice he has left firms to accept better positions, more lucrative positions. He is a member of the prestigious Downtown Athletic Club. He owns a boat, which is moored in fashionable Stamford, Connecticut. He is a name in his business, a professional in a demanding, complex industry.

I had come to talk of football, and to renew an old friendship. I wanted the memory of one game, one season, one moment of glory and disappointment. Jack Stroud played for the New York Giants in the 1958 championship game; indeed, he played for the New York Giants for a dozen years.

He played in the pits, on the offensive line, where men are anonymous, receiving recognition from the fans only when they miss a block or screw up a play or jump offsides. A great lineman receives status only among his own. The work is painful and long, the salaries painfully short. It has been said that only those who truly love the game can enjoy the offensive line. It has been said that only a masochist can truly embrace the offensive line and revel in its agonies.

It is thankless work, but invaluable. The swivel-hipped halfback would go nowhere without the drudges who toil on the offensive line, opening holes between tacklers with their heads and their bodies. The headline-familiar quarterback would be felled mercilessly by the roaring beasts of the defense if it weren't for the offensive linemen, the oxen, the blockers.

And Jack Stroud worked in the best tradition of such men. He sought no glory, and expected none.

"It was a job," he said, "and I did it because I have always had pride in my work. All the time I played I thought I was lucky to have the chance. I just loved football, and the people who mattered to me, they knew I did it well, and with pride."

But today Jack Stroud bears an unbearable sadness from which he can escape for only a few minutes or hours at a time. Jack Stroud's son—a fine, strong, athletic boy—died in 1970 in his eighteenth year. And when young Jack died, a part of Jack Stroud, Sr., died with him.

"Jack had won his own scholarship to Tennessee," said the father, who also attended Tennessee on a football grant. "He was an All-State halfback in high school in Tennessee. And a real fine athlete, a better athlete than his old man. He played basketball . . ."

Jack Stroud stopped, close to tears. Then he pressed on.

"He was eighteen. He would be twenty-three now. I didn't push him into football. In fact, I did just the opposite.

"A lot of people said, 'Gee, you know, he probably won't play football as well as his dad,' and I used to take him aside and say, 'Hey, you don't have to play football . . . I don't care *what* you do . . . just do something. You've got to do something in this life. But whatever you do—whether it's playing the piano, playing football, whatever it is, that's your business—just do it well, be proud of it.'

"But he had the drive, which was evident when he was little, he just hated to lose at anything. When he was seven years old, we used to take the kids over to the stadium on Saturday, you know, for a football game. Kyle's kid—we called him 'Rookie Rote'—and Frank Gifford's boy, Andy Robustelli's boy . . . they'd choose up sides. Well, this one day Jack's side lost the game. And he's walking off the field and there's tears in his eyes, so I walked up to him and I said 'What's the matter?' He said 'We lost.' He was really in tears.

"So I said, 'Look, you've got to learn to be a good loser.' You know, you've heard it all your life, you just say it off the top of your head.

"And Johnny Dell Isola, he was our line coach then, Dell grabbed me by the arm and he said, 'Goddammit, don't you ever say that to that kid again. You're not a good loser. You don't believe what you just said. Don't try to teach him that crap.'

"I looked at him and I said, 'You know, John, you're right.' He said, 'You show me a good loser and I'll show you a lousy athlete. It's all right, if you lose a game, you walk over and shake hands and say congratulations. But when you start meaning that congratulations you're in trouble.'

"But Jack . . . he was . . . he had everything going for him, and he, uh . . . "

Another pause. Another flash of private grief.

"He hurt the shoulder in high school, and every time he'd hit somebody . . . well, let me tell you this story.

"In his freshman year, I went up to Notre Dame to watch him against the Notre Dame freshmen. And after, he couldn't lift his right hand. I went to shake hands with him, and he just couldn't raise his hand. I asked what's wrong, and he said it was nothing, just a little injury, it happened in his senior year in high school . . . he had gained three hundred and some yards one night, and I was sitting right in front of a bunch of college scouts, and he had a hell of a night.

"It turned out that the socket, the doctors said it was destroyed. The orthopedic surgeon at Tennessee, who was the same surgeon who worked on me twenty years before, decided he should have it corrected. He was a very competent orthopedic surgeon. Jack just died. It was the anesthetic. Jack had a very rare reaction to it. That's all."

He stopped again, this time for good. And this time, the tears were so close that I turned away, feeling suddenly like an intruder.

This was the end of a two-hour conversation. Jack Stroud's memory is as good as a camera. He remembers details. It is the mark of an offensive lineman, whose assignments are intricate and precise, who reacts not by instinct but by observation.

Much of what a running back does is instinctive. He can free-lance, as the coaches say, once past the line of scrimmage. The receiver, too, can improvise, knowing the quarterback will be watching. If the sideline is covered, he can veer off into the middle. Defensive linemen are almost totally ruled by instinct. They must get to the quarterback, or stop the runner, but how they do it is their business, so long as they do it. They are all allowed the luxury of free-flowing motion, of following the ball, of moving in whatever direction might be dictated by the motion of others.

But the offensive lineman is a computer. On a given play he must know what to do, where to be, whom to block, where the runner will be, where the receiver will be going, what sort of help the quarterback will need. And when the ball is snapped, the offensive line must, as a unit, in concert, move as programmed. One man out of place, one man starting too soon, one man going the wrong way can destroy all semblance of order, of precision.

With an offensive lineman's acquired gift for detail, Jack Stroud went back to that afternoon in 1958, when the Giants met the Baltimore Colts.

"The first thing that comes to my mind, the first thing I think about, is that referee standing there, picking the ball up by his right foot, putting it down by his left foot. His right foot was toward the goal we were going to, and his left foot was the other way, and instead of making the first down by a foot and a half we were four inches short. He was standing right by the sideline, and his back was to the chains, and he looked back over his shoulder, took a reading and just put it down arbitrarily.

"That was in the final few minutes, and we had a lead, it was seventeen-fourteen, and we wanted to go for the first down, on fourth down, and we were mad at Jim Lee [Howell] because he wouldn't let us. We would have run our heads through a brick wall at that point.

"Marchetti broke his leg on the play, Big Daddy Lipscomb jumped on him, and I figured a quick dive with Webster over that same spot would get us a first down. It would have been a hell of a lot easier with Gino out of there. I saw him at the Downtown Athletic Club the other night, and I told him I didn't wish him any bad luck or anything, but if he was going to break his leg he could have done it in the first quarter and saved me a lot of trouble. I used to always wind up drawing him. I was still playing guard then, but one way or another we used to run short of a tackle when we were playing Baltimore and I was the third tackle, too.

"But even when I didn't, I'd play Art Donovan, who was a great tackle, so playing the Colts was no easy thing, it was a lot of work. But anyway, we were mad at Jim Lee for not going for it, because I had a feeling at that point that we should not let them have that ball back. In retrospect, I can't blame Jim. I'd have done exactly the same thing. Chandler punted it out of there . . . he got off a really good punt . . . and then we went into a prevent defense, which is something I don't agree with.

"I've never seen that defense work yet. Unitas and Berry . . . the extra time they had with only three men rushing . . . it was all they needed. John would plant that foot, and Berry would run his pattern and then come back, and those poor guys covering him had to overshoot him by two steps, and the ball was there. Wasn't anything the matter, they didn't have a chance to take the ball away. Of course, Berry always knew where he was on that field. You see a lot of clowns, they run down and they catch the ball and then they decide to run backwards to dodge somebody and they have a first down and end up losing it. Berry always knew where those chains were—so did Gifford and Rote—and he'd always fall forward.

"I saw Berry later, I guess it was '63. We were playing the Colts and they were down, and he caught a pass. He needed nine yards for the first down, and when he caught it he was about eight yards downfield and he got hit. And he spun around and dove with his hands outstretched, and he was looking right at the down marker when he did it. Where he came down, the ball came down, just over those chains. That kind of effort is hard to beat."

Effort was the word that marked Jack Stroud's season in 1958 as well.

"I tore my knee up three times," he said. "Each time I'd get it taped up and go back and play and tear it up again. So for that game I had a bad knee, plus I had been kicked in the ribs in Detroit so that I couldn't breathe, I could not stand up straight. I kept Marchetti from getting the passer, so I guess I had a good game. But I couldn't take a deep breath, and every time I hit somebody it felt like I was being jabbed with a knife. I guess it could have punctured my lung, or something, but you don't think about things like that, for God's sake. It was a championship game, and I was going to play if somebody had to drag me out there, if I had to crawl. I was going to play.

"If I'd have had a baseball bat in my hands, I could have done a better job on Gino, though. Or a small derringer . . . no, a large derringer. I don't think a small one would have hurt him."

Stroud had joined the Giants in 1953, when their home field was still the old Polo Grounds in upper Manhattan.

"In '55 we had played Washington and drawn only sixteen thousand people. George Preston Marshall . . . he owned the Redskins and he was one of the founders of the league, I think . . . he blasted the press and the fans and the Giants for not drumming up enough interest. You know, the lousy reception and the newspaper coverage and like that. And it was true.

"The next year, we moved across the river to Yankee Stadium and I think we averaged about forty-six thousand per game. Why? I don't know, really. People wouldn't go to the Polo Grounds because they thought they'd have their purse stolen, or if they drive maybe their wheels would be stolen. But a mile away, in the Bronx, that was okay. It was a good Jewish neighborhood, a lot of nice shops, and that year we won the championship, beat the Bears, forty-seven to seven. The next day, there was one column in each New York paper, telling how we lucked out. I think it was because only one or two of the sportswriters had picked us to win, so they had to cover themselves.

"Anyway, that was the attitude we faced. In '57 they kept writing we'd fall on our faces, so Jim Lee made us run . . . all year . . . he just ran us into the ground. I remember we were seven and two, chasing Cleveland, and we lost the last three games of the season, to San Francisco, Pittsburgh and Cleveland.

"We just ran out of gas. I think against San Francisco and Pittsburgh we fumbled something like six times in one game and seven in another . . . everybody was just worn out. And in '58 it started the same way. By the time the exhibition season was over we were just run into the ground. We were getting ready to open the season and Vince Lombardi [the Giants' offensive coach] scheduled a meeting on the Thursday night before the Sunday opener. We were planning on seeing a show, or just drinking beer or something to relax. Everybody grumbled and cursed, but at seven-thirty we showed up with our playbooks at our meeting room and one of the waitresses was standing there, saying, 'The meeting is downstairs.'

"It was a rathskeller downstairs . . . we were training at Bear Mountain. He had a three-piece combo, he had all the tables set up . . . he had kegs of beer . . . and he had a bunch of the waitresses for the guys to dance with. Jim Lee Howell went to bed at nine o'clock, but Vince stayed there. And about one-thirty in the morning . . . things were getting pretty noisy . . . he said, 'Okay, fellas, party's over,' and everybody scrammed. They had these kegs of beer with these big pasteboard containers, you know? So everybody ran over and filled as many of those gallon containers as they could, to take them back to the dormitory. What a night. I remember Phil King grabbed a case of bottled beer, and when we got back nobody had an opener, so he

The Game

There were two endings: one with 9 seconds left when Steve Myhra of the Colts (65) kicked the field goal that tied the game and another in overtime when the Colts' Alan Ameche galloped into the end zone untouched to win the game.

UPI

WIDE WORLD

Colts

After the game, the Colts kneel in prayer in their dressing room. Kneeling at left is Lenny Moore and standing at right is Raymond Berry.

WIDE WORLD

WIDE WORLD

Alan Ameche

WIDE WORLD

Johnny Unitas

WIDE WORLD

Raymond Berry

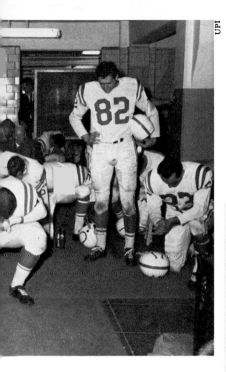

Lenny Moore

Gino Marchetti

Johnny Sample

Kyle Rote

Giants

After taking a handoff from Charlie Conerly (42), Mel Triplett (33) scores the Giants' first touchdown.

Rosey Grier

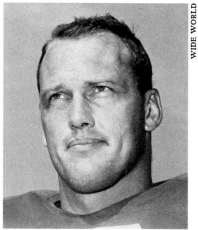

Andy Robustelli

Jack Stroud

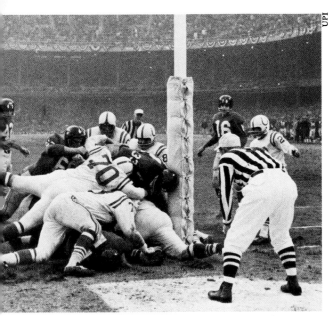

Alex Webster

Sam Huff

Charlie Conerly

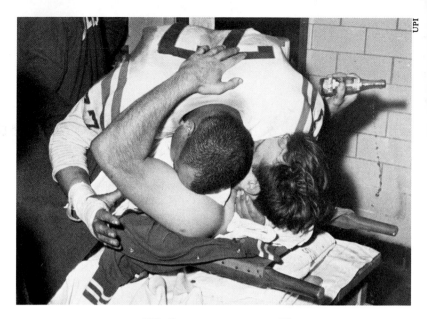

Afterward

Above, *Gino Marchetti, on a stretcher with a broken ankle, gets a hug from teammate Jim Parker.* Below, *John Unitas and Colt coach Weeb Ewbank, both with long careers ahead of them, smile for the camera the day after the game.*

Above, *Giant coach Jim Lee Howell discusses his team's loss.* Below, *twelve years later the coach is Alex Webster, whose teams never made it to the championship game.*

The Departed

Many of the participants in the game have died.

Vince Lombardi, Giant offensive coach

Emlen Tunnell, later a Giant coach

Big Daddy Lipscomb, Colts

Phil King, Giants

Jim Patton, Giants

smashed the bottles against the doorjamb and drank from the jagged edges. Only Phil could do that and not cut himself.

"And the next morning . . . boy, everybody was really dragging. But it broke the routine, the monotony. We went on to have a hell of a season.

"But that surprise party put us over the top, and when we started winning big that's when pro football fever hit New York. We got down to the end of the season and we had to play Cleveland twice. We had to beat the Browns the last game just to tie them for the Eastern Conference title, then we had this playoff game to settle it. Before the first game was over, people were lined up at the windows waiting to buy playoff game tickets . . . and before the playoff game was over, they lined up again waiting to buy championship game tickets. The second Cleveland game and the championship game we had a full stadium, first time ever.

"Something just happened. Football caught on. I knew, because all of a sudden all my friends wanted tickets, unlike the earlier years when we couldn't give 'em away. We'd tell people in restaurants we played for the Giants, and they'd give us this funny look and say, 'This ain't baseball season.' They didn't know there was a football team called the Giants. That was '53, and five years later we just didn't have enough seats.

"That was the year, '58, that pro football caught on in Detroit and Cleveland and Los Angeles, too, There had been interest all along in Chicago, and Washington. And for the first time, the columnists were writing pro football from coast to coast. And I can understand the owners, because from 1925 to 1958 they didn't make anything. It's been the last seventeen years, and I can remember one of the kids who was striking last summer said, 'Well, hell, they won't even open their books to us.' Well, why the hell should they? Did he think they owed it to him to keep that team going all those years?

"Is it part of the agreement to keep a kid on the bench and pay him fifty thousand a year? Do they want to share in the losses those men had for over thirty years? The most I ever made was twenty thousand, in my last year. My first year I made five thousand, and that was only because I made an agreement with the Giants when they drafted me in 1950, before I went back in the service for the Korean war."

But before Jack Stroud is accused of being a disgruntled old man, before he is labeled with the tag of "former player, now jealous," let us examine those feelings about today's athletes. "Hell, I don't begrudge them the money they're making," he said. "The more they can make, more power to 'em. What I do resent, and what I don't really understand, and never will, is when they make the money and don't want to put out for it. When I see 'em not really hitting out there, making errors because they're thinking about, you know, whatever they might be thinking about, that's what irritates me. I can't think of any team today that puts eleven good football players on the field at one time.

"In our season of '58, we had eleven real players on offense and defense. So did the Colts. And I didn't realize it at the time. I figured that was the way it was supposed to be. For example, I don't think I really appreciated how good Jimmy Patton was at safety. You just took it for granted that everybody would do their job. Today, the most glaring weaknesses I see are defensive backs who won't tackle. One of today's Giants, Spider Lockhart, he could play anytime. He'd have been great anytime. He's a little guy, a free safety, but he hits like hell.

"That's why you have so many thousand-yard rushers today. Once a guy gets past the line, his chances of getting rapped are very slim. Most defensive backs run along with them, like a damned escort, while they're looking for a soft place to hit him. It bothers the hell out of me to see the Giants do so badly now. I have a lot of ties . . . a lot of my old friends are still connected with the team.

"Everybody did his job when I played. Like Sam Huff. He wasn't real big for a middle linebacker. He wasn't real fast. But Sam did his job. If Sam was supposed to be in the five hole, he was in the five hole. He wasn't in the five hole two seconds late, he was in the five hole when he was supposed to be in the five hole. And when he got to the ball carrier, he hit the ball carrier. Hard. That whole defense did its job. The only guy who had any mental lapses, I guess, was Rosey Grier. He got a little sleepy once in a while. He'd throw somebody for a five-yard loss and then he'd rest for three or four plays. Sam used to jump all over him. The problem was he couldn't carry that much weight around, and he could not discipline himself, either. But when he didn't keep that guard away from Sam, he heard about it. From Sam. Sam took his job very seriously. Later, though, everybody fell in love with computer sizes. All the guys the Giants tried after they traded Sam away were bigger and stronger and faster. But they weren't nearly as good. Jerry Hillebrand . . . Henry Davis . . . I don't remember all the names.

"I remember talking to Harland Svare about that. It seems like the guy programmed into the computer, the best size and all, was Dave Robinson. But there was only one Dave Robinson, and he happened to be six-three and he weighed two-forty and he had hands as big as that television screen and his arms were about eight feet long and he was where he was supposed to be when he was supposed to be there. There are a lot of people in this world who are six-three and two-forty, but they are not all football players. That's where the computer fouled up.

"Sam Huff wouldn't have been drafted. And Nick Buoniconti. And Raymond Berry. And I don't care if Berry played fifteen, twenty years ago or today. He'd still be a great receiver, and there are guys running around now faster and bigger but he worked at it. He was devoted to it."

A feeling of togetherness, an aura of close-knit comradeship, permeated those Giant teams that Stroud remembers. But it wasn't all that peaceful and harmonious.

"We had individualists," he said. "I don't think I've seen a more diverse group. But we all knew our success depended on the other guys.

"Today they seem more interested in contracts and long hair and beards and mustaches and hair driers. We were the most critical of our teammates. We never covered up for a guy, we told him when he screwed up. We didn't wait for the coaches to see the films. The ones who didn't cooperate were the outsiders. In '64, when it all went to hell, the old guys still went out and gave one hundred percent—when they were allowed off the bench."

In 1964, when the old warriors were in their death throes, one incident revitalized the Three Musketeers feeling for one dramatic moment.

The Giants were in Pittsburgh. Young Lane Howell was at offensive tackle, playing defensive end John Baker, a six-six, 260-pound assassin. Baker broke through—to those who witnessed it, he simply walked through—and shattered Y.A. Tittle's ribs with one of the most violent, jarring tackles in memory.

The next week, against Washington, Lane Howell was being beaten by defensive end John Paluck.

"So Allie Sherman came up to me," Stroud recalled, and it should be noted that Stroud and Sherman were never the best of friends, "and, well, at least he could have been polite about it. After all, I hadn't done anything but sit there and get splinters. So he came up and said, 'Get in there, and you better do the job.' And I did resent that, because it wasn't me who let that guy hit Tittle the week before, and I had to sit there and watch that whole show. Well, I had played better games than that, but I got more publicity after that game than I had ever gotten before, because everybody was looking. I didn't let Paluck get to Y.A.

"I was an old guy with one leg, but I tripped him and I kicked him and I tied his shoelaces together . . . I did a lot of things to him. I never liked to block low. I liked to hit 'em in the head, because it hurt more when you did that. I'm sure I would have been cut that year [it was his last, in any case] but they knew they had two turkeys out there who couldn't play. So I guess I have to thank Baker and Paluck for giving me one more year, but the handwriting was on the wall. It was time for me to get out.

"I had had a run-in with Baker earlier. He was six-six and had arms out to here, but he was no ball of fire, if you know what I mean. So one day he's tearing up our tackle, and our line coach, Ed Kolman, says, 'Get in there and hit that son of a bitch.' I did, and do you know what? He quit on me. And his team, he was with Philadelphia, cut him the next week.

"But that '64 season was sad. When you trade away good players and don't get anything for them, you have nothing to trade back. They traded Sam Huff for two guys, Dick James and Andy Stynchula. James had been a good player for Washington. He did some running, played some defense, a good all-around guy. But Allie was going to use him as a heavy-duty runner, a fullback, and he just couldn't do it. And he replaced Sam with somebody who had never played the position. He just said, 'This guy's gonna be great,' and he expected him to be. I guess he wanted it so bad. Allie's problem, I guess, is that he thought we resented him. We didn't. I don't know what made him the way he was. But he was wrong, nobody resented him. We had a bunch of mature guys and somebody had to be boss. Okay, he was the boss. We didn't care one way or another about authority.

"We might not like everything he was going to do, but we'd do whatever he said to do. He almost tore the team apart in his first year, the '61 season. You could see it. There was a lot of dissension starting. We even had a team meeting. We said, "Hey, gang, enough of this. Only one way we're gonna win. Doesn't matter what kind of offense he puts in. Whatever it is, that's what we're gonna go with. We're gonna go out there and kick somebody's tail. And we're gonna win.' That's how the team got itself back together. And we won three championships in a row for him and he never appreciated it, I don't think. But I don't carry any grudges now.

"Football isn't like any other job, and I refuse to ever again feel the way I felt then. With the Giants, it wasn't just a nine-to-five job. You put your blood and gristle and everything into it, and you just felt a little more strongly about it. Teeth, knees . . . you give up a lot. I felt very fortunate that I was able to do what I wanted to do most and make a living at it. I didn't get rich. People asked me what I did with all my money, and I said I invested it . . . in the landlord, in the grocery store, in the clothing store. But a lot of people never get the chance to do what they want to do, and it lasted a lot longer than I ever thought it would. I was a twenty-five-year-old rookie from being in the service twice, and if somebody told me I'd play for twelve years, I'd have said, 'You're out of your mind.' I took it one year at a time. It seemed like every summer they had ten guards—big kids, faster— in camp, but every year it seemed like I was starting again.

"In 1960 there were like ten young guards, but me and Darrell Dess went all the way in a two-hour summer scrimmage.

"It was hot, and we were dead. I kept wondering where all those fine young guards were. Anyway, the last play Dick Modzelewski, the defensive tackle I was playing . . . he had gone all the way, too . . . he said, 'Hey, why don't you fall down and I'll fall on top of you and the hell with Jim Lee?' I said, 'Well, why not?' So I fell down and he jumped over me and grabbed Conerly and swung him around. And Jim Lee looked up and said, 'Stroud, what the hell kind of a block was that?' and I just blew the two hours I had played so well.

"I swore I'd get even with Mo, and I did. I used to take lots of health vitamins, especially vitamin E, and somebody kept stealing them. I peeked one day, and it was Mo, so I bought a big gallon jar of kelp pills, viler than hell, and Mo asked what they were. I told him they were the new miracle vitamin, kept your wind good, your legs strong, the whole bit. And I said you had to take a lot, maybe fifteen, twenty a day. Sure enough, he started stealing them. When the bottle was half empty, I said to him, 'Boy, would you believe some dummy is taking that kelp,' and he said, 'What do you mean? You're taking it.' And I said, 'Not me, you don't think I'd take anything that smelled like that,' and he got all upset. I said, 'Well, somebody was stealing my vitamin E so I put that kelp out there for them to steal it instead, and anything that smells that bad, it's just terrible for you. Smell comes out of your pores and everything.'

"He got all red in the face and said, 'You son of a bitch, it's me,' and I said, 'Yeah, and you screwed me in that scrimmage, too, remember?' Those were good years. I wouldn't trade them away for anything. And they're better than whatever else I'm doing now, because like I said, you can get that dedicated only once."

The years that went before were less good. Stroud's mother and father were divorced when he was young. His mother raised him in what was necessarily a tentative, day-to-day, hand-to-mouth existence.

"I grew up in the Depression," he said. "In California. I was born in Fresno, and my mother and I moved to San Francisco when I was twelve. This was in 1940, and she was a switchboard operator. She found an ad in the paper for a bookkeeper. The only thing she knew about bookkeeping was when she worked as an operator in a hotel in Fresno, the bookkeeper worked in the same room with her. She conned them into hiring her as a bookkeeper, and the difference was between making fifty dollars a month or seventy dollars a month.

"Our rent was thirty-five dollars a month, and I had a paper route which paid me ten dollars a month, and I graduated from that to busboy, and when I was sixteen I violated the draft laws, but differently. I got some draft card blanks and I forged one, because you had to be eighteen to work on the docks and I could make a lot more money on the docks than I could as a busboy. They needed every able body they could find, and I was larger than the average kid, so I spent all summer and weekends during school working as a stevedore. I'd work from Saturday morning straight through to Sunday night, four full shifts, but I'd come home with forty bucks for the weekend.

"But I can't complain. It wasn't an easy childhood, where I had time to lollygag around, but I didn't become a juvenile delinquent running around the streets of San Francisco, working the docks.

"What I became I owe to my mom. She wouldn't let me get away with anything. If she told me to be home after school, I'd damned well be home or she'd be on my behind. One of my duties was to come home and put the potatoes up to boil, and I was scared to death of forgetting and having her get there first. She was a disciplinarian, for which I was profoundly grateful. "One of the things I had enough brains to do before she died was to thank her for all she put up with from me. Because when I think of what she sacrificed, because I wasn't an easy kid to discipline . . . The first ruckus I really had with her was about playing high school football. She wouldn't let me, and I was fifteen and I finally said I'd forge her signature if I had to. She said if it meant that much to me, she'd do it, but she promised me I'd get all my teeth broken if I played.

"Then sixteen years later, after a Giant game . . . it was the one time all that season she came to New York . . . I was thirty-one years old, and I got my front teeth broken. I went back to the hotel where she was staying, and she saw my mouth all swollen. First thing she said was, 'Let me see your teeth,' and I picked up my lip and they're gone. She went beserk.

"It was sixteen years after I first started playing, but she started saying, 'I told you, I told you you'd get your teeth broken.' And I said, 'Mother, look at it this way . . . I got sixteen extra years' use out of them.' So she was right. Mothers are usually right. Even if they're late."

Stroud joined the Army at the age of eighteen.

"First thing I remember is eating whatever they put in front of me," he said, smiling. "I learned to do that at home, and it wasn't half bad to me. Worst meal I can remember in the Army, they put three different kinds of cabbage in front of me. Most of the guys got up and walked out, but I ate mine. I had the good sense to know that, number one, I was hungry, and number two, cabbage was good for me.

"I was volunteered for Officer Candidates School by the company commander. I went down for the test, and I passed everything, but I didn't want to do it. I didn't want to be an officer. I wouldn't sign the agreement that bound me to two more years after I became an officer. I went down and volunteered for the paratroopers instead. They didn't want to take me, but I insisted, and the guy finally said, "Well, if you want to be an idiot, here, sign this,' and I was a paratrooper. Then after jump school I failed the physical because I was too heavy. I weighed about two-twenty then, and their limit was two hundred.

"So then everybody got their orders. Except me. The next day I got mine. They were keeping me there as an instructor. I stayed there another year, then got out and went to Tennessee on a scholarship. I won eight letters, four in football, four in track. I threw the javelin, and I was Southeastern Conference champion twice, state of Tennessee champion four times. "Then I went back into the Army. I made the mistake of getting my commission in the R.O.T.C. In June of 1950 I was commissioned and in June of 1950 the Korean war broke out. So in 1951, when I graduated, I was on my way to Japan."

Two years later, Stroud joined the Giants.

Twelve years later, he became a Wall Street success.

"I got into this business while I was playing," he said. "For a time, I sold commercial printing while I was a player, and I really didn't enjoy it. I had had several offers to get into the brokerage business, but you needed a six-month training course and I always said I couldn't afford it. One day, one of my friends called me at seven in the morning and said, 'Hey, I got somebody who wants to talk to you about the brokerage business.' So I went down and talked to him. I still said I couldn't afford it, because I had an ex-wife and two kids I was supporting.

"But I thought about it all night, and I decided maybe I could afford it. I had a little money saved, and I discussed it with more people, and two weeks later I went to the school.

"It's been somewhat like football. No two days are the same. I am what's known as an institutional salesman, I sell research analysts a product for large buyers. I'm good at it. I enjoy it. It has its ups and downs, like what the government has done to the market, to the industry, which is a crying shame. In the name of helping the little guy, because he's paying too much in commissions, they've increased the little guys' commissions seventy-five to eighty percent since they set out to help him. And in the name of increasing competition by doing away with a fixed rate, they have already succeeded in eliminating about two hundred firms and there are about four hundred left, and if I have to guess, I'd say a year from now they'll be lucky if there are two hundred left out of that. But that's a whole long story, too. I feel very strongly about that. Let other people worry about the little guy. When the government starts to do it, the little guys get it in the neck."

There are three cats and a marvelous woman in Jack Stroud's life today. And he recently became a grandfather.

"Yeah, my daughter had a son," he said. "I'm too young to be a grandfather, aren't I?"

Jack Stroud drinks beer. He still works out three times a week, and he is in far better physical condition than men many years younger. He is quiet, as befits an offensive lineman, and he is staunchly loyal to his old friends. He fishes. He listens to music. He goes to plays and he is social-minded, socially conscious.

And on the mahogany credenza opposite windows looking out on the George Washington Bridge, there is a thick, white photograph album.

The pictures are of Jack Stroud, Jr.

There are newspaper clips, now yellowed from the years. There are photographs of young Jack, of his teams, of him with his dad.

There are black smudges on the white, padded cover, as from too many visits by a thumb, a palm, from too many quiet moments alone with the pictures and the memories.

"How often do you go to that album now, Jack?" I asked.

"Not that much. Few times a week, I guess. He was . . . I thought . . . yeah, that was the darkest day of my life. Not a whole lot else mattered when young Jack died."

Big Jack, who is becoming old Jack, has tried to make the most of the years since. The pain never leaves, he says, but sometimes it grows duller.

Football was kind to Jack Stroud, bringing him success and opportunities for prosperity. Life has been less kind. Obviously, he would trade all the football and the prosperity to have young Jack at his shoulder as he stares into that white album.

Raymond Berry

. . . Unitas to *Berry* plus 25 to 50, first down
. . . Unitas to *Berry* plus 15 to 35, first down
. . . Unitas to *Berry* plus 22 to 13, first down
. . . Unitas to *Berry* plus 15 for touchdown
. . . Unitas to *Berry* plus 21 to 43, first down

"As I ran off the field after that game, and it was unusual for me because I wasn't inclined that way, I was struck by . . . how much I had to be thankful for, to God."

WHEN PEOPLE LOOK at and listen to Raymond Berry, they think of Zane Grey, Gary Cooper, Clint Eastwood. Across the mind's eye flash scenes from *High Noon, Shane, Riders of the Purple Sage.* It must have been a man just like Raymond Berry who inspired the model for all those Westerns . . . slim-hipped, chiseled features, spare and lean, tough as nails. The perfect cowboy good guy. Texas, of course, is the only place Raymond Berry could have been born. His gentle drawl, sometimes so low as to be inaudible, is polite and pleasant, interspersed with "yes sir" and "no ma'am" and "thank you kindly." He seems never to swear, and he looks genuinely offended when others around him do. To the casual observer the stereotype is totally convincing. One simply sits and waits for a golden sunset, content in the knowledge that any minute now Raymond Berry will ride off into it.

But the reality is much more complex. Raymond Berry is not a cowboy. He is less dramatic and more thoughtful than our heroes of the screen. When he played football they said he was too small, too slow, too weak of vision (he wore contact lenses) to succeed. His successes were the fruit of painstaking practice, endless attention to detail, not blazing natural talent.

Berry doesn't even live in Texas. When I talked to him he lived amid the concrete and the smog, the poverty and crime of Detroit. He had a low-profile job, coaching the Detroit Lions' wide receivers and helping to plan the Lions' offense. (Since then, he has moved to Cleveland and taken a similar job with the Browns.) His interests outside his job are hardly cowboy naturals either—he is a religious man and is devoted to his family. So much for stereotypes.

Ray Berry was the best, the greatest pass receiver of his era. He did things no one had ever done on a football field, and he did them

131

because he didn't have the physical abilities to do the more commonplace.

To start with, he was too slow. Even in the 1950's, teams were looking for "burners," men who could cover half a football field faster than any opponent. They came up with men like Lenny Moore and Jon Arnett, Hugh McIlhenny and Del Shofner, Bobby Mitchell and the wondrously named Mac Speedie, Crazylegs Hirsch and Dante Lavelli. It was the age of The Bomb. Quarterbacks would fade, crank it up and launch those breath-taking passes way downfield, and millions thrilled to the sight of a burner ahead of the defender and stretching full out at top speed to catch the ball on his fingertips and streak across the goal line.

The masters of The Bomb were Johnny Unitas, Y.A. Tittle, Bobby Layne, Otto Graham. They called the plays, and they had the receivers who could score from anywhere on the field. Just half a step on the defender and it was over with the impact of a hammer blow and the cold and ruthless efficiency of a surgeon's scalpel. Defensive backs lived in fear of the throwers and the receivers. Unitas-to-Moore was an object lesson in helplessness. Del Shofner was a ghost, disappearing at the line of scrimmage, then reappearing downfield with a ball in his hands and a game under his belt.

And then there was Raymond Berry.

"It wasn't a question of staying with him," said one of the day's top defensive backs, Night Train Lane. "It was a question of slowing down enough so that he wouldn't stay clear in front of you. But then after you did everything you had to do, there he'd be with the ball in his arms. It got so I hated to hear his name."

We should be told that he was also too small. The roster listed him as six-two and one-ninety. The roster exaggerated. He seemed skinny, vulnerable, delicate. And because he wasn't fast, he had to be used on shorter pass patterns, not way out there, like Shofner and Moore. He was closer to the tackle, closer to the ball, and the patterns he ran were across the middle of the field, where the linebackers lived, dreaming of the chance to lay a forearm on the throat of a man who didn't weigh two-fifty, and who was hardly big enough to hit back.

Going into the middle where the arms were swinging, the knees and shoulders taking deadly aim, Berry had to maintain iron concentration and block out the threat of imminent physical harm. He had to sacrifice his body and still make sure, no matter what, that he caught the ball.

He had to catch the ball every time. That was all Raymond Berry could offer. There would be no room for someone too slow and too small if he couldn't catch the ball.

So he had two strikes on him. He was too slow for the deep stuff, for the flashing patterns downfield. And he was too small to be a tight end, the receiver who throws crunching blocks that can level a linebacker in his spare time.

But Berry had a third strike—a list of physical infirmities. Mostly, it was poor vision. Raymond Berry wore contact lenses during games. Without them, he would never be sure whether it was Weeb Ewbank or Big Daddy Lipscomb yelling at him. When he wasn't playing, he wore thick, horn-rimmed glasses, making him more like a schoolteacher than a professional football player. One of his legs was a little shorter than the other, so he also ran knock-kneed, not in the classic, flowing stride that eats up ground and outdistances fleet defenders.

If Raymond Berry arrived out of college today, he would not be drafted. The computer would reject him with haughty, solid-state disdain between snatches of hysterical transistorized giggling.

"If Raymond Berry were a horse," wrote John Steadman in the Baltimore *News-American,* "they'd shoot him."

But everything that worked against Raymond Berry worked for him as well. He studied. He concentrated. He created multiple-move patterns that had never been seen before, and used them with fantastic efficiency. He learned more about the league's defensive backs than their wives knew. He kept notes, volumes of diagrams and moves and steps and thoughts, a veritable instructional manual on the humiliation of the faster, quicker, stronger men who would defend against him. He knew which moves would work against which cornerback, against which zone, against which team. He knew the instinctive first move of every linebacker, and could exploit that split second of involuntary movement.

Raymond Berry was not an instinctive player. Instead, he made himself a machine, designed and equipped to overcome mere human failings. He designed a special corset to support his back, which was swayed to one side to accommodate his one leg being shorter than the other. He designed special shoes to compensate for the shorter leg. He even designed an eyeshade that would allow him to sleep in odd situations.

One day he noticed that the sun came over the rim of San Francisco's old Kezar Stadium at a crazy angle. The next time he played there, he might have to look back into that glare. He decided that he would be wearing special smoked goggles. Naturally, he was.

Berry smiles serenely as he recounts each edge he used, not boastfully but almost shyly. He is that way all the time, placid, calm. The only thing that can bring sparks to his light blue eyes is the suggestion that he was too slow, too small, too handicapped. Could he play against today's players?

"Oh, I don't think there's much doubt about that," he says. "The same requirements are still necessary as far as receivers are concerned. You got to be able to get open and catch the football."

How about his size?

"It's just not factual. I was six-two and between one-eighty-eight and one-ninety, and I was above average size for a wide receiver.

"And my speed was definitely an average speed. I ran a four-eight speed in the forty-yard dash, and nothing was going to change my four-eight speed. I wasn't going to be four-five, and I wasn't in the same speed class as Sonny Randle and Del Shofner and a couple others at that time who were tremendously fast, and of course there are so many of them today. But I found out in college about running. I ran track in college, worked with sprinters all the time, and I found out that even the best of those sprinters weren't going to run off and leave me all that bad. I could come out of the blocks with most of them, you know, and run forty or fifty yards with most of them, and the real fast guys might start leaving me after that.

"I felt like I could run good enough to do the job against any back I came up against. What I had to do was learn moves, finesse, technique . . . to get open. And that is still true today. A guy with a lot of speed still can't get by with just his speed."

And that meant study. Homework. Berry credits Bob Shaw, then the Colts' receivers coach, as his teacher.

"It was a real critical time in my career," he says, "and Bob really helped. He was a marvelous coach. He introduced moves to me . . . in 1957 and 1958. I had two or three moves, and I was using them very effectively, and he taught them to me. But it was not anywhere near what I had to start developing in later years.

"I learned most of my moves from watching other receivers. I used to study every film I could get. I became a composite of all the good receivers, but some of the things they did I just couldn't do. Physical ability enters in with all this somewhere along the line, but in many cases things I didn't think I had the ability to copy. You just don't ever know what you can do until you try harder than you've tried before.

"Up to the championship game of '58, which was my fifth year in professional football, I really was not a great move man at that particular time in my career. My development of multiple moves began later, in the '60's, and they were born of necessity because I began to have more difficulty getting open.

"But in 1958 so many of our routes had nothing to do with moves. If I just got a step or two on a guy, Unitas was such a tremendous passer, you see, so accurate, and such a good release, he got the ball to you so fast, that I didn't have to be that open on many plays.

"I just had a great quarterback throwing to me, and if there was just a little crack he'd get the ball in. I wasn't that much open in that championship game, either, but he'd drill the ball in there in such a way that if I didn't catch it, there wasn't anybody else was going to do it.

"But I did have real good hands. I could catch the football. And that was the great asset I had."

At practice, after practice, anytime the quarterback and his receiver could get free, they'd work together.

"We didn't need a defender around to time our patterns," he says. "We knew what we wanted to do, how we'd attack a particular defender or defense. Sometimes we'd stay out after practice. We worked a lot together."

The fruits of those long workouts were never more obvious than on that day in late December of 1958. Unitas, against the finest defensive team in the league, completed twenty-six of forty passes for three hundred forty-nine yards. Raymond Berry caught twelve of the twenty-six completions, and they registered one hundred seventy-eight of the yardage Unitas chalked up, more than half the total.

Was that game the greatest of Berry's career?

No. Well, almost.

"It's kind of tied for first place." He smiles. "The other one . . . it may sound funny, I know . . . it was my senior year in high school and we won the district championship.

"We beat Gainesville . . . I believe it was thirteen to seven . . . in the big game. My dad was the coach of our team, and we were basically a senior team. We played together four years, and it would be our last chance. The game was as close as this one, but it didn't have an overtime, of course. And winning that game in Gainesville, Texas, and winning that game in New York for the world's championship was exactly the same feeling.

"It was just utterly indescribable. We had worked for four years to win that high school game, and we did. I'll never forget the feeling, or the look on my dad's face. Memories don't have to be from a professional career to be important, and that one was as important as any in my time as a football player."

To those who witnessed it, their one lasting memory of the 1958 championship is the drive to the game-tying field goal. And when remembering that drive—a seven-play march with less than two minutes remaining—they mostly remember Raymond Berry.

Berry himself remembers the turmoil, the clutching, frantic New York defense. He remembers being sent into the middle, into the crowd of violent men because the Giants were expecting sideline passes.

"Going onto the field, with less than two minutes to play, I remember quite vividly thinking we had just blown the ball game. We had forced the Giants to punt, but we wanted to block that punt, and instead Don Chandler kicked a beauty. From his forty-three, it went to our fourteen. We were eighty-six yards away.

"We were losing, seventeen to fourteen, and early in the game we could have put it out of sight. That's how we blew it. I don't remember anything being said at all in the huddle. It was just a question of going to work then. He missed his first two passes, Unitas did, and we were down to third down. He completed a crucial pass to Lenny Moore, for about eleven yards, and we had another life. But that clock just kept ticking. Then he tried a pass to L.G. Dupre and it was incomplete. That, I guess, stopped the clock finally."

It did. And sixty-four seconds remained, with the Colts on their twenty-five. It was second down, ten to go.

"At that point, Johnny went to audibles. We didn't have time for a huddle. We just lined up after each play on the line of scrimmage and he'd audible another play. The first one he threw to me, for the twenty-five yards, was an audible. It was in-bounds, so we just ran back and lined up again. He threw to me, and I believe it was completed in-bounds also. And the clock kept running.

"Some people commented later that it was surprising we weren't going for the sidelines, and it was surprising. But I wasn't doing anything but following orders. John knew what to do. He outguessed the Giant defense by staying in-bounds. They were basic plays we were running all year. The third play was also a pass to me, another inside route, and we wound up on the Giants' thirteen and ran off the field."

Myhra kicked the field goal and the game went into overtime.

"I don't know if I can speak for the other guys," Berry says, "but from that moment on, there was no doubt in my mind that we'd do anything but win it. Our defense stopped the Giants' first drive, and my recollection was when we got back out that we were going to win it then. And it's kind of funny, because the Giant defense then was . . . well, it was a toss-up whether ours or theirs was the best in football . . . and they had held us to just that one field goal in the whole second half, and here I was supremely confident of scoring. I don't know how I got to feeling that way. I must say we were very fortunate to win the game at all.

"Old John never did get excited," Berry recalls. "He never did show any emotion. You'd think we were playing an intrasquad game back in Baltimore during summer camp. He was just a businessman, a professional, and it was time to go to work. He called all the plays. He knew what we could work against."

What he had to work with was Raymond Berry. And what he had to work against was the late Carl Karilivacz, the Giants' left cornerback. Berry embarrassed and humiliated him. It became necessary for the Giants to double-team Berry, using inside safety Jimmy Patton and the linebackers underneath.

And when a team goes into double-coverage, someone will be open. Unitas was able to hit Ameche on a flare pattern during that drive to the tying score because of the attention the defense had to pay to Berry.

Artistically, this was not the Colts' best game nor the Giants', in Berry's opinion.

"That's the whole thing about these championship games," he says.

"Both teams are great teams, and they're just not going to let you be too artistic. That's how they got there in the first place.

"I see that as a real reality of football. Nothing goes like clockwork. It just doesn't happen. When it does, it's kind of freaky. The momentum of that game went back and forth, and at one point if we had gotten in and scored from their one, it would have blown the game open. But they stopped us, and what could be more natural than to expect a championship-game team being able to score from the one?

"But they stopped us, and like three or four plays later they were in our end zone. Instead of us being ahead twenty-one to three, it was fourteen to ten. That's how quick a game can turn."

But the confidence . . . the enthusiasm . . . that had carried the Colts to the championship game carried them into the overtime. It had been building for a year.

"The season before, in '57, we had just as good a team," Berry remembers. "We just didn't have the knowledge that we could win. It hadn't dawned on us, how good we really were. The end of that season we went to California needing to win two games. We lost them both, and the reason was we didn't think of ourselves as being champions. In reflecting on that season, I think we realized that we were capable of being real good, that good. Our football team was matured and ready to go in '58, from the very beginning.

"It happens to young teams very often. They need a year of learning they can win before they do win. I read an interview with Lee Trevino a couple of years ago that just proved it so well.

"He made the statement that Jack Nicklaus once told him, 'Lee, your game is good enough now to beat anybody.' And then Trevino made this comment: he said, 'Suddenly, I realized I could reach the top.' To me, that was the key phrase. Something clicked in his head. I mean, he had all the ability before that, didn't he? The same thing happens to a football team. Suddenly, a team realizes that it can do it. They become a different animal after that.

"I wasn't aware of the impact it had made on the country," Berry says. "I was busy enjoying the impact it had made on me. I just didn't have the background and the experience to understand what that game meant. No way did I understand it. But looking back, I guess it's true. It was on national television, and it was so dramatic and so exciting, I guess it did make pro football an overnight hit. I heard many people say that, older people, men who had invested their lives in the National Football League. So I have always felt a sense of pride in that, too. Just to have been a part of it was very important."

Berry didn't realize that he'd one day reach the Hall of Fame, either. It came as a surprise.

"All the time you're a player, on the field, you're going through so much just to reach a goal. And especially when you reach your goals, you're used to being in the center of attention all the time. Now contrast that with the Hall of Fame, when you've been out of the game for at least five years, you haven't been in the arena, in the spotlight, at all. Then all of a sudden you're thrust right back into the middle of that thing. It was a little unreal to me, it was like they were talking about somebody else. The football was a long time ago. It was a very strange experience, going down to Canton, Ohio, for that induction.

"The other thing is just stepping back into the past when you've been out of it for so long. I never thought about the Hall of Fame when I played. Lord, no. I was just thinking about making the team. When I was a rookie I barely made it, and I was relieved only until the next year when I had to do it all over again. The Hall of Fame was probably the furthest thing from my mind. I was just glad to be around."

Raymond Berry played nine more years after that championship game, setting most of the Baltimore team receiving records before he retired. And with his logical, perfectionist's mind, he never suffered the withdrawal symptoms others do when football suddenly turns from a fact to a memory, when suddenly there is no football, after God knows how many fall days.

"I never had a problem, because of the way my retirement came about. I was spared the problem of having to be objective of myself, because physically I just had to quit. I used to evaluate every year, when I was done playing a season, and after my twelfth year I decided I had never been in better shape. But sometime between my twelfth and my thirteenth year, my body just went over the hill.

"In training camp that last year, I started having things happen to me that had never happened before, little things, injury-type things. I pulled a muscle in my neck . . . I got a muscle pull in my thigh . . . I never had these things. I always worked my tail off staying in condition, and I didn't change that at all. I just got old. It was the ability of the muscles to take that stress. I was thirty-four. My time had run out, is all. So after that summer camp, with all the annoying injuries, I dislocated my shoulder in the third ball game. I missed six weeks right then, and when I came back my knee started bothering me. No big deal, just swelling on me.

"That's when I realized I could never be counted on to play regularly any more . . . and I couldn't really perform up to my standards any more. It wasn't really sad. It was so clear-cut that it didn't leave me any room to entertain any doubts. I just couldn't play any more. "I never was interested in getting paid for doing something that I couldn't earn. I wasn't interested in getting out there and performing to standards that just weren't acceptable to me, and I wasn't interested in getting into a spot where the football team was depending on me to do the job and I couldn't. For those reasons, I was glad to say goodbye."

Retired, Raymond Berry cast about for something to do.

"I never did make any long-range plans," he says. "I was just anxious to make the next week as an athlete. But the one thing I never did want to do was coach. My dad was a coach in Texas high school football, remember, and I knew the pressures and the work load. I didn't think I wanted that. I knew all the demands made it tough to devote the time I wanted to my children, my wife, my family.

"So I looked around for a vocation. As a Christian, the number one priority I had, regardless of what I wanted to do, was that I had to determine what God wanted me to do with my life. I'd been asking Him for three or four years to give me some direction about it, and I just took it that I wouldn't be coaching because He didn't place any desire in me to coach. When the retirement became final, I had to determine which step to take. Two or three doors had been opened to me, a couple of them in business, one of them in coaching, and that's when I started to develop a really strong conviction, over a period of a month or so, that coaching was going to be my calling after all. It started coming through loud and clear.

"So I went to Dallas, to the Cowboys. I took up Tom Landry on his offer. And I began to enjoy it. But it was hard work. As a player, I shut everything else out of my mind except what affected my job. I didn't understand anybody else's job. Consequently, I had a lot of gaps to fill. It's a whole lot easier to play than to coach, no doubt about that. It's a lot simpler job.

"Just as I had no desire to be in coaching, I now have no desire to be a head coach," Berry says. "But I must face the possibility that if I stay in coaching long enough, I'm going to have that opportunity.

If the Lord wants me to be a coach, it seems almost inevitable that it will happen.

"I'm not interested in doing something I don't want to do. Money doesn't mean very much to me. What I like to do is be with my family. I've got three children, two girls and a boy, and it's a young family that needs a daddy. Whenever I get any time, I spend it with them. And it doesn't matter what we do. Just being together, going to church together, is what's important."

Religion has shaped and altered Raymond Berry's life since that day in 1958 and has helped put his life in perspective.

"I don't think I could have handled the hero thing," he says, "except for one very important fact. I came to experience the reality of the living Christ. He changed my life. I found out why I was a hero, and it didn't have anything to do with me.

"The ability I had was a gift of God, and the opportunity to use it also was no accident. Consequently, I realized I didn't have a single thing I hadn't received from Him, and it was just a simple matter of knowing what the source of it was. I discovered the living Christ about eighteen months after that championship game. As a matter of fact, during that game I was not a religious person, but it had a tremendous personal impact on me. As I ran off the field after that game, and it was unusual for me because I wasn't inclined that way, I was struck by the huge amount of good fortune I had to be thankful for.

"My most vivid memory of what happened after that game was when I went into that locker room at Yankee Stadium and I just felt, like, a presence. It was strange. I hadn't made any commitment at all, I was running my life pretty much as I wanted to, or so I thought. It just suddenly struck me how much I had to be thankful for, to God."

Many of us tend to be cynical about those who profess deep religious convictions. The first temptation is to think of it all as a charade. So many athletes today speak of religion and never live it, so many members of the Fellowship of Christian Athletes appear to be playing a role.

Who is this man fooling? No one. He has found that inner peace most of us seek, and fail to find, because he has found the courage of commitment.

"There's no doubt in my mind that God had His hand on my life at times I could have least suspected it," he says. "I look back on all that has happened to me and I'm more convinced of it every day. I frankly believe that no person is in this world by accident, that there is a grander scheme, a purpose, in everybody's life. He is the master designer, and He doesn't do anything as an afterthought."

There is no difficulty for Raymond Berry in handling the Godless players he finds today, and while he may be inalterably opposed to their life styles—alcohol, drugs, unfaithfulness—he insists he understands them.

"I was just like them," he says. "I had no interest in God at all, for many years. I can understand it. I wasn't a wild person, but only because I didn't have the time for it. I had this tremendous drive within me to become a football player. It wasn't by choice that I didn't carouse, I just didn't have time.

"Players will sometimes come to me now for advice, for guidance on things other than football, just to share things with me, problems, perhaps, or joys. And my main advice to them, to anybody, is to just tell them what happened to me. I can identify with anybody who's adrift, without purpose. I was like that for years. I tell them to look at Jesus Christ, examine His claims, and find out that what He says is true. We can't afford not to."

What of those who have found equal comfort in other religions, in other Gods? Can he feel comfortable with them, knowing they have found yet another way, another religion, another belief?

"I try to communicate, if I'm asked, that what a person has to face the reality of is that man cannot approach God on his own terms. He's got to approach God on God's terms. So it behooves man to find out what terms God has laid down.

"The claims of Jesus Christ are very narrow. They don't leave man any room to maneuver. Because He said, 'I am the Way, the Truth and the Life and no man comes to the Father except by me.' What the Christ's claim is, is that God has done something in history that man better pay attention to, and that's the Cross. And he did something there that man has got to recognize, one way or another. The main issue man has got to face is that he is separated from God, and how is he going to get reconciled to Him? There are basically two ways that man can get reconciled to God. One is by being good enough, by bringing his good works and saying, 'God, is this good enough?' and the other way is to bring absolutely nothing, and come just the way he is, His way, the Cross. One way he has something to

boast about, the other way he has nothing. And Jesus Christ said He
is going to accept only one way. Man cannot bring his good works
with him, it's not good enough. He's got to come by the Cross.
"And that's what Christ is."
I am a Jew. There have been periods in our history when to say that
was fatal. I wondered, when listening to Raymond Berry, whether I
was following the right path. I am Jewish. I am proud of that. But
is it right? Is anything about religion right? Or wrong?
There was much I wanted to ask Raymond Berry. Where was his
Christ during the holocaust? Was this some terrible vengeance for
millions of people who had chosen another way? Is Raymond Berry's
Christ interested only in Christians?
"The Jew, of all people, should very closely examine the claims of
Jesus Christ," Raymond Berry answered. "He claimed to be the
Messiah, and that's in the Old Testament very strong. A Jewish friend
of mine once asked if it would be very oddball for a Jew to become
a Christian, and I said a Jew who accepts his Messiah is just confirm-
ing that he is a Jew. I'm the oddball, a Christian who had to be shown
the way of Christ. The Jew who rejects his Messiah, he's the oddball.
The person who really wants to know God, he'll find out. Jesus said,
'If you believe Moses, you'll believe in Me, for Moses spoke about Me
when he spoke to you.' "
Berry finds the presence of Christ in the Old Testament, in the
stories of Passover, Cain and Abel, Joseph, Moses and the Ten Com-
mandments. And he sees signs of the teachings everywhere.
"The pastor of the church I go to here, his father and his mother
were Jews. He didn't hear about Jesus until he was twenty-two years
old, and he's the greatest Bible teacher I ever heard, and the minister
of a Baptist church. I'm not a Baptist, I'm a Christian. I go to that
church because they preach the Bible, preach Christ. They have a
tremendous program. I'll tell you, anytime I meet a Jew I'm very
excited, because I have a whole new concept about Jews since I
became a Christian.
"I was raised in a small town in Texas, and there wasn't any other
kind of people but like ourselves. Then I went to Baltimore, and that's
a real melting pot. It was the first time I ever had the chance to mix
with other people. A Jew should know more about his heritage than
anybody else, because there's no other race like it, and yet most Jewish
friends I have don't really know much about the Old Testament and

the Scriptures. I don't understand that. After all the Jewish people have gone through, I'd think today's Jews would want to feel proud, would want to know it all.

"What the Jews are going to have to decide is this: Is Jesus Christ the Messiah or isn't He?"

When I left the deserted Lions' offices after this interview, I was unsure of my feelings. I wanted to believe both of us. I wanted to be right, and I wanted Ray Berry to be right. The conversation had taken an unexpected turn, a football story had turned into something far more profound.

So I resorted to an inner flippancy, which I often do.

If Raymond Berry is right, I said to myself, still clutching the pamphlets he had given me ("Jesus and the Intellectual," "The Greatest Discovery," "Ten Basic Steps Toward Christian Maturity")—*if he is right, then I'll get a cab right away. This is a quiet section of the city, especially at night, and it's tough to get a cab without calling one, and I know I won't get a cab at all.*

And I walked outside and a cab was waiting.

I checked later. Ray Berry had not called one for me. It was just there.

Waiting.

Kyle Rote

... Conerly to *Rote* plus 14 to 48, first down
... Conerly to *Rote* complete, *Rote* fumble on 25, picked
up by Webster, goes to 1. Total 86 yards, first down.

"People still recognize me on the street. Not from the football, from the TV. The power of the medium is so strong . . . they know they've seen me somewhere. Maybe they don't know who I am, but they know they've seen me."

PEOPLE WHO KNEW him took his success for granted. That was the way it was supposed to be. It was said that Kyle Rote would have been a success at anything he attempted. Business . . . academics . . . coaching . . . broadcasting. He just happened to choose athletics. Of course he was a star.

There was a unique quality about Kyle Rote, a soft-spoken Texan who came to New York City as a football player and never left it. He was intelligent, he was resourceful and versatile as a player. More important, he was loved by everyone on the New York Giants. The offensive players absolutely revered him. The defensive players, who weren't sure they liked each other and never even pretended to like offensive players, admitted that Kyle—a star pass receiver—was a gentleman, a friend, one of the nicest men anywhere.

He handled his stardom with genuine humility. Autograph-seekers were never turned away. Reporters always got their interviews, honest, carefully considered answers to even the most inane questions. Players came to him with personal problems, and he helped them. Players came to him needing money, and he accommodated them. Players and their wives named newborn sons Kyle. At last count, there are ten such young men living their lives with his name. He went out of his way to assure others of his concern for them, of his willingness to help, to listen. He was a prince among men.

Rote had become a legend before he reached the age of consent. Down in Texas, where high school and college football is not a diversion but a religion, they spoke in awed tones of his abilities. At Southern Methodist University, where he ran in the same backfield with Doak Walker (one that may never be equaled for excitement and achievement), he was a demigod.

Today, nearly thirty years after he last played for the SMU Mustangs, Texas players with brilliant potential are said to be "almost as good as Kyle." Then he came to New York and his talent, personality and good looks helped bring professional football its new popularity. He had the world by the tail, swinging . . . swinging . . . swinging . . . Then what the hell was he doing living alone in a small, lonely Manhattan apartment? How did it happen that two wives decided their lives would be easier without him? What ever happened to Kyle Rote?

On my way into his building at East Fifty-eighth Street, the doorman asked me to take Kyle's tuxedo up with me. "He must have forgotten it last night," the man said. "He got in kinda late."

Sure. Up to the eighteenth floor, ring the bell. Nothing.

Ring it again. Nothing.

Back downstairs, to the doorman. Has Kyle gone out? He said nine o'clock. Is he there? Did he come home last night?

He's there, insists the doorman. Go try it again.

Up to eighteen. Ring the bell. This time the door opens, and there stands Kyle Rote, boyhood hero. His hair is ruffled, his face lined and almost gray. He stands in a blue bathrobe, with aged slippers on his feet.

"Did I wake you?"

"Yeah. I set the alarm, but I must've turned it off in my sleep. Sorry."

"You look like hell. Where were you?"

"I made the awful mistake of telling Toots Shor that I'd go drinking with him last night after the All-America Golf Dinner. That old man is amazing. I can't keep up with him."

Into the apartment now. Clearly, it has gone without a woman's supervision. Papers are everywhere. Mail is on the desk, unopened. Clothes are on the furniture. In one far corner is a small rolling bar, laden with extra-large bottles, mostly Scotch.

"Want coffee?" he asks as he heads for the kitchen.

"Sure."

Coffee comes. Instant. We drink it alike, black with sugar substitute. One small, futile guard against expanding waistlines.

And now, with Kyle Rote seated behind his desk, with the visitor perched on a chair in front of it, we begin.

He smokes continually, the hangover and too many cigarettes clearly audible in his heavy, throaty voice.

Where to start? With the football career? With the coaching career? With the broadcasting career? With the two marriages? All of them are over now.

Begin with the coaching career. There have always been unanswered questions, unconfirmed rumors of friction with Allie Sherman, the genius of offense who saw the Giants through the best times and their dismal worst.

Kyle Rote retired as a player in 1961. In 1962 and 1963 he was the team's offensive backfield coach. In each of those years the Giants won Eastern Conference championships. In each of those years, they lost excruciatingly close league title games, 16–7 to Green Bay, 14–10 to Chicago.

In 1964 Kyle Rote was gone. Fired.

"I was advised over the telephone," Rote says, "that I was no longer, uh, wanted as a coach. It was Al. His explanation was that he would require his coaches to work full-time now, and therefore he thought it would be better for me to plan on other things. He didn't ask me if I would be willing to make the transition and work full-time. That wasn't brought up.

"It wasn't much of a shock. There were different reasons, though. Not the full-time thing. Al thought I was trying to become the head coach. It got to the point where I had a discussion with him one day, I told him I wasn't interested in becoming the head coach of the Giants. I enjoyed my other interests . . . in radio, at the time, then television.

"Al felt I was a threat to him. I told him I wanted to clear the air, if there was any concern on his part. I don't know if that ever solves the problem, but I wanted to bring it out into the open, to tell him I didn't have that ambition. Which I didn't. I wouldn't have had the patience to be a head coach. I wouldn't have wanted the responsibility nor the discipline which is required for being a head coach."

But Sherman apparently still worried.

"Also, I had made a speech in Spring Lake, down in Jersey, right after the Giants had traded Sam Huff. They asked after the speech, what did I think of the Sam Huff trade? And I said, well, I didn't really want to address myself to the trade itself, because that could prove good or bad, like any trade. But I added that the only bad thing about it was the way in which they advised Sam.

"Sam was in Cleveland, I think, on business. And any player, especially getting to Sam's age and the length of his career, should be advised if you're going to trade him before it hits the papers, so that he can prepare his people for the news, and work out what will happen if he's traded. Before it becomes something that is embarrassing for him.

"And I made that comment. I told them my job is not only as a coach but I do some public relations, and while we tell you the good things about the Giants, this is one case where I think we should have taken the time to locate him, and advise him before it was announced to the papers.

"I don't think the Giants were too happy with that. I think it was a combination of that plus Al's suspicions. So in '64 I suddenly found myself out of football.

"I think Al was a brilliant football strategist. Designing plays . . . that type of thing. He probably knew football better than anybody I've ever known. I think if he had a problem at all, it was in handling people. For example. He would tell one player that he was going to start the next game. And I'm sure in an effort to bolster the kid's ego, to keep him going, he meant it. And the next day he'd do the same thing to another boy in the same position, not realizing, I assume, that these two boys would get off after a practice session and talk to one another.

"As a result, he lost some credibility. I'm sure his intent was not to hurt, but that was the result. I think Al was a sincerely loving type of guy, and wanted to make each player feel wanted and important. But the intelligence of that choice, to do it that way, has to be questioned."

But don't worry about Kyle. He'll be a success at anything he tries. Kyle Rote always has other irons in the fire.

"I had been working with WNEW radio since 1960," he explained. "By then, I was sports director. I did the locker room report after Giant games, and the evening sports news all during the year. So I just went and did more radio after that. I enjoyed it. I made good money and I was getting great experience. In the back of my mind, I had always thought about television. I knew I wanted to try that.

"It happened in '67. Chet Simmons, an NBC sports producer, asked me if I would be interested in coming to work for them. Which I was. I bettered my income, and it was something I thought I'd enjoy doing, commenting on television games. So we worked out a package of television games and sports news shows, and I took it. I stayed there from '67 through . . . let's see . . . my last season was '73 with them. "I had done news since '67, and wanted to give up the news. It was the six and eleven o'clock news, and I enjoyed it for a while but then it became a very confining activity. I asked Carl Lindemann if I gave up the news, would that endanger my doing the games. There seemed to be some concern there, because they wanted somebody who could do both.

"Quite honestly, I never did get an answer from him. But when I told him that, about three months later they began auditioning people for the news job. I had not given it up, I was still waiting on an answer from him. And then it was apparent they were going to replace me on the news. They did, with Dick Schaap. Then it was one or two seasons later they let me go as an analyst on the football games.

"That, I think, was just normal. Each year, as players retire, and are interested in doing television, they really legitimately can address themselves to the players on the field, guys they played against, or with, and it makes them more, I think, authoritative. I have no argument with that. As these players become available in the marketplace of television, any additional year you get as analyst—not professional play-by-play man—you're ahead of the game.

"I had understood this, and in fact anticipated it, and about two years before it actually happened I started with a friend of mine in an air-freight forwarding company, because it was only a matter of which year they were going to decide to replace me. The business is called Forty-Four Air Freight. Yes, that was my number with the Giants. So by the time they did replace me, our company had gotten off the ground. It gave me a place to go from there, from the television job. It was fortunate planning, anyway.

"And that's what I do full-time now. I didn't have to go scrambling around for some other job. It was a good thing."

So now Kyle Rote is divorced from sports. No longer a player. No longer a coach. No longer a radio or television personality. No longer that familiar face on the screen, that familiar, soft-gravelly voice coming through, incisively telling the viewer what he has seen, what he should look for.

He is just another businessman, neither a failure nor a great success.

"I have a tremendous love affair with this city," he said. "I really enjoy it. I have never felt compelled to go back to Texas. All my friends are in New York. Ever since I moved here, back when I was still playing, this has been my city. My home."

After our conversation, however, his first wife became seriously ill and Rote moved to Texas to provide a home for his twelve-year-old daughter. His love affair with New York continues. But, as he says, "You can always have a city. You can't always help your only daughter."

Rote was never the kind of athlete who resented the attention he received in public.

"I think, to begin with, people in our position were really privileged and fortunate," he says. "With that came the advantages. Getting a table in a restaurant . . . cab drivers going out of their way to do something for you . . . the men in the department stores and the little special attentions they gave us. All of that I don't think you earn, in a sense. It's a gratuity of the public to you. As a result, being stopped on the street, or being asked by someone while you're having dinner or a drink, for an autograph . . . that is understandable and something you should do. It's not an imposition on my privacy. I knew it would happen when I stepped out on the street, or in that restaurant. If you take the additional niceties that come your way, then those other things are obligations.

"It was all a lot of fun. It made it all seem like it wasn't a nine-to-five job, it was fun to be a part of one of the most vital cities in the world. I enjoyed it. Oh, I don't think it's realistic. I think that's the greatest danger of it all, trying to keep from being confined to living in that bubble. I was constantly trying to touch ground, to get some reality to it. But I think there are enough things that happen in a person's life to afford him the necessity of touching ground. Things happen to you. Real things."

But get to the real things carefully. Go slowly.

There was, on the Giants, an elite corps, a grander-than-grand segment of the team, men who were not only accepted as heroes but who lived the good life, the spotlight life. Kyle Rote was a part of this clique. He and Frank Gifford and Charlie Conerly . . . and Alex Webster, to some extent.

"I think it was the syndrome of the offensive player," he says. "That's strictly what it was. We had a much better defensive team than we had an offensive team, and we would have never come close if we had to depend on our offense. The problem is just human nature. People, historically, are attracted to the people involved in making touchdowns. Just like home-run hitters. People rarely take the time to think about defensive players, or good fielders in baseball.

"Also, we enjoyed Toots Shor's place. And when we did go into Toots's, the door was open to anyone else if they wanted to, if they elected to go in there. If they didn't want to come, they didn't have to, but we enjoyed it. We didn't consciously exclude them from our group. We'd go there and not know the others were going, too. Sometimes I'd go there with Frank, and we'd find Charlie and Alex. Or I'd go by myself, and find Charlie and Frank. The place was a blend of sports, show business, politics . . . that kind of crowd. If the defensive people resented that, it was more of a psychological thing than anything else.

"I noticed some resentment, of course, but nobody on the defense ever said anything out of hand. Jokingly, perhaps, or even semi-seriously, but they had a definite identity of their own, and if anyone had hang-ups, it should have been the offense. We knew they were a far superior unit to us. And I think that in itself should give them lifelong satisfaction.

"And believe me, my closest friends on the team were more than Frank and Charlie and Alex. There was Schnelker . . . Shofner . . . Rosey Grier . . . Rosey Brown . . . Jimmy Patton . . . guys we'd bounce around with. There was no elite, no clique. If there was, it was in other guys' minds. We never intentionally went off by ourselves. I like to think those Giant teams had great togetherness."

Football made Kyle Rote. Football, Texas-style.

"We didn't have any money," he remembers. "We lived in San Antonio, and the first job I can remember my dad having was during the Depression, when the WPA was formed. They decided to beautify the San Antonio River, and he worked at that. And later, he worked at other jobs. We had no real money. But I never did without food or shoes or shelter, and I had the kind of love that makes you not notice the absence of other things. The only thing I ever wanted that I had to do without was a bike, I think. But we had an abundance of love and time, time my parents made for us. If you have to do without that, you have a bad childhood, but I didn't. So it was a normal life, in that respect."

"There were a lot of kids in the neighborhood," he says, "and we lived near a vacant lot, and because I had an older brother . . . three years older . . . I was always playing with older kids. They seemed to be all his age. It was the normal pecking order of kids. I wound up centering for both sides before they'd let me do anything. Or catch for both sides. And whatever season it was, that's what we tried to play.

"I really didn't have exceptional athletic abilities. Hell, I didn't have normal athletic abilities. I remember in high school . . . it was 1943 . . . my dad had gotten a job with the War Department by that time and he had to travel a great deal. Anyway, it looked like he was going to have to go to Marshall, Texas, for a long time and my mother wanted to go with him. So I lived with another family, a friend of mine, for that one semester, so I wouldn't have to break up my schooling.

"It was my first year in high school. My brother had just gone into the Marines, right from high school. And this family I lived with . . . my friend's dad happened to be the college roommate of the high school football coach. And I'm sure that's the only reason I stayed in football that first year. The head coach kept me on the team as the fourth-string tailback. The freshman team, at Jefferson High School. They had never kept four deep at any position, but I'm sure that somewhere along the way my friend's dad got together with the coach and said, 'Look, if you don't let him stay on the team he's going to be impossible to have living at my house.' So they let me stay as the fourth-string tailback.

"The coach of our freshman team was a high school senior, a track star who used to play football. One time, when I thought I was finally going to get into a game, this student-coach slipped into the locker room at half time and put on a uniform. And when the third-string tailback finally went down, I thought it was my turn. But the coach actually went in and played instead of me. I guess I should have gotten the message. He showed great confidence in his fourth-string tailback, didn't he? At the time I was really crushed.

"What turned it around was this. When I was a senior, we had a really good basketball team. I was part of it. There were three seniors and two juniors, but none of us had any college offers of any kind. So we seniors decided we would 'post' for a year . . . you know, stay an additional year in high school, not graduating. Hell, I wasn't going anywhere. I wouldn't have been able to afford my own college tuition.

"Anyway, that year of maturity must have done a lot for me. We played football that 'fifth season' and we went to the state finals. We also went to the finals in basketball. We had good grades, it wasn't a question of flunking. In fact, two or three of us made the dean's list, or whatever they called it. We just decided not to take one final required English course as seniors so that we could stay another year. At that time, you were allowed to do that and still play.

"I had a good football year, and suddenly I was getting all sorts of scholarship offers. Once I sat down and counted them, and I guess there were forty, fifty of them."

And Kyle Rote chose Vanderbilt.

Vanderbilt? Wasn't he a legend at Southern Methodist? Yes. But that came after another emotional crisis.

"I went to Vanderbilt in the summer. Red Sanders was their coach then, and Tommy Prothro was an assistant coach. My dad really wanted me to go to Vanderbilt. At that time, if you went and registered for classes in the summer, you'd be able to play varsity as a freshman. So I did.

"I stayed there maybe . . . I don't know . . . four, five weeks. And I suddenly realized I was a long way from home, from where I thought I'd be making a living, from where my friends were. So I went to Red and told him I wanted to go back to Texas.

"I had not contacted SMU at all. They had asked me, but I had turned them down. Red talked to me until about two o'clock one morning, but he wouldn't give me the permission to leave. So the next day I just packed up and got on the train. The next day, those four guys I had played with in high school arrived at Vanderbilt, in Nashville. They didn't know I was leaving. They were coming up to talk me into going home, but I had already done it. So I got back home, drove on up to Dallas, walked into the SMU athletic office and asked if that scholarship was still open. It was. So I enrolled."

SMU . . . the rich kids' college in Texas . . . had a running back named Doak Walker. He was already a legend. Now he had company, for Kyle Rote became an All-America, nationally known, a hero who would be recognized far and wide.

"Again, it was the breaks. One of them was that we had Notre Dame scheduled in 1949.

"As it turned out, all the factors for making it a memorable game were there when we played Notre Dame. It was their last game of a four-year span that would have kept them unbeaten. It was also on December third, the week after almost every college in the country had finished its schedule. And it was one of the first nationally telecast college games.

"And Notre Dame always drew a fantastic audience. We were twenty-eight-point underdogs, and we had 'em tied, twenty-twenty, going into the last few minutes of play. They beat us, in the end, twenty-seven to twenty. A lot of people still think we won. I'll be out someplace and some guy will come up and say, 'I remember when you beat Notre Dame.' And I just nod, and say thanks.

"I had an outstanding game, statistically. It was an outstanding ball game. I scored all three touchdowns and I think I passed for over a hundred yards and ran for over a hundred yards and I punted for a forty-eight-yard average. Doak didn't play, he had been injured a few games before. We ran everything but the T-formation . . . double-wing, single-wing, Y-formation . . . slot . . . punt formation . . . anyway, it was a game that got me remembered by a lot of people."

The next year, Doak Walker went into the pros, with the Detroit Lions. He distinguished himself with uncommon splendor. Indeed, his number—37—has been retired by the Lions, and he is certain to reach the Hall of Fame one day soon.

"Pro football to us was something that was happening up north," said Rote. "We didn't have much television, and we never paid much attention to any of it until we started reading about how Doak was doing. That was 1950, and I first started thinking about a pro career then."

The next year, the New York Giants, having won the right to a bonus choice in the draft, claimed Rote.

"I wasn't even sure I'd ever play pro football," he said, "and then, to be the very first pick by a team in New York . . . it just surprised the hell out of me. I didn't know for sure the people in the East had ever heard of me."

Rote signed the first time Wellington Mara came to visit for a huge package by the standards of 1951.

"I got a three-year contract," he said. "No-cut. No bonus, either, but you might say one was built in. I was to get twenty thousand the first year, then fifteen for each of the next two."

Now, having become a professional, Kyle Rote was put to the test. He injured his knees in that first training camp, and although he remained at running back through the 1953 season, he never matched his magnificent performances at SMU. It was not until Jim Lee Howell took over as head coach in 1954 and put Kyle at wide receiver that the applause began again.

"I hurt my knee in Jonesboro, Arkansas, in a drill. We were there training for a game with Chicago.

"It was hot and we were tired . . . we had been on the field for three hours. Nobody even touched me. It just went out. And it went out again a week later. So for the rest of '51 I'd play until it went out, then I'd sit for a while, then go back. In March or April of '52 I was playing golf and it went out again. I contacted the Maras, they called a doctor in Dallas and I had an operation. Fifty-two, then, was just a so-so type of season. And in '53 I got my other knee hurt kicking off against Pittsburgh.

"In '54 Tom Landry was still a player-coach. He was a defensive back, and he felt I could run pass patterns fairly well. So he suggested the move to Howell, and I was moved out to flanker. That took a lot of pressure off my knees, and as a result I was able to add seven more years to my career. I never would have stayed around another year as a running back. I couldn't make the cuts, and I think I was endangering our own people, too."

Given new life, Rote gave the Giants new life in turn. He became one of the best pass receivers of his time, much like Baltimore's Raymond Berry, who, coincidentally, had graduated from SMU, had a marked absence of speed and had knee problems. In 1956, the Giants won the NFL championship with an effortless 47–7 rout of the Chicago Bears. In 1957, they slumped to second, behind the Cleveland Browns. And in 1958, they won their Eastern Conference title and played the Colts for the league championship.

"Two things stay with me about that game," Rote says. "First, of course, the fact that it was a sudden-death type of game. And also seeing Ameche go over for the touchdown that won it. I was just standing on the sidelines, helpless. It's a terribly frustrating feeling.

"Other than that, although people have picked up the phrase 'the greatest game ever played,' probably, play-by-play, you know, I just can't believe that it was. But I think the drive that Unitas and Berry put together, to get down after Chandler's punt, was probably one of the best drives I've seen. Especially under those circumstances, under that pressure. We had played as well as we could, especially in the second half, and in a sense I was relieved they hadn't scored a touchdown to win it in the fourth quarter.

"When they did tie us, we knew it would go overtime. Those were the rules. I don't think you can go into a game not knowing something like that, something that would affect your strategy in the latter part of the game.

"I was aware of the impact that game had made, but not just then. Upon reflection, it was the first time that Madison Avenue really projected itself into pro football. The Sam Huff television story . . . things like that. And they started using football players for commercials, endorsements . . . and because we were in New York, we fell heir to a lot of those assignments."

The year 1958 had seen many changes in Kyle Rote's life.

"After the '57 season, I went back home to Texas and just decided I'd rather move to New York year-round. I drove up here in January or February of '58 to look for a place to live. I found a place, moved my family up here and have been here ever since.

"In '64 I got divorced, and I sold my house in Scarsdale to Frank [Gifford]. He still lives there now. So I moved into the city, and I've been here since '64.

"I got remarried in '65 . . . got divorced again in '71 . . . and I'm not married now nor do I plan to be."

Kyle is aware of the hundreds of father-son situations in sports, in which the son is never capable of equaling the father's athletic prowess and, as a result, goes through life as "So-and-So's son." But Kyle Rote, Jr., became a star in his own right in a sport alien to the father.

"I'm a little bit surprised that it's soccer, because it's such a foreign thing to me," Kyle says. "I never saw a soccer game, I guess, until I saw him play in one. I really can't relate to playing that sport. It's a very difficult sport for an American, because we don't grow up with a soccer ball in our crib, you know . . . we never do learn to fiddle with our feet.

"But I always knew he was well-coordinated, and could do a lot of things. I'm really most pleased that he just flat did it all on his own. I say on his own . . . I'm sure with the help of many people, but not me. Maybe it's soccer because I was football, I don't know. But he was a very good football player. He won a scholarship to Oklahoma

State . . . he was a quarterback, and he broke his leg above the knee. And in rebuilding his leg, he began playing a lot of soccer. Postoperative rehabilitation, you know.

"Then he was up visiting me after his freshman year at Oklahoma State, and I sensed he wasn't that happy. I asked him did he want to go to another school, where some of his friends were . . . did he feel obligated to go to Oklahoma State because he got a scholarship . . . I told him to give it a few days' thought.

"So a couple days later he asked if I meant what I said, and I said yeah, and he said he would like to go to Sewanee . . . the University of the South, they call it, in Sewanee, Tennessee. Some of his high school buddies had gone to Sewanee. I told him, 'The first thing you do is contact Oklahoma State and tell 'em you're not coming back, and then you call Sewanee, and don't do it in reverse order. Do it in that order.' And he did . . . he called Oklahoma State, then Sewanee, and he drove down to Sewanee and enrolled. If I had known what college tuition cost, I don't know if I would have suggested it that strongly. Anyway, he played soccer and baseball and ran track, and thoroughly enjoyed his college career.

"When he was being recruited out of high school, a lot of colleges put pressure on me to sway him. Especially SMU. But I never did. In fact, I may have bent over backward to avoid doing it. My feeling is he's got to live with himself and that decision had to be strictly his, because he can live with a bad decision that way, but not with a bad one on my part."

Father and son, so closely aligned in their common love of athletics, both suffered from the divorce. So did Kyle's two younger sons and his daughter.

"I'm sure he was very upset by it," Rote says. "They all were. That's never a pleasant thing for anyone. It changed everything for me. Very much so. Very much so. But in the long run, it works out better. You just don't stay together for the kids. You're kidding everybody. But I'm very close to them now, and to their mother, and they feel very close to me, too.

"I don't know, I must be a tough guy to live with. You don't see anybody else around, do you? I must be. Must be.

"But people still recognize me in the street. Not from the football, from the TV. The power of that medium is so strong . . . they know they've seen me somewhere. Maybe they don't know who I am, but they know they've seen me.

"I would enjoy doing the games again for TV. I enjoyed it tremendously, being involved with football. But I'm realistic enough to know it won't happen. That's just one more part of my life that I have to forget. It won't happen again."

Kyle Rote, then, is a man of completed careers.

The player lasted eleven years. Age retired him.

The coach lasted two. Allie Sherman retired him.

The radio-TV commentator lasted seven years. The demands of the medium for new faces retired him.

And now Kyle Rote's youth has ended, too. He runs his freight-forwarding business from Dallas, cares for his daughter, visits with his sons, who are already as old as he was when he set New York on its ear. He smokes too much, visits the nightspots as if trying to recapture the moments at Toots Shor's with Frank and Charlie and Alex.

"He'll be a success at whatever he tries," they said. But it's too much even for this decent man to recover his star-spangled past.

Lenny Moore

... Unitas long pass to *Moore* complete on Giant 25, plus 60 yards, first down
... *Moore* around left end plus eight to Giant 2
... Unitas to *Moore* wide right plus 12 to Giant 3, first down
... Unitas long pass to *Moore* from Giant 42 complete on goal but ruled out of bounds

"They tried to pretend I wasn't black any more, so I made sure to tell them I was. A star and a nigger ... I never tried to pretend that becoming a star made me white."

LIKE COFFEE BREWED too long in its own dark essences, Lenny Moore is black and bitter.

For a long time he was bitter because he was black. But then, having grown proud of his blackness, he remained bitter because of what others had done to him because of his blackness. Eventually, he became cynical, because as a star he received the very liberties denied to other blacks. He saw what was happening. And he understood.

"Lenny Moore the star was cool enough for them to dig," he said. "Before that, it was Lenny Moore the nigger. It was sick, man, how much better it was to be a star.

"But they tried to pretend I wasn't black any more, so I made sure to tell them I was. A star and a nigger. They couldn't handle that. They were caught between hating me because I was black and needing me for their ego trips. They wanted me to be seen in their restaurants, their bars, their hotels. But they were uncomfortable when I reminded them why they wanted me there, why they needed to slap my back, throw their arms around me, introduce me to their friends.

"And you know what? I never let them forget I was black, and how they had treated me when I wasn't a star. I always made sure to tell them that I was still a man, always had been, and I wasn't going to change because they decided to like me. They were the hypocrites. Not me. I took whatever I could, because the same things were available to the white players . . . *all* the white players. I never tried to pretend that becoming a star made me white."

Lenny Moore, almost two decades later, still boils and fumes. His memories of prejudice experienced are no less sharp because they are properly verbalized, pleasantly modulated. He has had a long time to practice his bitterness; some say he wallows in it. For most of his life, it was all he had.

"I have been black a long time," he said. He smiled, only it wasn't really a smile, not with all those teeth flashing in a clench, not with all that emotion crashing through.

"I grew up in Reading, Pennsylvania, and . . . well, we didn't have much of any damned thing. I guess my old man made it to the point where we always ate. He worked in the steel mill and my mother did domestic work. We never had the things most kids had . . . we didn't always get that new suit, or those shoes when ours had holes in them. A new pair of shoes for kids like us was cardboard shoved inside, to keep the water and the rocks out. And we never had any pocket money, not ever, but the old man . . . he tried to get us a quarter sometimes for the movies. But we never had any of the luxuries kids look to, we were just poor. Nigger-poor. And I grew up that way. Poor and bitter, because I saw what other kids had.

"Like college, for instance. I never even thought about it, because I knew there would be no way I could ever do it, you know, financially. I became aware of college after the scholarship offers started coming in, after football at Reading High. But even then, I didn't really have grades . . . pretty much because my attitude was, you know, for what? I'm never going to advance any more than this. They had to take me in high school, but they sure as hell didn't have to take no black kid in some expensive college. I figured I'd probably go the same route my brothers did, which was to join the Army."

There were eleven children in the Moore family. Eight are living today. Of the eleven, Lenny Moore is the only one to progress past high school in his education.

"What the hell for?" he asked. "They went to the mines and the mills to put food on our table. When I went to college, I felt guilty. I still needed pocket money, walking-around money, and I knew how hard it was for my parents to get it to me. I knew what they were doing.

"There would be that extra money in the mail when I was in college, like two dollars, and that was big money for me. My mom would send it, and I knew she couldn't afford it. It was floor-scrubbing money. Where else would she get it? And my brothers would chip in and send me some shirts sometimes. They all rallied around me. It's something I'll never forget. I've tried to show them, in my way over the years, all the appreciation I had for what they did."

He attended Penn State on a football scholarship and proved to be an incredibly gifted athlete.

"Did I find prejudice in college? Sure. It was a kind of low-key prejudice, but it was there. Even at Penn State. It wasn't overt, but I was made aware of the fact I was black. Even some of the fraternity houses were problems, so usually it was only during open house that I'd get in a look around. But it wasn't bad there. I had a lot of good friends, white friends, and not because I was a football hero.

"But the road trips were something else. We were the first integrated team to play in Fort Worth, Texas. We played Texas Christian, and you could hear 'nigger' ringing all over the stands . . . and it was worse when we played down in West Virginia. But we were pretty much pre-notified as to what to expect.

"The team had to stay way out of town, way out of town. But that was pretty much natural, expected. And the blacks on the team were used to it. We accepted it, just because there wasn't any other way to feel. We knew what to expect, and those damned people never did let us down."

And still, there was the anguish of home.

"I came home from college this one time, and I had to go pick my mother up, and when I got to this house, you know, she was on her hands and knees scrubbing the kitchen floor for this white woman. It brought tears to my eyes. And I made a vow . . . boy, if I am ever fortunate enough . . . this time I had already started thinking into things . . . if I ever get into anything big, she'll never scrub another floor in her life.

"After 1958 I was in a position where I had a little money. My mother died that June. And I was never able to do a damned thing for her. She died as a domestic. I wanted to buy her a house, just so she'd never have to clean somebody else's."

Life had always been a search for money, for enough to live on.

"As far as I can remember, my mother was always a domestic, always cleaning other people's dirt. But she never complained about it. I never heard her say anything about it. It was something she just knew she had to do. Man, she only made a couple of dollars a day, but we needed it. It's hard to imagine now, but what she did was hardly worth all the work, all the years. But it put an extra quart of milk in the icebox. She had to do it.

"Even my old man, he did things on the side. Fixing radios . . .TV's

. . . to get extra pocket money. He was handy, and he worked all the time for the extra cash. I knew it bothered him, not for what he did but that my mother had to go out and clean. Like, maybe he felt he wasn't doing enough so that his wife could stay home with his kids. And it sure as hell bothered us, seeing her go out early every morning, walking miles sometimes to save the little extra it would cost for bus fare. It just wasn't any kind of way to grow up. The first thing you lost was your dignity. Then you lost your childhood, long before you stopped being a child."

But is not football, after all, a game for children? Isn't it an escape clause from the sadness of leaving childhood and growing up? Don't those who succeed in this boy's sport emerge into the real world as men bigger than life, propelled into cushy executive jobs, smart automobiles, expensive clothes, investments, money in the bank?

"Your ass," snapped Lenny Moore. "Football is great when you play it, while you play it. But the minute it's over . . . well, who the hell is Lenny Moore?"

What the hell does he mean, I should give him a job? Great career, Lenny, now go out and pound salt like the rest of us. Stick the Pro Bowl, Lenny. Jam the headlines, too. Sell the old championship ring if you can't find work. Now don't bother me. Tickets? Sure, I have season tickets. The company buys them. You want to see the game Sunday? Great. Here's a ticket. Now get the hell out of here. I'm busy.

And Lenny Moore, after a decade of incredible achievement . . . after a decade well enough spent to have gained him entry into the Pro Football Hall of Fame in 1975 . . . a decade of easing and pleasing men's lives . . . a decade of being sought by those who wanted autographs, who wanted to buy drinks and dinner . . . found himself out of a job, flat broke, and with no alternative but to return to the old bitterness with renewed fervor.

"Man, I never knew it would end so damned fast," he said. "It was the world's biggest comedown."

The beginning of the end was 1967, Lenny's final season as a professional football player.

"I heard from Coach Don Shula," he said, "and he told me the Colts thought I should give it up. Man, there was no idea in my head about that. In fact, I thought that I'd be tried as a wide receiver, instead of going back to halfback. And I still think I could have made it. I had my speed. I had moves. And I had all that experience. I could see on films my legs were slowing down a little. But I know I could have played.

"Let's face it. When they say you retired, that's a bunch of bullshit. They call you in and go over the situation with you. Shula told me the Colts were bringing in Timmy Brown, and I said, 'Hey, so what? Timmy can't beat me, you know?' My mind was telling me I still got it.

"But he said, 'Lenny, to be honest with you, you don't figure in our plans. So I'm asking you to retire.' It was kind of a shock. I wanted another year. And if I had gone out to flanker, man, I might still be playing.

"In fact, when Shula came in, in '63, he asked me if I'd like to go to flanker. I said, 'Man, that's like a godsend. Thank you. Now I can go out and get my shit together, you know?' But nothing ever happened. He either forget about it or decided not to bother. He left me in the backfield, blocking on those big linebackers, those beasts on the line, getting beat up every game. It takes something out of you. It shortens your longevity. I was no big Jim Brown type. It shortens the career. Anyway, I never got that shot to go out on the flanker. It would have just tickled me no end if Shula had said, 'Man, we'll give you a shot on the outside and see if you pan out.' I'm almost certain I asked about it when he told me about my 'retirement,' but in any case I guess he wasn't interested.

"So in April I made my little announcement. That was it. I was finished as a player."

And Lenny Moore had reached the most difficult juncture of all, that of player-turned-citizen. Many never attain a healthy adjustment. Many are unable to reconcile themselves to a normal station in life. Many have known no other station save that of Hero.

Too many expect and intend to live on past glories. They anticipate big jobs, offers from leaders of industry. Or they feel certain that their team—their former team—will reward all the years of accomplishment with an assistant coaching job or a scouting job.

And they sit back and wait. And wait. And wait.

The tragedy of such men is that they have spent their learning years playing a game, while others have been training for lifetime careers. It was big money for the athlete, while the budding lawyer clerked. It was national acclaim for the athlete, while the young doctor interned. The athlete today may earn $50,000 and $100,000 a year. But well before middle age, the athlete is washed up. The others are just taking off.

"All a retired player without preparation can really do is take advantage, somehow, of what he did," said Lenny Moore. "I mean, like he could open a restaurant or a bar in the town where he played longest. He could be a salesman in that town, playing on the fact that businessmen like to rub elbows with guys who were stars. He can go into broadcasting, but that's a long shot. There are too many guys who played the game and who can speak well. And there aren't too damned many broadcasting jobs."

Thus, abruptly cut adrift from not only an income but a sense of self, and of self-importance, the retired athlete founders. Too often he turns bitter, a complaining shell of a man who, if he lives long enough, becomes a dull storyteller, a bore, a relic of yesterday when all the premiums are placed on today and tomorrow.

Moore never saved money.

"Hey, listen, we never made that much. I was signed as a number one draft choice by Baltimore in 1956 for ten grand . . . that's salary, not a bonus. So when you talk about hitting the fifty-thousand-dollar level, that's a lot of years. If ever. You didn't get big raises, you know? Raises would be in the area of fifteen hundred, maybe two thousand. And you had to fight like hell to get them. The most I ever made was forty thousand, one year. It was a thirty-thousand face and ten in bonuses, performance clauses."

Lenny's first year of retirement was a snap. He chose television. Rather, television chose Lenny Moore. He was hired by the CBS network as an analyst, a "color" commentator, for each week's NFL telecast. He was close to the game he loved. He earned an income comparable to his income in football. And he was good at it.

"I worked hard," he said. "I was going to make TV my career. I studied. I would go on the road with the crew, and on Saturday nights they'd be partying and I'd be in my room learning the names and the positions and the statistics and the formations . . . talking to coaches, players . . . finding out what to expect. I knew it cold, man. I was the best prepared announcer in the world.

"And I listened to everybody . . . the technicians, the crew guys, the producers and directors and the other broadcasters. And they kept telling me I was cool, I had it down good. I don't know. Were they just pulling my chain? Was I a flop? I don't think so. But I can't explain why they didn't hire me back for 1969. And I never did get an explanation. It wasn't the blackness, because lots of black former players got hired, still do. It was just Lenny Moore luck.

"But they never gave me a reason, so I went up to New York and I stayed at the Hilton, right across the street from CBS. I got on the phone and I called Bill Fitts [then the network's top sports director] but he never returned my calls. So I went over to the office unannounced. I could look back in and see Bill back in his office. His secretary said, 'Mister Fitts isn't in,' you know, like that. Eventually, I did get hold of Fitts and he stumbled and fumbled on the telephone —never did give me the courtesy to see him in his office—and he says, 'Well, man, we just made some changes . . . you know, we never promised you the next year.'

"And I said, 'Yeah, man, I understand that, but what did I do wrong? Could you tell me that?' He couldn't. I said, 'Shit, the other guys are all back, Gifford and them.' No answer. And it wasn't anything personal. I didn't get into girl trouble or anything like that. I watched my damned self. I knew the score there.

"The guys had told me, you know, Gifford was horrible when he started, just horrible. And they told me I was way ahead of him. And then all the doors closed. I was jobless."

Lenny wanted work. Any work. He spent his last $5,000 on an extended survey of New York, checking all the talent agencies, advertising agencies, radio and television outlets.

But there was nothing. Nothing, for the man who even today holds the National Football League record for scoring at least one touchdown in eighteen consecutive games; the man who stands second to Jim Brown in lifetime touchdowns; the man who once scored twenty touchdowns in a single season.

Nothing.

"I went back to Baltimore, tried a little radio locally, made some speaking engagements, like that. But I just wasn't making any money. I'd get a hundred a week on the radio, maybe a hundred for an occasional speech. Nothing.

"So I went to the Colts in 1965. They finally said they'd co-sign a note for me to open a cocktail lounge in the city. Well, I figured I'd be that, a bartender, the rest of my life.

"And then one day a great break. A fellow called me from New York, wanted me to do a series of syndicated radio shows. Man, we had the thing, I think, presold in thirty cities. Then he found out I had the cocktail lounge. I didn't know it would be a hassle. But the guy called me and said, 'Lenny, I understand you're in the liquor business.' I said sure, it looked like a good thing, the Colts had co-signed the loan and all. And he said, 'Man, you just blew the deal. We're sponsored by a beer company, and they don't want to touch you now.' So I blew that whole thing because of my dumbness. I didn't know it would matter."

After that, nothing. The cocktail lounge failed, and the money disappeared, and no jobs were available. It was a down time for Moore, perhaps the most hopeless time of his life.

Friends assumed he was doing well. After all, he was Lenny Moore, Hero. Surely Lenny Moore would be raking it in. Surely nobody like Lenny Moore would need help, especially financial help. Vaguely, dimly, they knew about the TV work ... the radio shows ... the cocktail lounge. Nobody bothered to find out for sure. Nobody called. Nobody wrote. Lenny? Sure, he's doin' fine, isn't he? Look at him. Big hero. Had it made.

"It was exactly like that," he said. "Finally, it got so tough I went to Snelling and Snelling, a placement agency, and the guy said, 'Hey, Lenny, man, what the hell are you doing here?' I told him I needed work, man, and like he couldn't believe that. Everybody just assumes you're doing good, man. But I wasn't. The bread, it was almost gone."

But now, finally, the luck turned. The jobless star, the hero without work, saw hope at the end of the tunnel. Snelling put Lenny in touch with the Ayer Advertising Agency in Philadelphia, and that led to community relations work and appearances both in person and on the television screen selling the "New Army" recruitment program.

"That put me back on my feet," Moore said. "I was flat busted by then, and I needed anything."

Keeping himself in the public view made all the difference. In February of 1975, after three coaches, two owners and three general managers had passed through the Colts' offices, the team called back. The team remembered Lenny Moore.

"Joe Thomas [the latest general manager] called me. We met. He offered me a job, a good job. I'm director of promotions for the Colts, which is a great thing because it gets me back to my peers, keeps me in football. I make appearances for the team, set up the speakers' bureau we run, do public relations work. It's cool. And it has a lot of future, a good chance for advancement, promotion. I'd love to stay in football the rest of my life. Shit, what else do I know? It's basically getting out into the public, promoting group ticket sales, giving the team a good name, getting people excited. It's what I would have wanted ten years ago. It's what I've been waiting for, you know?"

We are sitting in the lounge of the Hunt Valley Inn, a swank hotel–restaurant–convention center in suburban Hunt Valley, Maryland, as far removed from the slums and squalor of Baltimore's ghettos as if we were in Beverly Hills or Scarsdale.

Lenny Moore, with a neat goatee, with a still-imposing body, attracts attention even now, out here in suburbia. Men cheating on either their bosses or their wives wander over to our table, drink in hand, smiling that tentative smile reserved for someone about to attempt conversation with a celebrity.

"Hey, Lenny, congratulations on being back with the team," one of them says, overly jolly. "Man, where you been all these years?"

A small smile, a sad smile. "Hey, you wouldn't believe it," says Lenny Moore. "But thanks."

Now a cocktail napkin is proffered. "Hey, man, would you sign this for my boy? He's still a Colt fan, and he remembers your name, you know?"

"Sure, chief. What's his name?"

"Greg. Greg, Jr. But just write Greg."

Moore does. The man leaves.

Moore smiles again. "For his kid, huh? It's for him, man. He's out here in the suburbs, raking it in, and he wants his friends to see that Lenny Moore signed something for him, with his name on it. Well, it's my job, now. It's cool. That's the guy who buys tickets. We need him."

The conversation continues, and it is no longer surprising that it turns back to Lenny Moore's problems with prejudice.

Even today, he is locked into the insoluble puzzle of figuring out how it might have been if he were white. Or if he were black in New York rather than in Baltimore. He is scarred, permanently, but the scars are those borne by most blacks.

Having experienced only a low-key bigotry at Penn State, Moore was totally unprepared for the more virulent form of prejudice he found once he joined the NFL.

"Oh, man, people just wouldn't believe what we had to take, and they still won't believe it now, man. But dig. When I came to Baltimore, we couldn't go downtown to the movies. We couldn't go to any of the eating houses. In fact, all of downtown Baltimore was taboo to blacks. We couldn't go anyplace . . . a clothing store, a diner, a tobacco shop. I had to live in a black area in northwest Baltimore.

"It was pretty much the same way at Westminster, where the Colts held their summer camp. It was a college, dig, and we were restricted to campus. We had to pretty much stay in our dormitory, but there were places we could go to for a sandwich. Oh yeah, we couldn't eat it there. We had to take it out. We couldn't go for a beer. There were only two movie houses in town and both of them were closed to us."

The eyes flash again, the teeth grind again, and he remembers, again, how it changed when he became a hero.

"How much of that was sincere, and how much of that was because I was Lenny Moore?" he asks. "You know the answer. We all do."

But Moore emerged as a superstar, not gradually but with a violent surge from his rookie year on. In 1958, his second year, Moore played a leading role in the rush toward the NFL championship, winning All-League honors and contributing 1,633 yards of combined offense, 938 of them coming on pass receptions. He scored fourteen touchdowns.

The Colts compiled a 9–3 record during that 1958 season, clinching the Western Conference championship with a dramatic victory in Baltimore over the San Francisco 49ers. That remains one of Moore's two most memorable games. The Colts were down 27–7 at half time and came back to win, 35–27.

"When we came back out for the second half, we played maybe the greatest half of football I've ever seen," he says. "And so did our defense. I mean, that day we could have done anything, beaten anybody. There was something almost magical about it."

And using that miracle comeback as a springboard, the Colts swept into the championship game against New York.

"The first thing that comes to my mind about that game," Moore says, "is just having been in it. The Colts had never tasted a championship before, and just to be there, just to be involved in it, was a great thrill. Secondly, the biggest thing was the overtime, that we were able to come back from behind, after we all felt we had it locked up.

"We were ahead fourteen to three at half time, and we were beating them pretty good. We were all pretty much shocked when the second half turned out the way it did. They scored twice, and we needed that field goal from Steve Myhra with just seven seconds left to tie it up. "I was on the sidelines when Myhra kicked the field goal. What was I doing? I was praying. Really. Steve hadn't been the world's greatest field goal kicker that year . . . and in a situation like that, any kicker could feel the pressure. When he finally kicked it . . . and there was some doubt he'd get it off at all because the clock was running . . . well, from the trajectory I knew it was long enough. But I had no way to tell if it was true enough. We didn't know that until we looked at the official. From our angle we couldn't really tell, it was kind of near one of the uprights, and I was just scared to death it would sail out at the last second. But he called it good, and we were tied. Then I knew we'd be in an overtime period."

"Running back onto the field," Moore says, "I just knew we were going to win. The strangest thing is that when we went into that overtime, it was just like the opening kickoff of the game.

"We had been dog-tired in the fourth quarter, but then the adrenaline started flowing again and we felt fresh and new. I know I did. I could have played another three hours, the way my body felt."

The Colts scored and won the championship. Moore had caught six passes in the game for 101 yards. His long-ball threat gave Giant defensive coach Tom Landry nightmares. The Giants double-covered Moore, making it easier for the other Colt receivers—Raymond Berry, in particular—to get open.

"Johnny kept sending me down deep as a decoy," Moore recalls, "and he knew I could beat my man when I had to. But he was working so well with Raymond there was no sense in it. Raymond had a super game. He was catching impossible passes, getting clobbered as he got his hands on the ball and still holding it. And I like to think they couldn't put more men on him because I was flying downfield, like I always did, ready to catch the big one, to break open the game. I always felt I could beat Linden Crow, and I usually did. I could handle him pretty easily, and he was one of the defensive backs in that game. As a matter of fact, I told John that whenever he was ready, I'd make the big play. I felt I could get open deep on him anytime it got to be a foot race. He just wasn't quick enough to cover me. I felt I could turn Linden Crow around anytime I wanted."

Once he almost did break the game open, taking a forty-yard pass from Unitas on the goal line. But the referee called him out of bounds. Moore almost got thrown out of the game for his protests.

"I was in bounds, I was, dammit, I really was," he says, still angry. But, of course the Colts won anyway.

The players still had to deal with the values of the 1950's, however, Especially the blacks.

"The next summer we played the Giants in an exhibition game down in Dallas," Moore says. "Remember, we were the world champs, and it was a replay of the greatest game ever, and there we were in Texas and, man, it was the same old shit all over again.

"When the plane landed on the runway at Love Field, the white players got off and boarded the charter bus. But not the blacks. Our general manager at that time, the late Don Kellett, took all the blacks aside . . . at that time, I guess we must have had eight or nine . . . and he took us all the way down the runway to the terminal. We waited for a cab, but they kept passing us up. Eventually, Kellett went to the phone and used influence . . . you know, the Baltimore Colts and all . . . and we got a couple of cabs.

"We were taken to a black area, and we stayed in a place called the Peter Lane Motel. No TV, no radio, just a room with a bed in it. No food, nothing. The rest of the team, of course, was staying down at the luxurious Sheraton Dallas.

"Well, we got a call from the blacks on the Giants. They were right up the street in a place called the Green Motel. We were all upset, and we met and tried to decide what the hell we should do . You know, should we hit the field and play, or just say the hell with it. The Colts tried to appease us with a couple of hundred dollars each . . . in fact, they even wanted us to come over to the Sheraton for meetings, but we said fuck it, we're not going.

"So we stayed out by ourselves, the Colts and the Giants, the black players. And the next day it was just the funniest feeling when we showed up at the Cotton Bowl for the game. We had decided to go on and play, that we wouldn't be helping things, really, by refusing. Anyway, when we walked into the locker room, you know how guys are carrying on, talking and mingling before a game . . . well, when that door flew open and we walked in, you could hear a pin drop.

"First guy to walk up to us was Raymond Berry. He was apologetic for us suffering the embarrassment and all we had to go through. I think he felt worse because he was from Texas, and he was just a super, super individual. Then Ameche came over to me on the field, and he says, 'Damn, Lenny, what the hell can I say? I know what you guys feel, man, and I don't even know what to say. It's got to be a hell of a shitty feeling, so let's just show these damned people down here in this game. What the hell can we do?' "

The Colts won the game, 28–3.

"But it was immaterial, man. What the hell did it mean? We blacks, on both teams, had been treated like animals. Like dirt. And we were the champions."

Moore's life has had its share of personal tragedy, too. He fathered a son while at Penn State but never married the woman. Then his first marriage ended in divorce. In July of 1974, he married again, and less than a year later was watching his new bride waste away with cancer.

"I'm not even sure how I feel about the Hall of Fame," he says. "I haven't really felt the impact. My wife is seriously ill. When the guy called me from the Hall of Fame, I was very, very excited . . . man, you never figure this is going to happen to you . . . but I couldn't really enjoy it, because of my wife's condition."

Baltimore sponsored a tribute to Lenny Moore in the winter of 1974, and his hometown of Reading, Pennsylvania, held Lenny Moore Day in May of 1975.

Too little? Too late?

"Let's let it rest," Moore said, sighing. "I've had enough of that. They wanted to do something for me, and fine, they did it. It was great. The thought was super. I don't want to smother everything that happens now with thoughts of things that happened years ago. I'm no different from any black. Things happened to me. Okay, that's the way it was. But I had it better than most blacks, too, and I have to be thankful for that."

So Lenny Moore carries on. Painfully, perhaps, and with no small measure of resentment.

"If I had come along ten years later, I would have been into the big money. Let's face it. I got nothing, really, for the way I played, for the years I had. But nobody else was making any big money, and there were lots of guys who should have. Look at that '58 team. Counting me, guys in the Hall of Fame include Jim Parker, Raymond Berry, Art Donovan, Gino Marchetti . . . and you know Unitas gets there the minute he's eligible. And from that game, you can add Andy Robustelli, Emlen Tunnell and Rosey Brown to the Hall of Fame list. And

I'm sure Frank Gifford will get in soon, and maybe Sam Huff and Charlie Conerly. How much do you think those guys would be earning today, as active players?"

But he has changed, inside, and he feels he is more a man, more an adult, because of it.

"I just want to let the rest of it slip away. I'm back in football, which is where I want to be. I had a lot of tough times, but maybe they hardened me, made me a better and more sympathetic man. There are a lot of great memories, too. I'd rather keep them fresh."

And so Lenny Moore paces through life like a sleek, black panther. Quietly, but not gently, nursing life's wounds to his magnificent pride.

He may never accept the cage, but there are moments when he manages to make the best of it.

Andy Robustelli

... Unitas hit by *Robustelli,* minus 11
... Unitas to Mutscheller pass intercepted by Karilivacz,
   pressure on Unitas by *Robustelli*

*"I thought it was a horseshit game for us. Because we lost, and I don't
think we played well."*

ANDY ROBUSTELLI IS at once the past, the present and the future of the New York Giants.

In the past, he was a defensive end. Some say he was the best in the history of the team. Others insist he was the best in the history of the game. In any case, he was good enough to earn election to Pro Football's Hall of Fame.

In the present, he is the team's director of operations, the head of an effort begun in 1974 to rebuild the once proud franchise. He has been charged by team president Wellington Mara with changing the dismally anemic performances of the team over the last decade.

In the future, he hopes to rule over a new dynasty. No, not hopes. Andy Robustelli fully expects to rule over a new dynasty in New York because he believes in hard work and dedication and blunt, outspoken honesty, and because he is old-fashioned enough to be tough and impassioned, modern enough to be ruthless and cold.

Tough . . . ruthless . . . cold. No one ever looked better for the part.

Andy Robustelli is a huge man, dark and swarthy. He has broad, massive shoulders. The hands are enormous, the forearms heroic. He has iron-gray hair, unsmiling eyes, a furrowed brow. He carries a look of constant weariness. There are bags under his eyes, always, and they are tinged with green, with black.

It is a cruel face, except when he smiles. And smiles are not normally part of Andy Robustelli's behavior. His voice is gruff and gravelly, raspy, hard. He speaks with a power that clips short his words. He even clears his throat in loud, harsh roars.

He speaks openly, directly. Sometimes too much so, by his own admission.

"Maybe it's stupid to be so honest," he says. "But if you start watching everything you say, start being careful of how it sounds, you'll never say anything at all."

At six-one and two-thirty, Robustelli strides with a big man's sureness in a variety of worlds. He has succeeded as a player and as a businessman. Now he seeks success as an administrator. He is Italian-American, and proud of that heritage. Indeed, he brings with him, every day, the finest virtues of hard peasant people. He is tough, wily, unyielding, accustomed to fighting and suffering for everything, wary of anything too easy, suspicious of rewards that are bestowed and not earned.

But the most outstanding characteristic of the man is his pride. He knows what he is and what he has achieved. He knows what odds were against him. And he is conscious of his worth. Such pride has not always been an advantage to him, but it has won the respect of many who would otherwise find him crude and unpolished.

"I thought I probably should have been named head coach when the Giants fired Allie Sherman in 1969," he says. "But I wasn't sorry . . . I wasn't angry . . . never bitter. I felt that if they didn't think I was good enough, then I wasn't. In their eyes. I thought I could have been a good head coach. I thought the qualities I had . . . even never having been a head coach before . . . were to have coached a pretty good defense three years straight, and played those three years, too. I think I would have been a good head coach."

Others thought so, too. But Robustelli required a lot in a coaching offer.

"I always had feelers," he confesses. "Every time a job came open, the Philadelphia Eagle job . . . the job at Iowa . . . the Yale job . . . But I never said yes. I felt I had to put myself in a position to have them come to me . . . make it so attractive to me so that I'd know what was there waiting for me . . . because even then I didn't think football was the end of the world. And even today. So I felt that rather than not have the situation in my favor, I'd stay here and do what I wanted to do, not what someone else thought I should do."

Pride. It surfaced, earlier, when Robustelli retired. It was 1964. The Giants were suddenly transforming themselves from champions of professional football to a joke, in a blaze of self-doubt and impatience.

"The Giants offered me a job as an assistant. It was a one-year contract. I wouldn't take a one-year contract. I didn't want to be a coaching bum. If you only think of me as a one-year coach, then I can't think beyond one year for you. That was my thinking.

"And I said to Al [Sherman], 'If you want me, get me a couple of years, and then at least I'll know where I stand. I don't want anything for nothing. You know me. If you don't think I'm doing a good job, you won't have to pay me. I'm going to quit. I'm not going to take anything that's not mine. I don't want it for security.'

"They turned me down. But when you say they . . . well, I think Al . . . I don't know . . . I never talked about it with anybody later. They never asked, I never asked. That's gone."

Robustelli's pride, and his fierce determination to win, became the trademark of the Giant defensive unit for eight years.

"When you're a player, you've got to be confident. You've got to know that when it's third and one . . . hey, don't even think about it . . . it's going to be a first. Take it.

"The spirit of our Giants . . . and again, this is something Al Sherman never realized . . . is that there are some people who never get credit. The credit they have is in association. And the credit that our defense never got was the pride, the competitiveness in saying to that frigging offense, 'You guys couldn't hold our jocks.' And it was a sensational motivation . . . we were sensationally motivated to knock the ass off our offense in training camp. Okay, but Sherman tried to lessen that. My point always was don't lessen us, fire up your other people.

"Al was afraid that we'd get so tough with our offense that they would quit. When I say quit, I mean depend on us. That's not the case. It would then be a crutch. When you know you gotta do it . . . and we never felt like we didn't have to do it . . . you do it. We were even hurt sometimes, when they were scoring forty, fifty points, because they took the steam from us. And we wanted to be the dominant part of that ball club.

"I mean, football is a selfish game. One of the things that I'm upset with the press over is if I say, 'Football is a selfish game,' then it is interpreted as me being a selfish guy. That's not the point. I think it's your responsibility as a writer to say, 'Well, what do you mean, a selfish game?' rather than let me go on speaking, because I know what I mean, but in the context that I'm speaking I can't explain to you what selfishness is. Ideally, you've got twenty-two selfish people playing for you, and if each of them does his respective job, completely worries about himself, it becomes a hell of a good effort by a selfish group of people, a team game.

"That's really what society should be. I mean, we should look at ourselves first. That's not to say a selfish person cannot give to other people. Once you've attained what you feel you have to, yourself, you can become part of a group."

Robustelli refuses to consider the 1958 championship game as a memorable moment in his life, as a game of magnitude in his career.

"I thought it was a horseshit game for us," he says. "Because we lost, and because I don't think we played well. You know, people have a tendency to make spectacular that which other people make spectacular. But I think when you realistically look at yourself and how you played and what the team did, not from a spectacular standpoint but what it really was, it was a game where we didn't make the first down with Gifford carrying the ball . . . the defense did not hold them the last series . . . had we been able to hold them, it would have been a game we won, a game we played pretty well. But Unitas killed us on square-outs, and when he had to come through he came through. The game stays with me as a memorable moment only because people constantly remind me of the game. The game that I remember as the best game we ever played was the '56 game against Chicago for the championship. You know, we had it . . . *boom!* . . . we dominated that ball game. It was forty-seven to seven, and that was a game we were good.

"But in '58 we were just not that good . . . in that game . . . I think I had a bad ball game. I think Jim Parker was a tough man for me to play against. And I don't mean to take away from what he did, or to take away from my ineffectiveness. I think you've got to try to understand the athlete, and very few people do. I believe that. The guy who knocks the athletes is the guy who gets the publicity, and I think that's so much horseshit.

"I love the English people, and their writers have class, even in defeat. They don't say the guy was a dog, they say he was very ineffective. They realize there might be more to it than a black-and-white picture. Why was he ineffective? It's a writer's duty to look at other things, to find out why, not to use just what he wants to, and interpret it just the way he wants to. They don't say, 'You dumb-ass, you're not a good football player.'

"Okay, so I look at that game as me having a bad game, personally.

And I can't ever remember a good game when I had a bad day. I'd be a phony to say I was happy to be in a game where I was lousy. But I'd also be a phony to say I was happy to be in a game where I played well and we lost, too. The combination of winning and you being the best that you could at that time is the ideal situation. Parker . . . I always had trouble with Parker, anyway. See, the strength I had as a defensive end was not to muscle people. And when the big tackles started to come into the league because of the four-three defense, they then had to turn out on the defensive end. And they could keep you out forever if you were just strong. Well, I could beat all the strong guys because I was agile. Work and work and struggle . . . well, Parker was almost as agile as I was, so me being agile against a big guy who was agile had no advantage. He was gigantic, like two-seventy, and I played at two-thirty.

"The only time we could be effective against Baltimore is when we could blitz. And in that game, every time we blitzed, Unitas would hit Berry with a square-out and we were dead. So Berry played the left end and I was on the left and Svare was behind me . . . and every time we started to come Unitas would hit Berry and *boom!* That meant every time we played the Colts I was ineffective, because if I got by Jim, which I did occasionally, that second damned back would be there to pick me up. Now, when we blitzed, that's when I'd get the quarterback. And I got Unitas in that game . . . in the last quarter . . . for a big loss, and then he came back and hit Berry with a spectacular pass and catch.

"So they made the big plays. We didn't. That's what the game was all about, and that's why I can't think of it as a great game. For us, it wasn't a great game. We lost, and there were very simple reasons why we lost. We didn't make the big plays."

The mystique of Sam Huff has been a controversy for years. Was the middle linebacker that good? Or was he simply the creation of an ardent New York press campaign?

"At that time," Robustelli says, "the middle linebacker was the most dominant part of our defense, and Sam Huff was the most. Again, don't misunderstand what I'm saying . . . he was not the best football player. But in our structure he had to be the outstanding guy. And very few people wanted to know why, or took the time out to learn why. Then they wanted to know what happened to Sam. He didn't change. The offense just started to catch up to the defense. And

once they did that, they forced you into things that . . . Well, we used
to have an inside defense. And nobody was better than Sam Huff,
because he was quick filling holes, he was strong enough to fill the
holes. So the offense went outside. Then our tackles would go outside,
and Sam would have to step up and fight the center. And, well, the
center was too big. The center would blow Sam the hell out of there
. . . enough so that the back could cut away. And that in itself was
enough to destroy our defense. Defense is a series of adjustments to
the offense, that's all. And by the time we made the proper adjustments to the new offenses, Sam appeared to become very ineffective
and Allie Sherman got rid of him.

"Al didn't know defensive problems, nor did he have the patience
to reconstruct. And really, that's what's been wrong with the Giants.
The coaches never had the patience to reconstruct. I tried to make Al
understand that in our defense it's a question of having faith in people.
That was the difference in our opinions. And the Giants did win
championships in his first three years, true. But the Giants could have
won those without Sherman. The Giants started to crumble when
Tittle got hurt, and when all of the old guys started to get old together.
They started to reconstruct, but it's a painful process.

"Al just didn't have confidence in the people he was using to replace
us with. If a guy made an error, you never saw him again. If a guy
fumbled on a kickoff, he was out of there, because Al didn't have the
faith that the guy wouldn't fumble again. I would rather have faith
in people and lose than not have faith in them and win, because then
you're just lucky."

But Robustelli's theories fell on deaf ears. Although he had doubled
as a player and defensive coach in 1962–64, he was, to the minds of
most, simply a former player with a bundle of thoughts on how to
coach, how to run a team, how to select talent. And every former
player has those ideas. Most of them couldn't apply anything more
important than a Band-Aid.

So Andy Robustelli retreated to his native Connecticut and began
building his businesses with the same hard-line, hard-nosed approach
that he used to emerge as a superstar football player. He became
owner of a chain of sporting goods stores and president of a chain of
successful travel agencies. But he never called on his football "connec-
tions."

"I've lost a hell of a lot of good business because I couldn't prosti-

tute myself as a person," he says. "I've never been a part of anything
... a joiner ... and I don't think I ever will be. I refused to use the
football contacts I had to give me the business advantages I could have
had. If I know a guy knew me because of football, I just cannot do
business with him. It wouldn't give me the satisfaction I need to prove
to myself I don't need the help. I can do it myself. I never had lunch
with people who could help me when I was with the Giants. I shied
away from those things. I never played that game, maybe the way I
should have.

"I guess that's the product of working for whatever you got, being
a little careful. If things came too easy, maybe they wouldn't be what
you wanted them to be.

"That's what I tried to instill in the defense when I played. I was
a little older than most of the guys, so I felt it was almost my duty
to help with a spirit kind of thing. I wasn't a fighter. Oh hell, I had
fights ... Rosey Grier, Rosey Brown ... but it was just stupid, I
must've been nuts. I think physically we were tough. We'd play with
pain ... we'd play with all kind of aches and injuries and needles ...
you know, all that kind of shit ... just because we didn't want to get
taken out of the line-up. I had come from the Rams. I was an All-Pro
out there. My first year with the Giants was '56, and we won the title.
So the guys who were sizing me up found out I could do all the things
people said I could do. I had a great season. It helped.

"But we didn't fight much among ourselves. Oh sure, there were
guys on other teams ... grudges, like that. A guy like John Henry
Johnson, for instance, we just couldn't wait to play him. There were
others ... Jim David ... Hardy Brown ... Johnny Sample ... but
Johnny was really mouthy. When the Johnny Samples started to come
in ... this was when the integration started ...

"Hey, I came in in '51, with guys like Tank Younger and Deacon
Dan Towler, black guys. And we went down south and we broke the
barrier in hotels ourselves. Kid wouldn't take their money, we'd say,
'Like hell, get this friggin' elevator upstairs.' Like the Stoneleigh Hotel
in Dallas, the Albert Pick in Little Rock ... they wouldn't let the guys
come in. But we broke that ourselves. I played fourteen years of pro
football with good people, and never one black-and-white situation.

"I still get letters to this day ... you know, 'You greasy Guinea'
... 'You wop' ... and I'd hope that we've grown beyond that, but if
not, the hell with it.

"But guys who were dirty, black or white, they were dirty. John Henry Johnson would throw elbows all over, and remember, we didn't wear face masks then. We'd break noses, jaws, you'd come off the field all bloody. Get even? We'd just knock the shit out of him whenever he had the ball. But he straightened up and became a hell of a player."

There is this about Andy Robustelli: he respects toughness, and he despises illegality. He is a product of a tough, poor, immigrant family that wanted to prosper honestly.

"I was brought up in an integrated neighborhood," he says. "Both parents worked, we didn't have any money . . . yeah, we were very poor. I was born in a house where we were the only white family. My mother was a dressmaker, my father was a barber. There were four black families and us in this house, and today guys come in and give me that shit about black and white. I'm forty years into that . . . I learned about good blacks and bad blacks, good whites and bad whites!

"There were six kids in our family, in a cold-water flat. It was in Stamford, where I live now. All there was to do was play football, tackle in the street, like that. We'd play football and baseball with a piece of rolled-up paper and put tape around it.

"I never got into police trouble, but I was pretty close a few times. What saved it was the strong Italian family customs. One thing, we'd have to be in bed early, our parents were pretty strict. So there was only a certain amount of time you could get in trouble. And we all lived around the church, which is probably what had the greatest influence on all us kids. I'm still a religious person, yeah, but not like I used to be."

Robustelli was seventeen years old when he graduated from Stamford High School, and he went for one year to LaSalle Military Academy on Long Island before going into the service.

"I wanted to enlist when I was seventeen, but my mother wouldn't let me, so I went to LaSalle for the football season. Then I joined the Navy for almost three years, and after that I enrolled at Arnold College."

Arnold College, no longer in existence, welcomed Robustelli as an athlete. He had built a mighty reputation in Connecticut as both a football and baseball star, and with the Navy years he had matured physically, as well. He was a twenty-year-old freshman.

"I didn't need a scholarship for Arnold, I had the GI Bill of Rights. And I couldn't have paid my way through college, no way. I remember in college, we couldn't go home on weekends because we didn't have nickels for the tolls on the highway. Maybe if we told our mothers we needed the nickel or dime, they'd give it to us. But we just didn't think we should take the money. When I was in the service, my grandfather died and left us some money and a house, so we moved closer to the church, bought a house, and my mother didn't have to work.

"But I played football, damned good football, at Arnold. Remember, this wasn't the big leagues or anything. We played Adelphi, Upsala, Wagner, schools like that. But the Rams drafted me. I don't know how the hell they found me, but I was drafted. I was the only Arnold player ever to be drafted.

"And in '51 I left my wife in Stamford and went to Los Angeles. L.A. was a loose place . . . that was sticky. Trying to keep your morals high in a place like that was a little difficult. I was interested only in making the team, and starting, and after the second game of that rookie season I was a starter. I even remember the name of the guy I replaced. Jack Zilly. He got hurt and I started and he never got back. I missed one game at the end of the season and then I never missed another one for fourteen years.

"In '56 my wife was pregnant and almost due, and it was summer and I had to report. I called and asked if I could get about five extra days to stay home, and Sid Gillman, the coach then, said no, I couldn't, and he said he'd fine me for every day I was late. Well, I told him I wasn't coming, and a few days later they traded me to the Giants for a number one draft pick.

"It was strange. While I was with the Rams, I always wished I was with New York. But when I got sent there, I was a little let down, a little apprehensive . . . depressed, I guess, too. It's tough to get traded, to know somebody doesn't want you.

"It was a psychological depression, I guess. I'm not an extrovert. I only like to do what I want to do. I only want to be with people that I want to be with. I don't make small talk, so I don't know how to get along. I don't have much of a social life. The friends I see are just the ones I've seen since I was a kid. The old neighborhood guys. I didn't really get close to any of the Giants . . . maybe Mo, but nobody else. I prepared myself. I knew once I was out of football it would be a tremendous letdown, so I didn't want to make it my life.

"For that reason, I never came around the Giants after I retired. And I never tried to live like a star. The night club scene . . . the flashy cars . . . I know that adds up to nothing. It never entered my mind. Money isn't important to me. The most I made as a player was eighteen thousand . . . we never talked contract. The problem now, when you talk to a kid, is he runs downstairs and checks with the other kids . . . we didn't have agents or attorneys or anything.

"Oh, sometimes Walt Kennedy advised me. I grew up with him. And if I have a friend . . . well, it's Walt Kennedy. If I go out to dinner with somebody, it's Walt Kennedy. And not because he was the commissioner of the NBA, because he wasn't when I knew him. And Howard Cosell . . . he used to live in Stamford . . . I don't know why Howard likes me. I like Howard . . . I like him, but I'd like to see him as a different guy. I'd like to see him happy, and not so uptight! And he's been particularly critical of the Giants the last few years. That doesn't bother me. It only irritates me when I know he's wrong. Howard will say to me, 'You football people don't know anything other than football,' but what is his life? Isn't it all broadcasting?

"Howard's a liberal guy, and he knows I'm not, yet his attitude to me was very tolerant, and for the life of me I don't know why I'm a friend of his. I'm a conservative. Definitely. We're different! But he's got a warmness few people have seen."

Robustelli views the world from a staunchly conservative position, and as with other topics he expresses himself with vigor.

"I have to go back to my environment. I think we're all products of the conditions we grew up in. You may be the product of an Orthodox Jewish family . . . and to me, I'm upset, because you don't practice it like your family did. To me, I still like to see the Jewish people up my way who walk to temple. That's beautiful. So I think the Orthodox Jewish family has to react differently from the liberal Jewish family that's been affected by the black movement.

"The Jewish person, psychologically, would like to see everybody liberated because it helps him become that much more liberated. See, I don't think there's anything wrong with being a slave. Maybe I'm just a different kind of a guy. Let me explain that. Some black people are almost ashamed that some of their ancestors were slaves. But to be humble, to be a servant to somebody, I think that's a pretty good quality. We couldn't live with slavery now, no way, but I think there are some terrific things we could learn from it. That was a culture of obedience, and I think those were good people. But if you make that bad, and use it to affect your life, I think that's wrong. You should be proud if your people were subjected, were servants, and did their job well.

"I don't think I have an ounce of racial prejudice, but I'm prejudiced against certain types of characters. I'm against welfare. I'm infuriated as a businessman when a girl quits and I know she gets unemployment for seventy weeks. That's what the college kids should be talking about . . . the structure of an organization. They're building a welfare state, and the welfare employee who sits behind the desk is not going to say, 'Hey, you shouldn't be getting this money,' because when he starts to cut all those people out his job is gone, so what he does is build up his job.

"In our day, it was demeaning to be a person who accepted welfare. But no more. For me it would be impossible, unthinkable. I mean, our parents . . . if they borrowed money, they'd suffer to pay it back. But we've allowed it to become different.

"A lot of things in our society are unpleasant to me now. And my kids are the same. Biologically, I think we're men and women. When you're a male, you've got male organs . . . when you're a female, you have female organs . . . and there should be a distinction. Well, whenever the distinction is not apparent, then I think something is wrong.

"I know that my kids are smarter than I was. I know that these football players are stronger . . . faster . . . tougher . . . but I don't know if they want it as much as I did. Look, I made a statement the other night in New Haven and, well, I'm sorry I made it. Public speaking is tough. I talked about the differences in the athlete today. To see a guy after a ball game with a hair drier . . . well, to me, I'm accustomed to seeing guys cry after a ball game. Do you know what it is to come into a locker room and get a feeling that these guys almost don't care whether they win or lose?

"I do know this. There's got to be more leadership on teams. If I was playing today, I'd have to try to change it myself, but I don't know that it can be changed. We're in a society where we've allowed people to do their thing. Drugs . . . clothes . . . hair. I say to my girls . . . they wear dungarees that rake the floor, they've got holes, they're scraggly . . . I say if you can just give me a reason. They say, 'I'm different if I don't, everybody does it.'

"So I say to them, 'Why don't you be different?' Don't do what they do because they do it, do what you feel because you want to do it. My father was not as tough as I am with the kids. We didn't see my father much. He worked from eight in the morning to eight at night, and we'd be in bed by nine. He'd come home, whistle, we'd go to bed, he'd sit up and have a few glasses of wine and then he'd go to bed. But I tell my kids we can only bring them so far, they've got to make a choice.

"Ultimately, I think we have to accept changes, like it or not . . . black marrying white . . . who would ever expect priests being married? It's got to come. Everybody's got to come together. But let's hope we never get conditioned so that we all drink the same coffee, for instance, because then we're being directed by someone other than ourselves."

Robustelli and the Giants, then, parted ways in the winter of 1964. Robustelli retired. He turned down the one-year offer as an assistant coach. He went back to Connecticut, and into business.

The Giants, meanwhile, continued their painful process of deterioration. The players were anonymous, most without talent. Allie Sherman was fired in 1969 mostly as the result of a weak, misdirected scouting department. Some of the blame was Sherman's, but he was also asked to make players of men who could never be players.

The shame built. The fans jeered. Alex Webster was hired, and only twice did Webster's team approach even mediocrity. Team president Wellington Mara, who a decade and more earlier had achieved a reputation as a sharp trader, had been passed by the tide of computer technology and the breed of bright young men who, as both head coaches and general managers, had left the Giant organization in the dust.

Trades turned into giveaways. Draft choices were bad jokes. Francis Peay . . . Don Davis . . . Bob Timberlake . . . Rocky Thompson . . . Eldridge Small . . . Larry Jacobson . . . Wayne Walton . . . all were high-round draft choices. All were mistakes.

Finally, the situation got to Webster. He announced his resignation before the final game of the 1973 season, a season in which the Giants were to finish with a horrendous 2-11-1 record.

Now Mara admitted his mistakes. And he promised to hire a football man to lead the team back. The new man, he said, would have total freedom, unquestioned authority, for every facet of the team's operations.

A director of operations.

And he called Andy Robustelli.

"After not playing for so many years," Robustelli remembers, "and after so many years of wanting to coach, at least in the back of my mind, one day Well calls me and says, 'Here's this job, and I want you to take it.' I didn't know what the hell to say.

"It wasn't retribution, or vindication, or anything like that. Well asked me because I think he knew what I could do. He sat in on a lot of our meetings when I was a player-coach. And he knew the kind of football player I was.

"If he hired me because I was one of the old group . . . if that was the case, then he was wrong to start with. You know, as I've said many times, I was not the old family kind of player. I really wasn't. I was never a part of anything. When he did call me, I knew the Giants really were in bad shape. And if I could do anything to help . . . well, that's all I really wanted to do. I don't want to come out of this thing being anything other than a guy who did his job. Help the ball club, that's all.

"I'm the guy between management and the football team. There's got to be a guy in between. I find it difficult to deal with today's players, because the only thing I really discuss with them is salary. We've got to stay within a budget . . . we're not gonna chop people to stay within the budget, but you've got to be realistic, start matching one guy against another one and see who's worth what.

"Maybe we made some mistakes with kids . . . maybe we stuck with Eldridge Small too long, for instance. But you won't know if a kid is going to make it or break it until he gets the chance. You don't find out in summer camp . . . in drills . . . you don't find out with a strike . . . you do it in a game, and if you don't do it, you don't and that's it.

"Look, we knew that first year [1974] would be tough. We wouldn't say it, because you just don't, but we knew it would be a bad season. We had a new coach and a new defense and new people, and we didn't have the kind of veterans who could fit into something new instantly. It takes time. Anything good takes time. We got close to winning some ball games and . . . I don't know, maybe it's better we didn't win 'em. Everybody would get excited, and everybody would expect you never to lose again.

"Winning some would be a plus, though. It all depends how you handle it. If we had won some games, and did so knowing it wasn't a good team, it would be important how the coach handled the players. You can tell a player all day, 'Well, we won, but we were fortunate to win,' and he's gonna say, 'Shit, the coach is blowin' us down now, we're really pretty good.' You know you're good when you romp that guy's ass off the field, and we didn't romp people's asses off the field."

Andy Robustelli, tough and hard, old-fashioned and conservative, has thus defined his job.

He must find people who can romp other people's asses off the field, and if he has to romp a few off the team, well, that's football. The strong survive, the fittest rise.

And when he gets that team of ass-rompers, he'll know it. All he'll have to do is close his eyes and picture Huff and Landry and Katcavage and Madzelewski and Svare and Tunnell.

And Robustelli. He was the best ass-romper of them all.

Johnny Unitas

. . . *Unitas* to Berry plus 15 for touchdown
. . . *Unitas* to Berry plus 25 to 50, first down (1:04 to go)
. . . *Unitas* to Berry plus 15 to 35, first down
. . . *Unitas* to Berry plus 21 to Giant 43
. . . *Unitas* to Berry plus 12 to Giant 8, first down
. . . *Unitas* handoff to Ameche, touchdown at 8:15 of
  sudden death

"A defense always gives you something, any defense. You just have to pick and scratch until you find it."

MOST MEN ARE both victims and prisoners of what-might-have-been, raging at the seeming conspiracies of fate.

The word *if* does it all for them.

If I had gotten a better education . . . *If the boss didn't move his son up over me, I deserved the promotion* . . . *If I didn't marry that woman* . . . *If I did what I really wanted to do* . . . *If I didn't have to worry about mortgages and bills* . . . *If I had* . . . *If only* . . .

Athletes, too, use the magic word.

If I had been drafted by a team that needed a fullback . . . *If the damned coach gave me a real chance* . . . *If I didn't break my damned leg* . . . *If the stupid receiver had held that pass* . . . *If I had* . . . *If only* . . .

A superstar doesn't need the *if*. But for the men who passed him up, the word rings over and over down the years.

Johnny Unitas is followed by a horde of men mumbling *if* . . .

Notre Dame had a skinny kid from Pittsburgh on its campus. He had come in search of a football scholarship. He had made an impression on many college scouts, including the one from the most storied of all football schools. But the Irish turned him down, sent him home because he just wasn't heavy enough, strong enough, solid enough . . .

The Pittsburgh Steelers own a worthless contract dated 1955 and signed by John Unitas. Is is tucked away, no doubt, in some dusty, embarrassed basement file. They had drafted him on the ninth round of the 1955 draft, but the head coach, Walt Kiesling, found himself with four quarterbacks in training camp. He would keep only three —Jim Finks, Ted Marchibroda and Vic Eaton. The one he would cut would be Johnny Unitas . . .

The Cleveland Browns, too, are haunted. Unitas was scheduled to try out for them in the spring of 1956. But then the head coach, Paul

Brown, called back. He had persuaded Otto Graham to postpone retirement for one more year. Would Unitas wait until 1957 before reporting? No, dammit, he would not. And the next season the Browns introduced a fullback named Jim Brown to the world . . .

Johnny Unitas has never had to say *if.* He knew what he could do, and given the chance, he went out and did it.

But in 1955, Johnny Unitas was just another almost. He had had his chance and he had been cut, released, dismissed as not good enough, sent away with little hope.

He was working in construction and playing football on weekends. Then the Baltimore Colts called in February of 1956 and asked him to come down.

"Don Kellett was the general manager," Unitas recalls, "and he said, 'We need a backup quarterback for George Shaw and I noticed your name and checked on you and we'd like you to come on up and have a tryout.'

"I said fine, and he said he'd send me a contract for seven thousand dollars . . . no, six thousand. Pittsburgh, when I signed there, was going to pay me five thousand. So I said hell, I didn't do bad, I received a thousand-dollar raise and didn't even play.

"So I went up there in May and had the tryout, and then I came back for summer camp and that was it. One nice thing . . . that summer we played the Steelers in an exhibition game and I had a really good day . . . threw a couple of touchdown passes and had over two hundred yards passing. Kiesling was still the coach, and it felt real good."

Unitas' childhood helped instill the toughness, the sense of realism and the determination that were so valuable to him.

It was Pittsburgh, steel country, not much money and too much work.

"I have a brother and two sisters," he says. "My father died when I was five [in 1938] and my mother didn't remarry until all the kids had grown. Her second husband, my stepfather, died about five years ago.

"She's a hell of a woman, my mother. She was hit by a car about a month ago . . . broke both legs and her right arm. She's seventy now, lives in Pittsburgh close to my sister, who has five boys. She's a strong woman.

"We never had much money in the house. She'd leave the house at seven and come home at five. She used to scrub floors at night in downtown office buildings, and in the daytime she'd work in a bakery. And in her spare time she went to school, and after so many years she took a civil service exam and passed it with the highest score, and she became a bookkeeper for the city. She also sold insurance. And at the beginning, she ran my dad's business when he died. He had a little coal business, trucking business. He was thirty-seven when he died . . . he was putting some coal in for some people in the rain, and he caught a cold, and that developed into pneumonia, and his kidneys locked, resulting in uremic poisoning, and he passed on.

"She hired somebody to drive the truck and she'd take coal orders and he'd deliver the coal. But we always managed to eat. She always had a big garden out back and she was always canning tomatoes and peppers and whatever we could raise. We always managed to eat . . . it wasn't steak and roast beef, but we ate a lot of Spam and gravy and potatoes, lots of cereal. There was always enough in the house.

"I worked during high school, too. At night I'd go over and clean up a little plastics shop. If I'd see a load of coal on the street, I'd stop and ask the lady if I could put it in [the basement] for her. Plenty of times I'd be walking home from school and see a load of coal and ask if I could put it in. I'd make three, four, five dollars doing it, and it wasn't hard work. I didn't want to have to fool around trying to borrow some money from Mother, which she didn't have.

"Sometimes I'd come home from a ball game all beat up and she'd say, 'You know Mrs. Rigby up the street?' and I'd say, 'Yeah, I know Mrs. Rigby up the street,' and she'd say, 'Well, she has three tons of coal sitting on the street, see that it gets put in.' And I could hardly move and I'd say, 'Ma, it's raining.' She'd say, 'Yeah, it's raining. Go do it.' So I did it.

"And those are the kind of things you remember . . . at least I do. Nowadays people complain and I say, 'You don't know how easy you have it.'"

High school for the pencil-thin Unitas was tiny St. Justin's, which had "about three hundred kids." He played well, and scholarship offers were tentatively tendered. Notre Dame . . . Pittsburgh . . . Louisville.

"I went out to Notre Dame," he says, "but I was such a skinny kid, five-eleven, maybe a hundred thirty-five, they changed their mind. Then I flunked the entrance exam at Pittsburgh, so I couldn't go there.

"Then I went to visit Louisville, and had to take the exam there. I flunked it, too. I wasn't a good student in high school, never studied or anything. But then I talked to the board at Louisville and they let me come in on probation, to see if I couldn't do the work. I finished that year with a B standing, and they took me off probation and let me take as many hours as I wanted. I graduated in four years, without any problem. I had never really taken the time and effort to study in high school. I was always out in the streets somewhere . . . never at home . . . and I should have studied. I regret not doing it."

The voice on the telephone said to take the interstate out of Baltimore to Highway 83–North. Then look for a cutoff near a red brick church and turn into the first driveway after the church.

There is no name on the mailbox. But the property has a name: Sunning Hill. And the house cannot be seen from the road, because there is a twisting, uphill drive that bends for a quarter of a mile through heavily wooded grounds. It is fall. The leaves are gold and red, rust and purple, flaming orange and umber bronze.

He is already waiting at the door, a trim, solidly built, smiling John Unitas. Successful businessman, television personality, entrepreneur, restaurateur, gracious host.

We sit in an office overlooking the hill, a large window facing the purple-orange-red-yellow-gold dance of autumn, the room itself crammed with the trophies and plaques and awards and game balls, wall-size photographs and framed proclamations from various politicians and municipalities—the residue of his football accomplishments.

Unitas is poring through stacks of canceled checks, occasionally setting one aside to verify it, to confirm it, sometimes shaking his head, mouthing a silent exclamation at the amount. His desk telephone, encased in a dark wooden box to look like an expensive cigar humidor, rings frequently. He smiles apologetically before answering, and keeps the conversation brief. "I have somebody down from New York, talking," he says.

This is the private John Unitas. He is happy here, tucked away in the hills of rural Maryland, in his house on the hill with a new wife, a new child and a new career.

"I've been here in this house, oh, going on four years," he says. "The five kids by my first wife all live with their momma . . . they're twenty, nineteen, seventeen, fifteen and almost eight. And the baby is nineteen months. I always see my other children . . . the youngest spends a lot of time here, weekends . . . I take him fishing . . . movies . . . sometimes he goes to the Sunday games with me.

Unitas still draws deferred salary payments from the Baltimore Colts and the San Diego Chargers. He owns a restaurant, with former teammate Bobby Boyd, in Baltimore, "the Golden Arm."

"We've had it eight years, and we've been very fortunate because it's doing well," he says.

He also owns a hotel-restaurant, the Sheraton-Orlando Jet Port Inn, twenty minutes from Disneyworld. He has real-estate holdings throughout Florida, mostly situated in the Deltona-Sanford area. The land developments are sold off in parcels, with water, piping, roadways all built in.

"But they aren't selling at all," he groans, "nothing much is these days."

And he works with CBS as an analyst for NFL football.

"I really enjoy the television work," he says. "I wasn't afraid of it or anything. It was just a matter of getting an idea of what they wanted. After that, there wasn't any problem, because I know the game forwards and backwards. There's some homework, you have to keep up with who the players are, what they're doing. I go to my game on a Friday or Saturday, depending on where it is. Then we generally have a production meeting with the staff and the crew, decide what we're going to do and say. I work it out with my play-by-play man, the guy I'm working with now, Gary Bender, he's a super guy, really good.

"Then it's just a matter of doing the ball game, and you just do the game like you're playing. You take it piece by piece. And it's a lot of fun . . . I enjoy sitting up there and watching, I get an entirely different perspective. The big thing is that you're not on screen, just your voice. The way I look at it, you get in, make a complete thought and get out. You don't want to talk too much. People don't want to hear all that, they want to watch the game."

There are many sides to Johnny Unitas, and he is a man of strong feelings, feelings he is not at all reluctant to state. The current unrest between the players and the team owners, for instance, bothers him deeply.

"The kind of things they want are ridiculous," he says, "just plain stupid. Like no curfew. You have to have that. And it was part of our life, sneaking out if you wanted to risk it. It was a hundred-dollar fine if they caught you, and let's say I got away with it more times than they caught me. I played that '58 season for twelve thousand five hundred dollars. I know rookies who don't play who make three times that much now. I get tired of hearing about the strike . . . this guy's going to do this, that guy's not going to do that. My feeling is they ought to cut 'em back to thirty-three players and make 'em play football. It's crazy. There are guys who get seventy-five thousand and don't really care to play. They don't like to get their faces busted up. Me? I never had to worry about my face. Maybe getting it busted up would help.

"But I have no regrets about not coming into it today for all the big money. I did all right. And I enjoyed football. I enjoyed every minute, every game, every practice. Everything I've ever done in football I enjoyed. It was fun. I don't think they have any fun now. It's run as a real big business and the attitudes of the guys don't permit them to have any fun. If anybody had more fun than we did I'd like to see them.

"I'm still close with a lot of the old Colts. Sure. Bobby Boyd and I are in business, and I see him nearly every day. I see Art Donovan. Gino, of course, is out of town so I don't get to see him. Bill Pellington owns a restaurant right down the street here, so I see him a lot. We play golf together. Mutscheller is my insurance man, so I got to see him, right? Tom Matte is still here in town. Bobby Vogel lives up in Havre de Grace. Freddie Miller I see a lot. He lives up in Hampstead, which is in western Maryland . . . he has a big farm up there, and every Fourth of July we all go up there and have a big outing so everybody can get together. We play ball, bring all the kids, have a good time."

An elder statesman now? A graying former athlete? It doesn't seem fair that we can no longer see number 19, dancing back in that unique, tiptoe way, cradling the ball halfway between his ear and his shoulder, eyes scanning every player, brain whirring like the most sophisticated computer, arm cocked, ready to throw.

"Playing against him," said John Symank, who played briefly as a first-rate defensive back, "was like being the turkey in a turkey shoot. You knew you had to get hit, you just didn't know when it would happen. John created intimidation. He had Berry and Moore and great protection. He could sit back there and wait and wait and wait.

He always kept you off balance, always called the unexpected play at the right time. When you woke up on a Sunday morning and realized you had to cover Berry . . . with John throwing to him . . . it took all the pleasure out of the day."

John Sample, once a teammate of Unitas' in Baltimore, recalls the day he played for the New York Jets against the Colts in Super Bowl III: "In the fourth quarter they finally put Johnny in. He had had a bad elbow and didn't play much all season. Now, dig. I knew we were going to win. I knew we were ahead and that we were dominating the game. I knew we had stopped everything they wanted to do. But when I saw him walk out onto the field, my knees started shaking, and I knew that if there was any man in the world who could turn it around, I was looking at the cat who could do it. And he damned near did it. I'll tell you, he scared grown men, just by taking the snap and looking your way."

In the 1958 championship sudden-death game, Unitas scared the New York Giants silly. It was his game, more than any other man's. His two late drives—the one for the tying field goal with scant seconds on the clock, and the one for the winning touchdown in the sudden-death period—were works of art, as real and as solid as a painting or sculpture.

"The man was a fucking genius," said Giant middle linebacker Sam Huff. "I never saw a quarterback that good in those two drives."

Unitas smiles. "Nah, that wasn't our best game. It was a fine ball game to win, to participate in, but it should never have been so close. I was sorry the thing went so long. We should have blown them out. But we didn't get in on that one particular touchdown drive, and that turned the game around."

It was midway through the third quarter. Baltimore, holding a 14–3 lead, moved from its forty-one yard line to the New York three. It was first down. Then in three plays, they gained only two yards. On fourth down the Colts spurned the opportunity to kick a field goal. It would be a touchdown or nothing.

"One thing to remember," Symank said, "is that John always had a garbage play, a gimmick play. You knew he'd use it, you just didn't know when. But you worried yourself silly waiting for it, and then he'd spring it on you at the most unlikely time and beat you with it anyway."

He picked this crucial moment to use the garbage play against the Giants. And it should have worked.

"It was a pitchout to the right," says the master, "and it actually was supposed to be a pass. Ameche was supposed to pass to Mutscheller in the end zone. I pitched it to him, and Jimmy was standing there all by himself. But Ameche started running, and they stopped him. Alan never did explain why he didn't throw. He knew that was the play."

Eighteen years later, Unitas can still play through that game in his head, remembering nearly everything about it—especially the Giant pass defense that collapsed under his attack in the final minutes.

"They were just giving us certain things, and we were taking them. Berry was working back there on Karilivacz, I believe it was, deep on his outside, and then we'd come back inside and work on a linebacker. They were just leaving it there, so we kept going back to it, taking advantage of it. We could just as easily have gone over to the other side, but when you get something going like that, you just don't give it up.

"We were also beating the linebacker, Svare. We'd beat him deep . . . go behind him . . . and then we'd throw it in front of him next.

"Sam Huff was concerned about that little quick slant-in on the weakside. He was trying to help Svare and Karilivacz. But he should never have gotten out of the middle. If you can take care of your own responsibilities first, and then go back and help there, too, fine, but he couldn't do both things at the same time. He never should have gotten so far out of his position. When he did that, he just left open the big play for Ameche [twenty-three-yard gain on a quick trap up the middle, the play that sealed the Giants' fate in the overtime]. It was a very simple matter of checking off the play, making sure the offensive tackle could get over to block Sam. And Sam was deep enough where he could. A defense always gives you something, any defense. You just have to pick and scratch until you find it.

"Anyway, we got down and Myhra kicked the field goal, and I knew we had a sudden death. Tired? No, you don't get tired in a game. You collapse later, maybe, but not in a ball game like that.

"The game caused a hell of a lot of excitement later, but to me it was just another game, one we had to win. People still talk to me about it today, though: 'Hey, I saw that overtime game, and I sure hated you in '58.' And I say, 'Well, it was my pleasure.'

"The biggest thing I remember about it is that there was some drunk running up and down the field, and they called a time-out while the police were chasing him, and somebody kicked the plug out of the wall in the TV booth. It was off the air for a while. Anyway, the police finally caught this guy, and they're getting ready to take him away, and he yells, 'God-dawg, shouldn't be gettin' me, should be gettin' that number nineteen, he's the guy that's killin' us.'

"But the game, to me, wasn't any big thing. Hey, a championship is something you work for all year, but I was just concerned with winning it and getting out of there. And when Alan scored the winning touchdown . . . all I tried to do was make sure of a solid handoff . . . I knew he was going to score. They weren't going to stop him that late in the game, on the one yard line. When I saw he had scored, I just hightailed out of there, because all those people started running down on the field and that's a lot more dangerous than playing. You never know what they're carrying, and all that back-slapping and head-slapping and all, that's not something you want to go through.

"A field goal was never my decision," Unitas says. "It was always the head coach's responsibility. If he sends a field goal in, I go off. Even in that sudden-death drive, it would have had to be a fourth-down situation, and we didn't come up to any of those. We were controlling the football, moving it on the ground . . . there wasn't any sense in it. Why try to kick a field goal? No reason for it. Besides, I always hated to see the man send a field-goal team in there. I figured I could always get a touchdown out of any drive. Quarterbacks have to think that way."

John Unitas became an institution in Baltimore, a god in a hard-working, hard-drinking town. Part of his appeal was that he was only a few years removed from the same hard work himself.

"I was working for a construction company as a pile driver," he reminisced in his elegant study, playing back his job as he would a football game. "I was what they called the monkey man on the pile-driving outfit. I had to get to the top of the thing . . . I worked a hundred and twenty-five feet in the air . . . always keeping everything greased up."

He enjoyed the memories, going into detail, describing the physical details with his hands: "Connected to the hammer was a cone-shaped thing that fit in there, and an oak log, about that wide, about that

round, set in the bevel part of this cone-shaped thing, so that the
hammer was not hitting directly on steel, it was hitting on that wood,
which would drive the dick into the boot which would drive the steel
into the ground.

"Well, the wood thing would burn out, depending on how hard you
were driving, because every time the hammer would hit, it was equiva-
lent to eight tons, and so that would pulverize that wood thing and
it would burn out. And, depending on how hard the ground was
where you were driving, if the damn thing was not going in very good
you may be a hundred feet or so up in the air when the son-of-a-gun
jammed. And I'd have to climb there and pick it up and throw it out
. . . the thing weighed about a hundred and twenty-five pounds . . . and
get the crane to bring over another one. So that was my job . . . I had
to change those oak things and also keep everything greased up good."

That kind of hard physical work and earthiness was what made
Unitas and the Colts favorites in Baltimore. The city tolerates its
baseball Orioles, but it is not an easy tolerance, and the Orioles,
despite years of winning, have never been box-office smashes. Football
is this city's game, hard and basic, direct and often brutal. Life is like
that in Baltimore, and its citizens can identify with bloody nose far
more easily than they can with a double-steal or a suicide squeeze.
And from 1956 on, whatever else went wrong with the Colts, there
was Johnny Unitas, crew-cut and slender, dancing back behind the
line ready to work his magic.

But things changed. Carroll Rosenbloom, who had owned the franchise since it was deposited in Baltimore in 1950, sold it to a Chicago
refrigeration tycoon named Robert Irsay. In 1971, Irsay brought in
a busy little general manager named Joe Thomas, who claimed credit
for building championship teams in Minnesota and Miami.

In his first off-season, Thomas traded no fewer than nineteen of the
revered Colts, doing so because "we need to clean house in order to
build from the foundation." The fans, at first unhappy, became furi-
ous. But they assumed Thomas would never mess with Johnny
Unitas.

In January of 1973, Thomas did just that. He traded Johnny Unitas.

"I wasn't surprised at all," says Unitas. "I knew that's what they
were going to do. The only thing that came as a surprise was the way
they did it, that's all.

"We had had meetings before. They didn't want me to play here any longer. And I said, 'Well, I feel I can still play . . . and I'd like to still play . . . and I've played here all my life . . . but if I can't play here, I want to play somewhere.'

"The situation was just no good. They sat me down on the bench that season and I just didn't play much at all. So when I got with John Sandusky, who was the interim coach at that time . . . he said no way would I play another play with the Baltimore Colts unless the kid gets hurt and I have to go in. But listen. This is all old stuff, and I'm tired of hearing about it, and as far as I'm concerned it's over and done with.

"As far as the trade's concerned, they talked about where. 'Suppose we trade you to Boston?' they asked, and I said I wouldn't go to Boston. I knew the Redskins were interested in me, and I would have liked that, but I knew they'd never let me play for George Allen. George said he had talked with Thomas but there was no way they'd trade me there. I knew that. Ain't no way they'd send me sixty miles away and there I am, haunting them. 'If you want to trade me, I have no objection to being traded,' I said, 'but you find out who's interested in having me, and then you tell me and I'll tell you whether I'll go there or not.' And that was the agreement they made.

"So I left the meeting . . . their lawyer and my lawyer . . . we left that meeting, it was right before Washington was playing Miami in the Super Bowl, and about ten days later I got a call from a writer here in Baltimore, Larry Harris. And he says, 'What the hell you doing going to San Diego?' I said, 'I'm on my way to Florida, I got a speaking engagement, not San Diego.' So he says, 'Uh-uh, they just traded you to San Diego.' I didn't know anything about it. They didn't tell me after all, and we had an agreement, I thought.

"We settled the matter of my contract, my deferred salary, and it's all over with as far as I'm concerned. I don't care to talk much about it. I hope they win, because to me you hurt the economy of the whole city by not being winners. I'm sure they cost the city three to five million dollars a year. I'd love to see the kids play and have a good team. It's good for the town, for everybody.

"Hey, I'm still a Colts fan. Oh, sure. Of course, I don't get to go, because I work with CBS every weekend. No, I haven't done a Baltimore game yet, but I would."

Unitas went to San Diego. He played. But it wasn't the same. He was on the other end of the world, as far as the Colts could have sent him. Ironically, Harland Svare was the coach and general manager at the time. Unitas played the first three games of the '71 season, then sat on the bench while young Dan Fouts played quarterback.

"I said, 'If that's what you want, it's your business, nothing I can do to stop it. I'll do what I can to help you in any way you want me to do it.' "

But after that first season the Chargers hired a new coach and then Unitas retired as a player amid controversy about fulfilling the terms of his contract.

"I was ready to fulfill my contract any way they wanted. Any way possible. But I had a long siege with them . . . finally got it worked out all right. They wanted to set me back for the money I earn from CBS. I didn't think that was right, but I don't like lawyers and legal things and I agreed to the set-off just to get away.

"Litigation and courts and things like that just isn't my way. If I can't sit down with somebody and straighten things out, what good is it?"

It was not the way for this man's career to end.

And now he mulls his future.

"I think about it a lot," he says. "Sometimes I think I'd like to stay in television. It's a good field. Maybe I'd do more things . . . different things. I don't want to coach, but I'd maybe work in the front office of a team, even be part of a group that buys a team, I don't know.

"But you need to have something to do. Can't just sit around. Can't do that. But I'm not so sure I'd want to own a team these days, not with the players' attitudes what they are. It puts a different taste in your mouth.

"I don't blame some of the owners I've heard who say they want to get out, it's no fun any more. You can only go so far with these ridiculous demands and all . . . you're going to kill the golden goose, you know. At the same time, the owners can't take the attitude of Well, we'll just sit around and wait. If they've got a problem with the players, they've got to sit down and resolve the problem, not wait until the season starts. Because then they're fooling with the people who count, the fans. And the fans are damned fed up with listening to some guy making forty, fifty thousand dollars for a six-month period, hollering poor-mouth. 'Cause if the fans stop coming the TV won't be there and then they'd be back playing for a hundred dollars a game."

John Unitas had played for a hundred dollars a game and he knew firsthand about the rewards pro football offered. The game had been good to him, a forum in which to prove his intelligence, his awe-inspiring abilities as a passer, his courage.

It seems only fair to add that the greatest quarterback of his time had been good for football, too. As the architect of the two dramatic marches down the field of Yankee Stadium, he earned the gratitude of all the great players who came after. It is his special mark that, although many are compared to John Unitas, John Unitas is never compared to anyone else.

John Unitas is John Unitas.

And that's all that needs to be said.

Charlie Conerly

... *Conerly* to Schnelker plus 17 to 39, first down
... *Conerly* to Schnelker plus 46 to 15, first down
... *Conerly* to Gifford right sideline, touchdown
... *Conerly* to MacAfee plus 15 to 39, first down

"I don't know if that was the best game ever played. It's getting better, though, as the years keep going. That happens when you get older."

THE FACE IS unique. Matchless.

There is a ton of living in Charlie Conerly's face. It is lined and leathery, weather-beaten and weary. It is a man's face; indeed, it was the first Marlboro Man's face back in the Fifties, and thus it became a national face, the face of the lonely cowboy on horseback with endless skies over his shoulder, gazing across limitless plains.

It looks old, this face, but it is the face of a man quick to laugh. The laugh lines at the corners of the mouth seem poised, anticipating the next chance. It is the face of a man who has seen much, sometimes too much. But it has taken everything it has seen and accepted. There is that, too, in this face. An acceptance of life, whatever its nature.

It can be a face ominous and sinister, set with inner determination, unyielding, hard, cruel. On another body, housing another brain, it could have been the face of a Southern sheriff. It might have been the face of a movie actor. It was once the face of a Marine.

And today, incredibly, it is the face of a shoe salesman. Well, not really a salesman. It is the face of a man who owns shoe stores, seven of them; a comfortable, successful businessman.

Even now, Charlie has a muscular quarterback's body. Though he is past fifty, he still walks with an athlete's grace, a quarterback's confidence. He is still at playing weight, even now in playing trim. He strides smoothly, almost bouncing, clearly recognizable.

He is still The Quarterback, a man accustomed to total authority, acclimated to the role of leader, comfortable with the adulation of others, composed and poised in the face of any crisis. In the caste system of professional athletics, he is an aristocrat, not so much because of his statistics as because of his demeanor. He lives with a bearing of nobility. His mien exudes royalty, the jocks' royalty.

He never made an effort to learn the names of the rookies each year.

"I don't bother none with them," he said, " 'cause they ain't going to be around anyhow."

He never joined in conversation for conversation's sake. If you had something to say, he'd listen. And his response would be one part care, one part terseness. If you came to chat, he had no time at all. He never spoke first, never volunteered a thing. Men of few words were as chattering fools next to him. It was his nature.

His closest friends among the New York Giants were Kyle Rote, Pat Summerall, Alex Webster, Frank Gifford—the elite.

"Sometimes," Rote remembered, "we'd go out and old Charlie wouldn't say anything for hours. But we knew he was having a good time, 'cause he didn't leave."

A grim picture, then? A difficult, distant man? Not at all. Charlie Conerly is delightful, more so now that he is no longer a player, burdened with the pressures a quarterback must bear.

Conerly never really did have the fans on his side. He was a victim of the strange chemistry between a star and his local following. He seemed remote, out of reach. When the Giants were losing, the fans jeered Conerly. And the longer he resisted a show of emotion, the more intense became their outcries.

"They did get pretty rough," he says now, sprawled on a hotel bed in underwear and black socks. "But what the hell. They were paying their money. I figured they could do what they wanted to do. Didn't bother me none."

Not true. The pride of Charlie Conerly was cut. There were welts on his ego. But he bore the problem silently. It was his way, and he'd be damned if he'd show those rubes they had gotten to him.

And the fans' fury grew. The jeering turned vicious. Signs hung from the rafters in the Polo Grounds in the early Fifties, before the team moved to Yankee Stadium across the Harlem River and became champions. The signs: GO BACK TO MISSISSIPPI, YOU CREEP. CONERLY MUST GO. WHO NEEDS CHARLIE? CONERLY STINKS.

"I remember once, a group of us went to a hockey game, or maybe it was basketball, in Madison Square Garden. The announcer introduced us to the crowd—and the crowd booed. It was embarrassing, out there like that in public, but what the hell, I was the quarterback and they figured it was my fault.

"Also, I was quiet. I didn't talk to many people much. The first four, five years were kind of rough years. We weren't winning and I was getting the blame, which quarterbacks do. So we didn't socialize much. Sportswriters . . . well, I never knew them well. Maybe that would have helped, I don't know.

"But I never talked a whole lot to anybody. I didn't have anything to say. And in the bad years . . . well, the booing never really bothered me. At the games, heck, that's all right, but not walking down the street, not in restaurants. I didn't want my wife to have to put up with that.

"So we didn't go out too much. Oh, there were a couple of places where we went, where we knew we'd be left alone. I spent a lot of time at Toots Shor's and P. J. Clarke's. Toots was always a great friend of the Giants, and Danny Lavezzo, who owns Clarke's, he was always very nice to us. It was a place where we could go and, you know, let our hair down. Nobody would bother us, and the gossip columnists wouldn't write anything. Nobody would bug us, and that was good because we needed a place like that. We had to find a place to relax, to go out and not be bothered all the time."

There is a story about another flamboyant quarterback who once went to Shor's, got a bit loud, and was escorted out by ponderous Toots, bartender to the stars, with a curt question: "Who do you think you are, Charlie Conerly?"

Conerly chuckles. "Yeah, I heard that, or I read about it somewhere. Toots was always very good to us."

But there were years of glory, too. There was 1956, when the Giants won their first championship under Conerly. It was a 47–7 thumping of the Chicago Bears, and that game stays with this gray warrior "because we won. I guess the '58 game was a good one, too, but I'll always remember the one in '56. It was our first championship, and that meant a whole lot."

The 1956 season ushered in a period of domination by the Giants. They just lost out to Cleveland in '57, then played Baltimore for the championship in '58 and again in '59 in a rematch that was anticlimactic. The Colts won that '59 title, 31–16. In '60, Charlie's Giants finished second to Philadelphia.

And the following year brought much drama to New York. Head coach Jim Lee Howell was replaced by young Allie Sherman. And Allie Sherman soon made a trade for Y.A. Tittle, a quarterback of consummate skills who had played for a decade with San Francisco.

The first challenge to Charlie's authority was at hand. But he didn't see it in that light.

"In '60, I had missed a few games with a bad elbow or something," he says, "and I was getting old and tired. Anyway, I had told Jack and Wellington [Mara] that I was about ready to quit. Truthfully, I didn't care much about playing in '61. But we didn't have anybody. I think we had Lee Grosscup, and maybe we had another quarterback, I don't remember.

"Then, luckily, they made a trade for Tittle, which was great with me. It just turned out fine that he played so well. I never felt bitter or hurt. I was just glad he played so well, and that we were winning. I did get into a couple of games that we won. But I wasn't hurt. I never saw a guy play as well as Tittle did in '61. I know he played well in '62 and '63, but I wasn't there then. Hell, I just figured I couldn't play any more."

Much happened in that '61 season between Charlie Conerly, Y.A. Tittle and Allie Sherman. Most of it went on behind closed clubhouse doors and did not become public knowledge until much later.

This was an old team, a close team, a proud team. Despite the fact that he had once been an assistant—indeed, he had been hired by the Giants in 1949 to instruct Conerly in the workings of the T-formation —Sherman was to a large extent an outsider.

And now he had taken the team's most cherished man, quarterback Charlie Conerly, and decided to ease him out in favor of Tittle. For that, all along, was the intention. Sherman had been a quarterback. He was a student of the passing game, a veritable genius with a chalk and a blackboard. And Charley just didn't pass well enough any more.

The whole team was tense, awaiting the outcome of their first confrontation. It took place at Fordham University, which the Giants were using as a temporary training base.

"We were in a tiny dressing room no bigger than a small office," Sherman recalls. "Just the three of us were there—Y.A. and Charlie and myself. I shut the door, locked it, and then started to talk to them. 'Guys,' I said, 'there are three men on this team who can decide the future of all the rest. We can win a championship or we can be broken into factions and cliques and bicker back and forth all season. The three men are in this room right now. I need your help. I am in my first year as coach. Y.A. is in his first year with the Giants. Charlie has been the Giants' quarterback for a dozen years. But I'm going to have to make a big decision, and I want you both to understand. I am going to have to pick one of you as my starter, and I don't know when I can make that decision. It might be in a week or it might not be until the middle of the season.'

" 'All I ask is that the both of you be ready to play, be prepared to play and be prepared to sit on the bench. I know that's a lot because you've both been starters for a long time, but the Giants can win a championship if I make the right choice, and I'll need all your help and understanding to make that choice and stick with it. Okay?'

"Y.A. looked a little pale and nodded his head. But Charlie, bless his heart, he just smiled that crooked smile and drawled, 'Sheeit, Al, you know all I want to do is win. Go ahead and do your damnedest. I'm always ready, and if old Y.A. here beats me out, I'll shake his hand.' It was what I had hoped he'd say. I knew then and there we would win it, because men like that, both in their late thirties, are just not supposed to be that cooperative."

Conerly started the first game. And lost. Conerly started the second game, and he was struggling and behind. Tittle was sent in, and he completed his first eight passes, finished with ten of twelve and pulled out the game.

The third week of the season found the Giants in Washington. Conerly started. Conerly was losing, and then he threw an interception.

"Then he took me out," Charlie says, "and I got a little hot. People heard me say something, I guess, but I was a little mad about the way he took me out, after an interception like that."

What Conerly did was stride to the sidelines, throw and then kick his helmet, and sit off on the end of the bench. Alone.

"But as you probably remember," he says now, "Tittle came in and he just played great. We won. I was sorry I had acted like such a damned fool. Allie had Tittle warming up, and I didn't see it. I thought it was a quick hook because of the interception. But the next day my wife told me she could see Tittle warming up from the television, and that afternoon I went to Al and apologized."

And twice during that last season of Charlie Conerly he bailed out the Giants, two victories that were mandatory to stay ahead of the onrushing Cleveland Browns.

Against Los Angeles, the Rams had fought back from a 10–0 deficit to take a 14–10 lead with 3:45 to go in the game. Tittle was terrible. Sherman sent in Conerly.

"We need it, Charlie," he said.

Charlie smiled. "Coach, you got it."

He proceeded to throw a thirty-seven-yard touchdown pass to Kyle Rote to put the Giants ahead. Then he hit Del Shofner with a minute to play to assure the victory.

"I honestly had chills," Sherman says. "I had been in a lot of big games, and they never affected me. But I got chills for that old man. What he did is what makes sports so great. It was a miracle, and that old man lived up to everything he was ever taught."

Much later in the season, Conerly was called on again. It was in Philadelphia, a dreary, foggy, murky city that day. The Eagles took a 10–7 lead, and with Tittle being hounded relentlessly, Sherman called for Conerly.

"Really," Sherman says, "I had intended to let Y.A. look at it for a few minutes and then go back in. But the old man got hot, and when he started picking them apart like he was doing, I just couldn't take him out. There was no way I could put Tittle back."

Indeed, Conerly was hot. He threw five straight passes and completed them all, the fifth for a touchdown. He added two more touchdown passes. The Giants won, 28–24.

"Hey, listen, those two games are way up there on my list, too," Conerly says. "I knew it was going to be my last year, and I knew that for most of the season I was just extra. I held the ball for extra points and field goals. That's all. So when I helped win those two games, it made me feel like I was still contributing. It was good to get back on the field, in the middle of an important game, and be able to pull it out."

The Giants won their Eastern Conference championship and lost the league title game to Green Bay. Then Charlie Conerly retired to his hometown, Clarksdale, Mississippi.

"I never had any trouble being retired," he says. "I really was looking forward to it. I was forty years old and every fall since I was a teenager I had been a football player. I'd made up my mind I had just had enough. Jack Mara asked me to come back and I said no. He asked if I wanted more money, and I just said I'd had enough. I wanted to get home and do something else."

But doing something else is easier said than done. There was nothing Charlie Conerly could do, so for the first two years that is exactly what he did. Nothing.

"I owned a farm outside Clarksdale that my mother and father lived on," he says. "It wasn't making enough money for me, but I had ... which I don't think is any secret, I'm sure they still do it ... I had deferred payments from the Giants for two years. I was looking around, but I lived in a farming area, and hell, I wasn't qualified.

"You know, what the hell could I do? I had played football all my life. So I think it was maybe the second year, after I was out, that a friend, a guy I grew up with ... we got into a Standard Oil distributorship. We had that for a year. It wasn't worth a damn. So then it turns out that some friends of mine in Memphis whose family had been in the shoe business asked me if I'd want to go into a shoe business in Clarksdale.

"I said I didn't know anything about the shoe business. But he said, 'Well, we have all the money, we have all the shoes, and we'll go in partnership.' So I got my buddy and we decided to try this thing. It went over very big. We bought these people out about four years ago, and now we have seven stores in Mississippi.

"I'm lucky as hell. We just grew into it. I had to try something. I didn't know what I could do, but if anybody told me I'd wind up owning some shoe stores, I'd have looked at him like he was crazy. Shoes? No chance."

From time to time, Conerly still models as a Marlboro Man.

"I went in 1974 out to Colorado. It was the first time in six years they'd called me. They use guys I've met, the same guys all the time. One of them, big guy with a big mustache, he was a ranch foreman in California. Now he's done so well with Marlboro that he owns a ranch in Montana. But those guys are cowboys. They can ride and rope and that stuff. I never made much money from it ... just like two hundred dollars a day ... except one year, when they used my ad on television and I got a lot of residuals."

Money, however, has never been of paramount interest to this man. Not really.

"I never made all that much with the Giants," he says, "but to me it was a lot. I liked the game, I really did, and I never did have any complaint with the money. I was making twenty, twenty-five ... I think my last year I made thirty thousand ... and I guess I was one of the top players. I don't know. I never knew what Gifford was making, and Gifford and I were close together. We just didn't talk about it. They might talk about it nowadays, because they're getting so much more money, but we never did . . . and I never cared.

"I hope Jack Stroud made a lot of money, for example, but, you know, I never asked him, and he didn't ask me. I guess they assumed that Gifford and I and Rote made some more money, but that's the way they paid. It sure wasn't much, though, when you look at it now. Television has helped so much. But I think all the guys I played with, they liked to play.

"I look back and . . . being around in '68, when I did the radio thing with the Giants . . . I know it's a different age. Things have changed. But a lot of guys seemed to me like they just didn't want to play. I really don't know, but that was the way I felt. I knew a couple guys then with the Giants that liked to play. But some of the other ones . . . I don't know, maybe it's just me . . . but I just don't understand it. I know it's a new life style and everything, but I just never could understand it. You know, they're getting good money, and it's just like anything else. If you're taking somebody's money you ought to give him your best effort.

"But maybe, I think when we were playing, we ran a little scared. You know what I mean. It wasn't a cinch. I had a five-year contract with a no-cut when I signed, but I didn't know what the hell that meant. I was always scared . . . what would people say if I had to go home, didn't make the team? I don't know if guys nowadays care about that, or if it's money they're concerned about."

He doesn't understand a lot about today's pro football players, because today's players are nothing like the players were in Charlie Conerly's days.

"I guess I'm glad of it," he says. "We had guys on the team we didn't like. I guess there were guys who didn't like me. It's hard to find forty guys who are going to like each other all the time. But it was our job. To play, I mean. I might not like a guy six days a week, but on Sunday I'd just love the hell out of him if he helped us win the game."

Sports was the ruling factor in Conerly's life from his childhood days in Clarksdale, during the Depression. Sports broke the monotony, provided the fun, compensated for the absence of almost everything else.

"I can remember the Depression. My daddy worked for the railroad, the Illinois Central, and then he got laid off, rolled, as they called it in those days. Then he worked for Clarksdale as a garbage collector, you know, anything. But looking back, nobody else had any money who I ran around with, so it didn't make any difference. All we had was baseball . . . football . . . basketball. We didn't have any organized things, like Little Leagues they have now in every town. Everybody's organized now, Babe Ruth Leagues and all that.

"We'd just get up a team . . . you know, hit the ball, and catch it, and pitch it. As I grew to a teenager, it was the same thing. We had a team, the Roaches, and after that everybody called me Roach. We'd go and play other little towns on a Sunday . . . get on a bus, or a truck. But we had no cars and stuff, and all my friends, the guys I played with, they were all busted, too, but we didn't know any different.

"My daddy never made much money, but I don't remember ever being hungry. I had a good childhood. When I was about sixteen or seventeen, my dad, he got to be a deputy sheriff, in the county jail, and we lived in the jailhouse for four years. They had living quarters, I don't mean we stayed in cells and stuff. Then when they got a full-time sheriff we moved into a house and my daddy was on the city po-lice then.

"I went to high school and played football and baseball and basketball. Sports was all we knew. I heard from Ole Miss and Mississippi State and I think LSU or Tulane, but I knew I'd go to Ole Miss. It was only sixty miles from home.

"I was a tailback at Ole Miss in the single wing. I'd throw some, but it was a wing formation. I ran a whole lot more. I stayed at Ole Miss for my freshman and sophomore years, then I went into the service for three years. In '41 and '42, I was a freshman and sophomore, then I went to the Marines and didn't come back until '46.

"I never will forget. It was '44, and I was on the island of Guam in the South Pacific, and the Redskins sent me a telegram saying I was drafted by them. My mother sent me the telegram. My college class was graduating, I guess, so I was eligible to be drafted by the NFL teams. I didn't know what that meant. I knew where I was then, and

I'd 've tried anything to change it. But there I was. Then I came back to Ole Miss in '46 and '47, and finished up college.

"By then, the Redskins had traded me, I believe for a boy named Howie Livingston, Cliff Livingston's brother. Cliff was with us for a while on the Giants. But the Redskins had also drafted Harry Gilmer and they still had Sammy Baugh, so they didn't really need another quarterback.

"So I was a rookie with the Giants in '48. I had done a lot of passing when I came back from the war. We had a boy named Barney Poole, big boy, not fast but good for ten, twelve yards for a hook pass, and we set a collegiate record my last year at Ole Miss. He was a nice big target, and we didn't have a running team so we threw a lot.

"When I got to the Giants . . . Steve Owen was the coach . . . I started off in the A-formation. Then he tried a winged-T . . . I was running left halfback, and Paul Governali was the quarterback, and he'd hand the ball off to me and I'd throw it. Then we went back to the A-formation. And I believe the next year Sherman came in and he put in the T-formation.

"That was '49. I guess somebody talked Steve into it. He never was much of an offensive coach, anyway. But I'm glad they put it in. I know I couldn't have played very long unless they put in the T. Running backs off the wing used to get banged up.

"But it was kind of hard, too, because I had never played T. I was always back, getting the ball on a direct snap. I had to learn about handoffs and all that. It was something different. But it worked.

"I really don't know if I was a good passer or not. I know I had the knack . . . I could see the field. I don't know if it was peripheral vision or what, but I could see a second or third receiver. I thought I was average, I really did. I could pick certain plays . . . I couldn't throw a ball all that far, and I'm not complaining, but I never did have anybody who could go that deep, anyway. I was an average quarterback."

In '54, Charlie was given a companion. His name was Don Heinrich, a quarterback, and after a while Heinrich would start, play a few minutes, perhaps the first quarter, and then give way to Conerly.

"I never did know why they did that," Conerly says. "Don would keep the ball on the ground. I didn't mind throwing it. They said Don would go in to see what the defense was doing, then come out and tell the coaches and they'd change up and I'd go in. Didn't make much sense to me. You always see more when you're in there. But it was working, and we were winning. Maybe they felt like . . . I was getting to be thirty-five, thirty-six years old . . . maybe they felt like I couldn't play the whole game. I think maybe they were trying to make it easy for me."

Indeed, Heinrich started the 1958 championship game. He played the first three series, fumbled once, completed two of four passes and then came out.

"Yeah, he started," says Conerly, "but it was my game. It was one of the outstanding games I played in. When it went into overtime, I was let down. I just felt like we were beat. It looked like we had them beat, and then we let them tie it. I think the punch was all gone from us. We had played as good and as hard as we could, and then they just walked in.

"After the game was over and they had beaten us, I really didn't feel all that down. We played as well as we could, maybe a little better, and we were downcast by losing, but just being in a game like that . . . it was very exciting that way.

"What was amazing to me is how they moved the ball there, late in the fourth quarter. They hadn't scored a point in the second half. Our defense had played such a great game. But Unitas started throwing the ball and I guess we were playing loose on Berry, because he caught most of the passes. And I figured we'd win, because that was the season we had to win five games in a row . . . couldn't lose a game . . . and we had to beat Cleveland twice, once at the end of the season, then in a playoff game, just to play Baltimore.

"I guess the instance I remember most in the game was right before it was tied. They had an award . . . you know, for the Most Valuable Player . . . and here comes Bob Daley [then the Giants' publicity man] telling me I'd won it. That's kind of a little early, and some way I expressed my feelings, told him it was too early. Sure enough, it went overtime and Unitas won it. I think he won a car. But they had voted too early, before the thing was over. I said, 'Please, Bob, this thing ain't over, go away until later.'

"I don't know if that was the best game ever played. It's getting better, though, as the years keep going. That happens when you get older."

It came down to that one play. Late in the fourth quarter, the

Giants are running out the clock. It's third and four on the Giants' forty. Gifford gets the carry . . . pile-up . . . the ball is inches short.

Conerly, as always, is resigned to history.

"I really couldn't see the play that well. Frank always seemed to think he had the first down, though. That was my call, it didn't come off the bench. Looking back, maybe I should have given it to Webster, him being bigger than Frank and all. But we never thought about going on fourth down. Chandler made a hell of a punt. They were down on their fourteen with two minutes to go. They got eighty-something yards to go and the defense had held 'em all the second half. It looked impossible to me.

"I was standing on the sidelines watching it. That's when Daley came over and said, 'You won it,' and I said, 'Won what? It ain't over yet.' We were just pulling as hard as we could for the defense to hold 'em. We were standing there, the offensive men, and there wasn't a thing we could do but watch.

"I was never thinking they'd make it. But it started to look like they would . . . the defense had been so good, and why all of a sudden should it collapse. Tom [Landry] was the defensive coach, and I'm thinking, well, maybe let's do something different. But they'd done so well all the game, I'm sure they were trying as hard as they could. They knew the Colts had to throw the ball, and they were playing mighty loose, not to let anybody get behind them. I know I'd have done it that way if I was on defense.

"Unitas just put together a great series of plays, perfect. He never threw to the sidelines to stop the clock, and he called a few traps up the middle with Ameche when it looked like it was pass. But it really wasn't that big a disappointment.

"We had changed our offense during half time, scored a few points and fooled 'em pretty good. In the first half, they were looking at Gifford all the time on pitchouts, and they were coming up. So we used a lot of plays that came off a fake pitchout to Frank. I'd fake to him and then just drop back and throw the ball. I remember I hit Schnelker with a long one . . . maybe Rote, too . . . on fakes like that.

"It was a veteran team, more or less. We knew what we could do. I'd listen to all of them in the huddle. If a guy told me he could get deep, I'd call it for him. Once I learned I could believe them, I'd let them get their plays. They knew what they could do."

Conerly admits to a rivalry between the offense and the defense.

"They'd kid us a lot, because we really didn't score a lot of points. They won some games on their own, and we won a few just with Summerall kicking . . . field goals.

"I remember once we won a game thirty to nothing, and somebody said, 'Well, Summerall kicked ten field goals.' Those defensive guys used to tell us, 'Get in there and hold 'em a little, we need the rest.' But it never got nasty, no fights. I never seen a football player yet that could fight. I think it was all good-natured. I don't know, maybe somebody didn't like somebody else, but it never got in the open."

Not much did with Charlie Conerly. He was a quiet man, with likes and dislikes kept inside.

Conditioning, for one, was a dislike.

"I never did like training camp," he says. "It was boring, hard work. You know, twice a day, in the hot sun. And there isn't a hell of a lot you can do with a football. That was the toughest part. Baseball, now, it's fun to hit it and I kind of like to catch a baseball. But football is so repetitious, same plays over and over. It's something you have to do, and you have to get in shape. But twice a day for three or four weeks was brutal, because I'd try to do some running at home every year, but soon as I'd break a sweat I'd get tired and I'd quit. And it's just tough as you get older.

"I never had to run a lot, any way. It was mostly my legs, my timing. And drinking . . . well, we'd drink mostly beer, really. I drink a bottle of beer now and then, but I must have drunk so much I just don't want any more now or something. That used to be a real social event for us at camp. We'd practice and then head for the beer place. Wouldn't drink any water after practice. We used to have our Monday nights when the season was on. We'd go out and make a few of the joints. But I've heard some guys talking about drinking it up on Thursday and Friday nights. Well, that just doesn't make any sense to me. It goes back to taking people's money. You owe them, too.

"And I wasn't a wild sort, either. I didn't fight, and I didn't get drunk, and I didn't run around. One time, I remember . . . this goes back to the Polo Grounds . . . some big tackle from the Cardinals hit me with what I thought was a late tackle. So I tried to scratch him in the face . . . and I might have gotten thrown out, I don't remember. But it was dumb. Here I was, six feet and one eighty-five, and he's like two-fifty. It was nuts. I'd bitch at my guys, at the linemen when they missed their blocks, but I left the other tough guys alone.

"Those were good days. It was fun. Frank and Rote and Webster and Heinrich, we'd get out and have a lot of laughs. And in the off-season I'd go home. And I'd do nothing. What could I do? I never even thought about living in New York. I love it when I come up to visit, and I enjoyed it when I played there, but I don't want to live there now."

Charlie Conerly appears to have life figured out. "I was a hero, and I enjoyed that, but not too many younger people know who I was, so it doesn't matter any more. I still find guys who remember. I was on a plane not long ago and some guy in jeans, with a big beard, introduces himself to me. We flew together, and he tells me he wrote *The Summer of 'Forty-Two,* the book and the movie script, and he's always been a Giant fan, from all the way back.

"He says now he's working on a movie . . . *Ode to Billy Joe* . . . fifty miles from where I live . . . and Max Baer, Jr., is the producer and he's the writer. He said, 'Hell, I'll write you a part in it,' and I said, "Man, I don't want to be in no movie,' but he was a football bug and he remembered me. I really enjoyed talking to him, and his business was interesting to me, and I'm sure I enjoyed being a hero. I didn't think people were a pain. I appreciated the attention. Anybody who tells you they don't enjoy it, I think they're lying a little. It's nice to be recognized.

"I did a lot of things in New York, when I played. I remember I did some modeling work for Thom McAn, and some cigar ads, and I posed for Arrow Shirts . . . and the Marlboro Man thing, of course. I remember at the time thinking it was a kind of bad ad for kids, you know, seeing an athlete smoke and all, but I did smoke. I remember once they did some film of me and Paul Hornung and Frankie Albert, smoking in a locker room, and I didn't think that was good. They finally took that out."

Conerly was an observer, a man who enjoyed the antics of his more ebullient teammates, but quietly.

"Once, Cliff Livingston showed up at an airport . . . we played an exhibition game in Dallas, and old Cliff got lost someplace that night, after the game. And he lost his pants and his money and everything . . . and he came into the airport, we were waiting on him, and he shows up with his dark glasses and a pair of swimming trunks. And nothing ever happened. The Giants were a pretty strict team, but nothing like that ever happened before. We never did fine him . . . I mean, he didn't miss the plane or anything.

"I never would have showed up like that. I'd have missed the plane, bought me some clothes and got back by myself. I couldn't have done that. I was the quarterback. But Cliff sure was a funny guy."

One point that Conerly is reluctant to explore is racial prejudice. He is a Mississippian.

"I never did go to school with any blacks," he says, "but I played with some when I was a kid. I never even thought much about it. My rookie year, '48, Emlen Tunnell was on the team, and I know he was the first black to play with the Giants. There was Tunnell and Bobby Epps and Rosey Grier and Rosey Brown . . . but hell, they were good football players, and I'd rather have them than some white boys who can't put any money in my pocket. And they were really nice guys, too. I still see 'em all the time, and I'm glad when I do.

"I'm from Mississippi . . . and people from Mississippi get a lot of knocks, which they shouldn't sometimes . . . but I never did think about playing with blacks. When the older people back home asked me about it, I thought it was kind of a dumb question. I'd kid Rosey Grier, for instance. I'd tell him to come down to Mississippi . . . I said, 'You'd be *big* nigger down there,' and he just laughed and said, 'Oh, Charlie, I ain't never goin' down there.' Anyway, a few years later when he started his singing career, I saw that Rosey Grier was going to be at a club in Memphis. And I said to myself, this is an all-white joint, what's Rosey doing there? Sure enough, my wife and I went up to see him and it was all white people there and he was glad to see us. It was a strange place for him, and I guess he was a little lonely. But hell, I didn't care what color a guy was, if he could play his position."

In the mysterious hierarchy of the Giant family, Charlie Conerly is still a favorite son. He still visits the team office whenever he gets to New York, chatting with Wellington Mara and nephew Timmy Mara and former coach Jim Lee Howell, who is now part of the team's scouting department.

"Football is what made me a business success," he says. "I never would have known these people if I wasn't a player. And the Giants gave me the chance. And those were good years. I have a lot to remember."

He was not the best quarterback of his time. But he had a toughness, a quality of class, that made it all work.

"I can remember," Vince Lombardi once said, "when I coached the Giants' offense. Charlie was the quarterback, of course, and it always amazed me how when he spoke everybody else would shut up and listen. He never had a lot to say, but they all knew when he did it was important. He had a way about him. He was the boss, they all knew it. And if they didn't know it, they felt it. There was nothing I told Charlie that I ever had to repeat. He remembered it all, and he'd work and work and work at perfecting it. He set a great example. I guess that's what all the great quarterbacks do. They have that special something. It cannot be defined."

But it can be seen. And felt.

Postscript

THERE WERE SO many others who played, who were part of the drama in Yankee Stadium that day in December of 1958.

Some have prospered.

Jim Parker, perhaps the finest offensive lineman in the long history of professional football, is a successful businessman in Baltimore.

Jack Kemp, a reserve quarterback for the Colts, went on to a long career at Buffalo in the American Football League. After retiring from the game he was elected to Congress, as a representative from the district that includes Buffalo. He is a conservative Republican.

Don Maynard, a young kickoff-return specialist for Baltimore that day, blossomed into a magnificent wide receiver for the New York Jets. Before his retirement, he shattered Raymond Berry's league record for career receptions.

A few have remained in the public eye. Pat Summerall has become an important sports broadcaster for CBS television and radio. Harland Svare became the youngest head coach in NFL history with the Los Angeles Rams, and after subsequent coaching positions with the Giants and Redskins he became head coach, then general manager, of the San Diego Chargers.

Some have found times harder. Sherman Plunkett, a rookie in 1958 with the Colts and later a member of the New York Jets' Super Bowl team, drives a messenger-service car for the State of Maryland, plying back and forth between Baltimore and Annapolis. As we have already seen, John Sample and Lenny Moore also struggled.

But of all the athletes overlooked here, none stands out so noticeably as Frank Gifford.

He was New York's Golden Boy, a multiple-threat halfback around whom other teams mapped entire defensive game plans.

He ran the ball with strength, grace and deceptive speed. He caught the ball by employing precise and intelligent patterns; paradoxically, while Gifford the running back was a notorious fumbler, Gifford the receiver was applaused as the most sure-handed of men, famed for one-handed, behind-the-back, diving-and-falling circus catches. Frank even passed the ball, a skill acquired as a collegiate quarterback, and this ability caused teams to fear the nearly indefensible option passes which were thrown while running. Gifford was, early in his career, also a sometime punter, sometime defensive back for the Giants.

He is a national celebrity now, part of the three-voiced team that made ABC's Monday Night Football a prime-time television miracle. He is seen daily on television selling various products, from washing machines and refrigerators to apéritifs.

Gifford was friendly and helpful, but he was also reticent. There were many areas of his life he chose to veil; hence, one must write more about Frank than with him.

But Lord, what a football player.

Frank played only for the Giants. He played from 1952 through 1960, then again from 1962 through 1964. The missing year, 1961, was spent recuperating from a serious head injury which threatened his life and his career. But he recovered, and played three more seasons while adding to the long list of team records he still holds.

On the morning of the championship game, Gifford was chief among the concerns of the Baltimore defense.

"We were told to key on Frank," says defensive end Gino Marchetti. "We were told to follow him wherever he went . . . to come up fast, never losing sight of him, when a play began to develop. Listen, there were a hundred ways Frank could beat you. We had to be worried about every one of them."

Indeed, the Giants' marked lack of offensive success in the first half of that game was directly attributable to this overreaction on the part of Baltimore's defense. When, during the half-time break, the coaches made the decision to use Gifford as a decoy, the game was significantly changed. That single decision placed the burden on the Colts. They had to isolate Gifford anyway, preparing for the moment when the Giants would go back to him.

The game was grueling for Gifford, perhaps even more so when he became the second-half decoy.

"Being a decoy . . . faking the run . . . faking a handoff . . . it sometimes is more difficult than actually taking the ball," he explains. "If your fake isn't perfect, they [the defenders] just won't pay attention to you. If it's convincing, they hit you just as hard as if you had the ball. Nobody likes to decoy, but I knew it was our only chance. We were playing a better team that day, and we needed every advantage to stay even."

This attitude is characteristic of Gifford.

"We were all beat up, going into the game," he says. "Hell, Charlie didn't even practice that week. I had a couple of broken ribs. I think Alex had a sprained back and he couldn't even walk real well. We had other guys who were hurt . . . but nobody ever said they couldn't play. We didn't do that in those days. It was too important to us. And, you know, the Colts were rested. They had clinched it with two games to go, and then they had a week off when we played Cleveland.

"We were just all dead. I was really surprised we played as well as we did."

Losing that sudden-death game hurt, of course. But Frank was able to put it in its proper perspective faster and more intelligently than most other Giants.

"We were playing a better team, yet we made them work harder than they ever did before they were able to win.

"I was as proud of our guys as if we had won. Maybe more. The challenge of competition is to put every ounce of energy into your job, to keep fighting until there's no more time left. I don't think those ideals were ever reached quite as completely as we reached them that afternoon."

There would be other championship games for Gifford and the Giants. There was a rematch with the Colts in 1959, won by Baltimore. In 1960, with the Giants battling the Philadelphia Eagles for the Eastern Conference crown, a jarring tackle by the Eagles' Hall of Fame middle linebacker, Chuck Bednarik, almost cost Gifford his life. It did cost him the entire 1961 season, which he spent as a team scout.

"We had another game with Philadelphia the week after I got hurt," Frank says now, chuckling. "Bednarik was terrified that he killed me, so all that week when he kept calling the hospital I refused to talk to him. I didn't blame him. It was a clean tackle. But I figured if he was that worried he might not play well the next Sunday, and we'd win the thing anyway."

Gifford's return to the field in 1962, after exhaustive tests conducted by specialists, marked his assignment to a new position: wide receiver.

"I just didn't think I should ask for the pounding a running back has to take," he says. "I was well again, fully recovered, but you never know. I wasn't gun-shy, just cautious."

Nevertheless, Gifford as a wide receiver was just as good for the Giants. He became one of the league's most respected pass-catchers, recording many "impossible" receptions in what always seemed to be the most crucial part of a critically important game.

In some respects, Gifford was too good and too spectacular. His circus catches on the field and his aloofness off it made him the focus for the resentment of the great Giant defense. Sam Huff recalls that the defense used to psych itself up at practices by focusing its hatred not on next week's opponent, but on Frank Gifford, the personification of offensive football, the recipient of the glory that the defense had earned.

"I understand Sam, and all that stuff," Frank counters. "It's a resentment you really saw for the first time when writers came into the game . . . media people who really understood the game. And they understood that defense is really a lot more important than offense in football. To me, too. If I were to build a football team, I wouldn't take Namath, I'd take Joe Greene.

"The defensive guys, like Sam . . . they knew this. And I knew it. I was a defensive player to begin with. You win on defense, you don't win on offense. And a lot of media people . . . when pro football first grew up, they'd send out a baseball writer who didn't have the foggiest idea what was going on . . . I mean, technically, which is not all that complex anyway.

"I used to kid Jimmy Patton, who had the locker next to me. He was a very proud guy . . . and guys like Huff and Robustelli . . . all of them. And they should have been, they were really a much better unit than we were.

"Yet they'd pick up the papers and see Charlie throws three touchdown passes and Gifford scores this, Gifford does that, it's automatic resentment.

"I grew up in the limelight . . . where Sam Huff grew up as a left offensive guard from West Virginia . . . so I was a lot more conditioned to realizing that was a lot of crap. But they started to read about it, and they started to form a little nucleus that said, 'What the hell's going on here? We're doing all the work and they're getting all the glory.' And it was the media's fault.

"I used to tell Patton, 'Hey, I played defense before you got here, I know you guys don't make enough money.' I really liked Jimmy ... he was a tough little guy ... a tragic little guy. But I couldn't kid around with Sam ... look, Sam was really a good football player, better than people realize, but he was a victim of those media people. He wasn't what the media made him. Sam was really a solid football player, but he wasn't vicious, and he wasn't tough, and he wasn't strong, and he wasn't any of those things. Somewhere along there he realized he had to twist somebody's head or make a late tackle to get recognized.

"Sam was also Tom Landry's man, the focal point of the 4-3 defense. Tom did that with defense, with his middle linebacker. Look at Lee Roy Jordan [in Dallas]. Lee Roy Jordan is a fine athlete, but he would be nothing compared to what he is with other teams. And that stuff about the defense shutting us down in scrimmages, getting 'up' for us ... yes, it's true. Look, you go through six, eight weeks of training camp and the defense knows everything you do. Everything.

"Harland Svare used to eat me alive in scrimmages, and Harland Svare was a lot smarter than Sam. He played the right-side linebacker and I was the left halfback. I couldn't do anything against Svare. To us ... to the offense ... it was kind of a joke. We knew we weren't trying to beat the defense, we were trying to get ready for our next game, not beat Svare, or Huff.

"I know Sam and some of them called me things like 'Hollywood' and 'Glamour Boy' and 'Tippy-Toes.' I couldn't change the way they used me. I had the respect of the few people I cared about: that was Charlie, who was the inspirational heart of that team; Jim Lee, the coach; and Vinnie Lombardi, the offensive coach. I would have done anything I had to do ... I would have gone head-to-head with Sam if I couldn't avoid it.

"But I understand Sam. It's the whole background. You know, poor boy out of Farmington, West Virginia ... never expected to make the team ... tried to quit as a rookie ... had to be begged to come back ... changed positions ... I understand Sam. I stayed in New York every year, started doing a radio show in '57, had my own TV show in '58. The other guys mostly went home and just crapped around the house. Not only Sam but a lot of the guys felt I had more opportunities, because I was on offense, was kind of the glamour boy of the team. Bull. I just happened to be Vinnie Lombardi's guy. He went up to Green Bay and made Paul Hornung his guy. But I wasn't paranoid about the resentment. Frankly, I didn't give a damn."

Gifford may have been resented and maligned by the defense, but his contributions to the Giant successes of the '50's and '60's could hardly be denied. He was never a fan favorite, being as reticent and circumspect in public then as he is today. But he had a certain sense of confidence—in himself and in the team—that caught the imagination of players and fans alike. When he took a handoff or went out for a pass, he *knew* he would succeed. His fumbles were only passing misfortunes.

His role in the 1958 game illustrates his odd situation. Although it can be argued that he brought on the defeat with two disastrous fumbles, it is clear that without him the team would never have had a chance. He was a weapon whether he was used or simply played the decoy. And, despite tributes paid to the defense, a team needs an offensive threat as well. So Gifford was the logical man to take the blame for offensive failings *and* be the indispensable part of the offense at the same time.

His bearing made him a man to admire—in a special way and at a distance. Frank Gifford never asked nor gave the opportunity for the public to be close. Perhaps the ultimate irony is that a man who has succeeded in the media lives with an abiding suspicion of it and insists on keeping it at arm's length.

A surprising number of participants in the game have died prematurely. And it is with them that we conclude.

Big Daddy Lipscomb was a six-foot-six, three-hundred-pound tackle for the Colts who seemed to embody all that was violent and larger-than-life in pro football. He died of an overdose of heroin in 1963 while still a member of the team. Several of the players I talked to mentioned Big Daddy—Lenny Moore, John Sample, Johnny Unitas. Let Big Daddy's best friend, Lenny Moore, tell the story.

"We've been pretty upset about that whole scene. They just closed the case. Daddy wasn't on dope. He lived with Sherman Plunkett [then playing for the Colts]. So Sherman saw him every day. And if he didn't, I did. Listen, just to get him to take a damned cold shot, you had to track him down and corner him. And it used to take six or seven of us to hold him down to give him a shot of Novocaine. "There is no question. He was killed. They set him up. He had played softball that evening and then he went over to a place in east Baltimore, and he was playing shuffleboard and drinking . . . and, of course, when you mention the chicks, Daddy wants to be around 'em, you know. Daddy used to have a bad, bad habit, and I used to get on him many times about it. He'd pull his roll out and . . . you know . . . 'Set everybody up,' and I'd say, 'Man, hey Daddy, you don't have to do that.' But that's the type of guy he was, 'Give the boys a drink on the Daddy,' you know. And he'd just throw them shots down with everybody else.

"Now, the needlemark was in his right arm. Daddy was right-handed. So he's gonna mainline himself with his left hand? No way. I just can't see Daddy stick himself with a needle.

"And he always wore the old raggedy Sloppy Joe cut-off sweat shirts. Would he do that if he had tracks on his arms? I never knew him to have enemies, but there were people envious of him, I guess, because of his position. But you find that anywhere. But no outright enemies. He was a lovable dude. He was too nice. He was the party at parties, if you know what I mean. And being big, and he could dance, everybody just used to get a big kick out of seeing the dude.

"It's one of those things. I assumed it was a money thing. I can't think it was anything but that."

Bobby Layne, the original Free Spirit quarterback, grew close with Big Daddy when both played for the Steelers. "I never saw a man that big," he says, smiling. "The Steelers didn't sign him, they treed him."

At his funeral, attended by thousands, all three of his former wives showed up. Big Daddy always had problems avoiding alimony payments, and each time he got to California there was a summons waiting for him for nonpayment.

Of one of his wives, he once said: "I didn't mind losing her so much, but I sure minded losing my '56 Mercury to her. I loved that car. It was the best car I ever owned."

Big Daddy died at thirty-two. Somewhere, someone knows why.

The Giants' reserve fullback, Phil King, distinguished himself in the 1958 championship game with a fumble. In 1973, he died of a self-inflicted gunshot wound. A Southern businessman and a friend of

Charlie Conerley, he was mourned by many of the Giants of the era. His death was ruled accidental.

Ironically, death has struck hardest at the Giants' defensive backfield. Of the men who faced Johnny Unitas' passes that afternoon with uneven success, three are dead.

Jimmy Patton, a great safety for the Giants from 1955 to 1966, died on Christmas Eve, 1972, in a one-car accident in rural Georgia. He was on his way home to Mississippi.

Carl Karilivacz, the man victimized by Ray Berry and Unitas in the decisive moments of that championship game, died of a heart attack in 1970. He had been traded after the 1958 season and never played another game for the Giants after the overtime.

The most affecting loss, however, was that of Emlen Tunnell. Tunnell was thirty-four when he played for the Giants in 1958; he died in 1975, at the age of fifty. He was a member of the Pro Football Hall of Fame, the first black man to be elected, and was a scout for the Giants at the time of his death. Indeed, he was at the team's summer training camp in Pleasantville, New York, attending a scouting meeting.

Tunnell, who had played college football—briefly—at the University of Iowa, left school to join the Navy. Then, in the spring of 1948, he walked into the Giants' offices in Manhattan and asked the late Timothy J. Mara, founder of the team, for a tryout. Ray Walsh, currently the team's vice-president, secretary and general manager, was then an administrative assistant, and he remembered Tunnell's name. He recommended that Mara sign him, or at least grant a tryout. Mara did. It was a most fortuitous decision.

By the time Tunnell retired, after the 1961 season, he had established himself as the finest safety ever to play in the NFL. He went away with many of the more notable records as well, including career interceptions (seventy-nine), most punt returns and most yardage on both interceptions and punt returns.

"He was the greatest safety of all time," Howell says. "But his real value was as a person. He was a genuinely funny man, always coming up with something that would make everybody laugh, that would relieve the tension that always builds during a football season.

"He coined the phrase 'Different strokes for different folks' and I think it became a recording later on. He once told a guy he'd never cheat on his wife, but 'there's nothing wrong with reckless eyeballing.' He was a little moody as times, but you just had to like him.

"He had the greatest natural ability of any defensive back I've ever seen. He was trim and very fast and he could always get the jump on the ball. He could anticipate . . . I mean, actually how he did it he couldn't tell you . . . but he could always get to the right spot at the right time. He was the forerunner of the free safety type, where you just let the man roam free back there. He made very few mistakes.

"The '58 game was his last for the Giants. We traded him to Green Bay for the '59 season, because Vinnie [Lombardi] had just left us to become the head coach out there, and he wanted someone who knew what we were doing, who knew what Tom Landry [the Giant defensive coach] was doing, someone who could help him teach defense to a new bunch.

"And Em had those 'soft' hands . . . I can still see him catching punts, like Willie Mays used to catch a baseball. He'd just reach up and take the ball, all hands and wrists, and I don't remember ever seeing him drop one. It was very unusual. And he had such great moves. He'd catch the ball and somebody would be right there to nail him and then somehow Emlen would get clear and start moving up the field. He was a natural runner. And on defense he'd really hit. He was a big man, six-one and about two-fifteen, two-twenty. He sure hurt when he hit guys.

"I don't know . . . he never told anybody how sick he was. I do know that he used to get fat . . . he'd balloon up and his arms would get big and heavy and he'd perspire more than usual. But he never let on, and in the last few months he had lost a lot of weight and he looked really good.

"He knew everybody . . . everywhere he went. He was a great guy, nobody ever had a bad word about him. He'd go to a place in Harlem, the Red Rooster, when he was a player, and he'd just buy everybody a meal or a drink or something. He was that kind of guy, everybody loved him. It's hard for me to think of him as dead."

The Minus Funeral Home is in the center of a black, poor ghetto area in Ardmore, a near-suburb of Philadelphia. It is a small converted home, far too constricted for the crowd that showed up to pay last respects to Emlen Tunnell.

Police cordoned off a four-block area, and estimated that five hundred people attended the funeral. Emlen's pallbearers were former teammates Alex Webster, Rosey Brown and Jack Stroud, and then-current Giants John Mendenhall, Carl Lockhart and Henry Reed. Tunnell had scouted the latter three and recommended they be drafted by the Giants. Lockhart and Mendenhall had become All-Pro choices.

Scores of former NFL players, among them Gino Marchetti, and John Sample, were in the throng outside. Most of the Giants' "official family" appeared, including team president Wellington Mara and director of operations Andy Robustelli. And fans and friends, hundreds of them.

Em Tunnell was a personal friend of mine. I can remember him once saying, as a chartered jet cut home through the darkness, "I played so hard for so many years . . . I always finished a game dead tired . . . I don't see how it can't but take some years off my life at the end."

It did.

The sadness is as great as Emlen's friendship was to me. I'd like to think he got every minute's worth.

And so this has been the story of men, a diverse group, fighting as you and I against the intrusion of years. They have attempted to relive what was, for most of them, a better time.

There is sadness here, but a sadness familiar to all of us. We can none of us win the war, defeat the calendar. Time is always a mightier opponent.

The men are different now, diminished. The arrogance and verve of youth has been tempered by the advent of middle age, the forced acceptance of change. They have a tendency to look back, perhaps too often, to remember the glory and the cheers. It is a happier alternative than to accept the reality of now.

When once they never thought of anything but life, they must admit that death has touched them. Emlen Tunnell . . . is he really gone? Yes, he is. Can it be true that Phil King and Big Daddy Lipscomb, who lived life as few of us ever have, are dead? Yes, it's true. Alex Webster and Rosey Grier are grandfathers. Think of it.

Years whirl past faster than we can know, and where we were and where we are is separated by a blurring, fading vortex of half-remembrances. Our images are colored by sun, not shadow. We see what we would rather see.

But it is this way for all of us, and it has always been. Old men remember each other as classmates, and refuse to see each other as old men.

Many years ago, Oliver Wendell Holmes was asked to deliver the welcoming address for the fiftieth reunion of his Harvard class, a class special for the prominence of its members. He chose to compose a poem.

As he looked out at the audience, he saw gray heads and white beards. And he saw empty chairs. And he asked in his poem (as we ask of the men in this book) if these gray heads could really be the boys he knew. He concluded:

Then here's to our boyhood, its gold and its gray,
The stars of its winter, the dews of its May!
And when we have done with our life-lasting toys,
Dear Father, take care of Thy children, The Boys!

About the Author

DAVE KLEIN writes a sports column for the Newark *Star-Ledger* and the Newhouse Newspapers. He has covered the New York Giants for fifteen years and has written articles for many national sports publications, including *Sports Illustrated* and *Sport.* His newspaper articles have appeared frequently in *Best Sports Stories of the Year,* and in 1974 he received the best-in-book award for his coverage of the Bobby Riggs–Billie Jean King tennis match.

Mr. Klein lives in Scotch Plains, New Jersey, with his wife, Carole, and their children, Aaron and Mindy.